Writing

and

Workshopping

Poetry

A CONSTRUCTIVE INTRODUCTION

Writing

and

Poetry

A
CONSTRUCTIVE
INTRODUCTION

Workshopping

**STEPHEN
GUPPY**

broadview press

BROADVIEW PRESS— www.broadviewpress.com
Peterborough, Ontario, Canada

Founded in 1985, Broadview Press remains a wholly independent publishing house. Broadview's focus is on academic publishing; our titles are accessible to university and college students as well as scholars and general readers. With over 600 titles in print, Broadview has become a leading international publisher in the humanities, with world-wide distribution. Broadview is committed to environmentally responsible publishing and fair business practices.

The interior of this book is printed on 100% recycled paper.

Library and Archives Canada Cataloguing in Publication

Guppy, Stephen, 1951–, author
    Writing and workshopping poetry : a constructive introduction / Stephen Guppy.

Includes bibliographical references and index.
ISBN 978-1-55481-308-7 (paperback)

    1. Poetry—Authorship. I. Title.

PN1059.A9G86 2016   808.1   C2016-906727-0

Broadview Press handles its own distribution in North America
PO Box 1243, Peterborough, Ontario K9J 7H5, Canada
555 Riverwalk Parkway, Tonawanda, NY 14150, USA
Tel: (705) 743-8990; Fax: (705) 743-8353
email: customerservice@broadviewpress.com

Distribution is handled by Eurospan Group in the UK, Europe, Central Asia, Middle East, Africa, India, Southeast Asia, Central America, South America, and the Caribbean. Distribution is handled by Footprint Books in Australia and New Zealand.

Broadview Press acknowledges the financial support of the Government of Canada through the Canada Book Fund for our publishing activities.

Funded by the Government of Canada | Canadä

Edited by Karen Taylor
Book design by Michel Vrana

PRINTED IN CANADA

Contents

Shaping Fire

The genesis of our best poems is often mysterious. Perhaps we find some image, phrase, music, or story that intrigues us. We can describe that image in words, try to embody that music in rhythmic language, recount the storyline, or elaborate that interesting phrase into a stanza or even the rough draft of a complete poem. Sometimes the creative process is less easily defined. On some occasions, the language of the poem finds *us*: whole lines, phrases, rhymes, or images appear in our minds in response to circumstances or simply "out of the blue." Traditionally, poets have spoken of this process of unconscious creation as "inspiration." In Norse mythology, the god Kvasir was killed by two dwarves who then mixed his blood with honey. Anyone who drank this "mead of the gods" was filled with poetic inspiration. In the ancient Greek myths, inspiration is the province of the Muses—nine sister goddesses, each of whom is patron of a particular art. Celtic poets spoke of *Awen*, which was both divine and poetic inspiration. *Awen* was a multiform property or identity, reflecting the diversity and richness of artistic creation.

Though poetic inspiration is an important aspect of any poet's practice, too stubborn a belief in the idea that poems begin in the subconscious or, at any rate, "outside" our conscious minds can be a trap. When we start writing poetry, many of us have the impression that "talented" poets simply conjure up poems out of thin air. They enter a state of poetic inspiration, and their poems come to them unbidden. This concept of "outside" inspiration is mirrored by the idea that poetry erupts spontaneously from the inner self without the mediation of the conscious mind. That notion comes from various sources, notably the introduction to the *Lyrical Ballads* of Wordsworth and Coleridge, and has proven remarkably durable: even a couple of hundred years later, the conviction that "poetry is the spontaneous overflow of powerful feelings" is common among poets, particularly relative beginners. Another common misapprehension is that poetry, unlike other forms of writing, isn't necessarily *about* anything: it's an expression of feelings, and it doesn't connect to the events of the world or to history, the other arts, or science. These related myths are appealing in a romantic way, but they can prevent us from developing our craft and from writing as much or as well as we might have written.

In order to create worthwhile poems on a reasonably regular basis, we need craft as well as inspiration. The repertoire of techniques that make up the craft of poetry shouldn't be restricted to editorial strategies: before we edit and polish our work, we have to build our fragments of vision and intention into reasonably complete structures. Accomplishing that task involves not only learning new skills but also pushing our limits and stretching our imagination. Poets are the masters of language, and learning about the place of poetry in the wider field of language and culture is an essential step for any aspiring poet. Poets are also the heirs and heiresses of a rich tradition—one that embraces not only the history of English but also the history and potential of all cultures. In order to build our poems from inspiration to final production, we need to make ourselves aware of that cultural surround, which is usually the work of a lifetime of reading and writing. Most important, we have to be prepared to *think like poets*—to engage our imagination and to take risks with thought and expression. We'll be exploring some ways of achieving those objectives here and in the chapters that follow.

POETRY AND LANGUAGE

Most written and spoken communication is intended to convey a message. Think of language as a wagon and the message as the goods that the wagon delivers. If you're waiting for an important parcel, you're probably not going to pay much attention to the appearance or construction of the delivery wagon. Similarly, if you're reading an engineer's report, you're not much concerned about the elegance of his or her prose style. You want to build a sturdy house or bridge; you need the engineer's advice to accomplish your objective; and you don't care if the language of the report is dull, as long as it conveys the message clearly. In a good poem, the language is just as interesting as the message it communicates. A poem can't be paraphrased or summarized: it's not the message alone that matters; the message and the language that embodies the message are inextricably melded. As the poet Paul Valéry said, "To summarize a poem or put it into prose is quite simply to misunderstand the essence of an art."[1]

To a poet, language isn't simply a code for transmitting messages. It's a material, a substance made of sound and graphic figures, and it can be patterned and played with just as we'd play with clay or paint or the sounds of a musical instrument. Poetry shares some characteristics with other literary genres, but it differs from most other genres in that it foregrounds the material of communication—the texture and structure of the language itself. In a nonfiction document (and to a significant extent in most fiction), the language is primarily a medium of communication and representation; we look *through* the

1 Paul Valéry, *The Art of Poetry*, in *The Collected Works of Paul Valéry*, vol. 7., ed. Jackson Mathews and trans. Denise Folliot (New Jersey: Princeton UP), 147.

words into the lives of characters in a story or history or into the concepts and examples in a theoretical work. A poem, on the other hand, invites us to look *at* the language as well as *through* it. To quote Monsieur Valéry again, "The essence of prose is to perish—that is to be 'understood.'"[2] That's not entirely true of poetry. A poem can be a transparent window into a world of people, things, events, and ideas, but it's also a stained-glass window, one that invites the reader to be aware of the materials of which it's composed.

A poem cannot be paraphrased, but it can be engaged and explored by attentive readers, and it can be "reverse engineered" by poets who wish to understand how it was made. We'll be looking at examples of poems from the various subgenres of poetry in order to see how they're constructed, and we'll have the opportunity to apply the techniques we find in those poems to our own original work. In order to engage the examples we'll be reading, we first need to consider some general ideas about poetry.

Poetry uses all the resources of language. We can get a sense of the range of those resources by looking at the listing for almost any word in a good dictionary. A typical listing will tell us quite a few different things about the word:

- graphic symbols (i.e., the arrangement of letters that forms the word—put more simply, how it's spelled)
- syllable breaks in polysyllabic words
- stresses
- pronunciation (i.e., the sound of the word and any variations of sound in different dialects)
- meaning (denotation and connotation; literal and figurative)
- derivation (English combines Latinate and Germanic roots, and many ideas can be expressed in either Germanic-derived or Latin-derived words. English also includes a large number of "loan words" from other modern languages as well as some invented words—"coinages"—quite a few of them dreamed up by poets.)
- syntax and usage (the way the word is used in larger units such as phrases, clauses, and sentences)

As poetry engages the resources of the language so completely, *everything in a poem has meaning.* That the words of the poem are meaningful is obvious, but it's also important to keep in mind that other elements of the presentation communicate meaning. The length of lines, line breaks, stanza breaks, syntax, rhythm, the visual design of the poem on the page, punctuation or lack of

---

2 Valéry, *The Art of Poetry*, 146.

punctuation, and sometimes even the font in which the poem is printed are important nodes in the web of signifiers that make up the complete poem. Writing poetry well requires an acute awareness of the technical resources at our disposal. That awareness is developed through reading and writing: if you want to write poetry well, you have to be prepared to study and practise.

The craft of writing poetry is difficult both to teach and to learn because there are so many different ways to write a good poem. One of the exciting things about participating in a writers' group or poetry workshop is that we're likely to encounter poets whose taste in poetry differs radically from our own. The genre embraces a wide range of forms and styles, from the delicate three-line haiku to the book-length epic and from traditional rhymed verse to concrete poetry, sound poetry, and hypertext poetry. Most poets prefer one or two of these possibilities over the others, and most will choose to work in one style for a lengthy period of their writing life, perhaps even for their entire careers. It's possible, however, that the first style of poetry that engages us may be a flirtation or a summer romance and not the "love of our lives": it's a good idea to encounter as many subgenres of poetry as we can so that we can discover which style or styles suit our turn of mind.

So what do all good poems have in common?

The stock answer is that poems are written in verse, while stories, novels, and nonfiction books or essays are written in prose. People often consider "poetry" synonymous with "verse." **Verse** is writing that's organized into lines, in other words writing that doesn't go from left margin to right margin and then carry on to the next line without any break. (Writing that *does* go from left to right and then wrap onto the next line without a pause is called **prose**.) The *poetry* = *verse* formula isn't entirely adequate. Some very good poems have been written as prose paragraphs, and there are also sound poems and concrete poems that can't be described as verse, and the emerging genres of motion poetry and hypertext poetry don't fit comfortably into the existing categories. We also need to consider what makes some documents **"poetic"** and others **prosaic**. Understanding the importance to poetry of musical composition and analogical thought will shed some light on that complex issue: we'll get to those ideas in later chapters.

Alternate possibilities aside, it's true that *most* English-language poems are written in verse. That is, the language of the poem is divided into rhythmic or syllabic or visual units signified by line breaks. As far as English-language poetry is concerned, poems written in paragraphs of prose instead of lines of verse are relatively rare and considered by some to be a bit of an acquired taste. (The **prose poem** is more popular in some other European literatures than it is in English.) Much of this book is devoted to the art and craft of writing verse. Prose poetry will be discussed in a separate chapter, though many of the skills involved in writing verse poems also apply to prose poems. We'll also consider subgenres such as concrete poems, sound poems, motion and hypertext poems, and aleatoric poems elsewhere in the book.

THE ROOTS OF POETRY

Poetry is an ancient art, as ancient as anything in humanity's repertoire of skills and obsessions. The history of poetry stretches back into the oral prehistory of literate societies, Western or otherwise, and poetry still holds its place as a central art form among the world's purely oral cultures. Within Western civilization, poetry has become something of a hybrid form, one that exploits the possibilities of print technology while retaining the qualities of pure orality. In the modern world, a verse or prose poem should "work"—in the sense of creating emotions and ideas in the reader or auditor—both as spoken language and as a written text.

One way of understanding the mechanics of song and thus of poetry is to consider the function of poetry in a preliterate (oral) culture. In a world without writing, how would we preserve information from one generation to another? How would we keep our traditions and history from being forgotten? For one thing, we might arrange our information into stories with memorable and interesting plots. This narrative craft might help us to remember the outline of historical events, but it wouldn't be much use when it came to remembering specific ideas. (What do you remember after reading a novel—characters certainly, the plot-line perhaps, a scene or an image or two, but can you really remember any passages of the novel word for word?) In order to preserve language more precisely, oral cultures made use of some aids to memory such as rhyme, rhythm, parallelism, and repetition. Put these techniques together, and you'll be creating poems or songs, not narrative or expository prose.

It's impossible to draw a neat line between an oral phase and a literate phase in the development of Western culture. Oral forms—song, chant, prayer, rant—didn't evaporate with the rise of literacy. For centuries after the advent of reading and writing and even centuries after the invention of moveable type in the Renaissance, the majority of the populace created and consumed poetry as "folk" songs, mnemonic "nursery rhymes," rhymed proverbs, epigrams, and so on. Perhaps surprisingly, this is still the case today. The only verse poems that the average citizen of an English-speaking country enjoys are the lyrics to popular songs. Some of these are imaginative and memorable enough to be called poetry and not just pedestrian verse—song lyrics are, after all, a form of "folk poetry." A couple of hundred years ago, songs were often written by the common people, people who were uneducated or illiterate. Print poetry belonged to the educated classes and not to the society as a whole. Today, most people enjoy songs for both their music and their lyrics, and some—a much smaller demographic—read and write poetry.

WHY READ POETRY?

Traditionally, poetry found an appreciative audience because it was *memorable, musical, witty,* and *wise.* Robert Browning combined some of these essential qualities in a couplet: "Grow old along with me! / The best is yet to be." These lines may stick in our minds, as they have remained in the memories of four or five generations of readers, largely because they make use of a couple of **mnemonic** devices: predictable rhythm and end-rhyme. They are, in other words, both memorable and musical. They are also, of course, arguably "wise" in that they give voice to an attitude we may consider both reasonable and enlightening. The most passionate young lovers will someday grow older, so why not embrace that process? Poets today still write memorable, aphoristic lines and stanzas. Here's American poet Amy Clampitt: "Love is a climate / small things find safe / to grow in. . . ."[3]

Browning's poems and Clampitt's may include ideas that strike us as "wise"; their work, and the work of a great many other poets, can also engage us through a comic image or an ironic turn of phrase. Wit in poetry can take many forms: a joke, a riddle, a pun, a parody, a *double entendre,* an inventive choice of diction, even a clever inversion of our expectations of poetic technique and form.

On a technical level, most (but not quite all) poetry has the following characteristics:

- It's *musical,* as we've said, sharing at least some of the properties of a song, or at the very least paying attention to the inherent musicality of language.
- It contains or consists of *concrete images.*
- It involves **analogical** as well as *logical* thought processes.
- It's constructed around a *simple* **rhetorical strategy,** usually **narrative** or argument, or perhaps it's purely descriptive, consisting of an image or a number of juxtaposed images. In other words, most poems do one or more of the following:
  - tell a story
  - argue a theory
  - paint a picture

Longer poems, of course, may explore all three of these options.

---

3 Amy Clampitt, "The Smaller Orchid," in *The Collected Poems of Amy Clampitt* (New York: Knopf/Borzoi, 1997), 44.

A poem has unity, coherence, and sense of purpose. It's intended to tell us something, presumably something of reasonably wide interest and something important enough to make it worth the time we're going to spend reading it. A poem should be accessible to a sufficiently wide readership. Abstract "language" poetry might seem to be an exception to that rule, but in fact an abstract poem communicates a message through its very abstraction: it tells us that it resists the function of language as communication in order to foreground the nature of language as "material." (This is true of all poetry, but the abstract poem makes the materiality of language the subject and raison d'être of the poem.) The refusal to communicate, paradoxically, communicates a political or aesthetic message. Similarly, a "sufficiently wide readership" may be defined differently by different poets: for some, that readership should be any reasonably literate person; for others, it's a small coterie of initiates into an artistic school, religious faith, or political constituency. Every poet defines his or her audience through his or her choices of subject, style, and form. The core objective will always remain: a good poem has a readership that finds value and enjoyment in the poem. That's a very broad criterion, but it does exclude the poet who writes only for him- or herself. There's nothing wrong with writing for yourself; it might be a useful form of meditation or therapy, or you might simply wish to keep a diary in verse or to entertain yourself by writing in challenging poetic forms. It should be obvious, however, that you don't need a creative writing class or a book about ways of developing your skill as a poet to accomplish those goals. This book is addressed to poets who want to improve and refine their abilities and to address an audience of readers, as is any worthwhile poetry workshop; poets who write only for themselves can do so without advice.

WHAT MAKES A POET?

In order to write poetry well, we have to possess or cultivate some special abilities:

- Perceive or visualize concrete objects, persons, or scenes and record them accurately in descriptive imagery.
- Hear and appreciate the "music" of language and construct that music from the **phonological** resources of language; this process will involve, for example, being able to hear stresses and keep time, being able to hear the similarities and differences between groups of vowels and consonants, and being able to hear pauses of varying duration.
- Construct arguments around such elementary logical operations as comparison, causal analysis, thesis and refutation, exposition and resolution, definition, listing of examples, and enumeration of categories and subcategories.

- Recount a simple but interesting narrative and recognize the relationship between the complexity of the story and the scope of the poetic form.
- Think analogically by perceiving the common qualities of apparently unrelated objects or phenomena; this ability will allow us to construct metaphors and employ parataxis.

Anyone who is reading this book has the abilities listed above. If we didn't have any inclination towards metaphor or any ear for the musicality of language, we wouldn't be interested in writing poetry. All of us, regardless of our natural aptitudes, can benefit from refining and developing our talents. That's our objective here.

TAKEAWAY

- Poetry is an ancient and universal art form and has its roots in oral cultures.
- Poetry foregrounds language to a greater degree than other literary genres.
- There's no single "right way" to write a good poem, but all good poems have some characteristics in common.
- Poets possess abilities common to most people, but they may possess them to a greater degree than most, and, more important, they're willing and determined to cultivate and refine those abilities.
- A good poem combines wit, wisdom, and musicality. A good poem is also memorable in whole or in part: successful poetry stays with us and continues to enrich our lives long after we put down the book.

TERMS TO REMEMBER

- analogical
- mnemonic
- narrative
- phonological
- poetic

- prosaic
- prose
- prose poem
- rhetorical strategy
- verse

CHAPTER ONE

Finding the Materials

Anything, however small, may make a poem;
nothing, however great, is certain to.[1]
—Edward Thomas

Understanding where our poems come from is important to our practice as poets. Those moments of inspiration when an idea comes to us unbidden are certainly welcome, but we can't depend on that sort of visitation consistently enough to write poetry on a regular basis. And, of course, if you don't write regularly, it's difficult to develop your skills. The one-poem-a-year poet is unlikely to perform much better than the one-game-a-year athlete.

A common complaint among writers—particularly beginners—is that they can't produce anything new because they're suffering from "writer's block." In fact, this malady is more myth than real affliction. If we can't think of anything to write about, it's probably because we haven't developed that side of our practice sufficiently; we can't find inspiration because we don't know where to look. We need to develop a repertoire of sources and methods. If one well-spring of inspiration dries up, we can then look to other sources for our ideas. A poem can begin with an image, a sound or a rhythm, an emotion, an idea. Poems begin in dreams, in everyday occurrences, in articles in newspapers, magazines, or on TV. Some poems begin as memories; we recollect the past and try to evoke it for the reader in a poem. By recreating our past experience in language, we attempt to give it structure, shape, and meaning, to make sense of the fragmentary images and voices that live in our memory. Poems can have their origin in *observation*, *remembrance*, *reflection*, and *research*. Many poems involve some combination of those factors.

WRITING FROM EXPERIENCE AND OBSERVATION

"Write what you know" is one of the most durable clichés among aspiring writers, and there's a certain wisdom in that idea, particularly as it relates to poetry. Poetry is one way of distilling into language our perceptions of the events and emotions we encounter in our everyday lives. The "write what you know"

---

1 Edward Thomas, *Maurice Maeterlinck* (Methuen, 1911), 28.

formula can be overstated: some writers may feel that only those people who have had extraordinary lives can write worthwhile poetry. That's clearly not true. Some poets have indeed lived lives of adventure and excitement; other equally productive and gifted poets have been recluses. Emily Dickinson crafted poems that touch on the most essential themes while living with her family in a quiet town in New England; toward the end of her life, she rarely went out in public and preferred to conduct her social relationships through the mail. At the opposite end of the scale, poets such as Lord Byron and Lady Mary Wortley Montagu enjoyed flamboyant lifestyles. The moral is clear: it's not the sort of life you lead but your ability to observe carefully and think deeply about your life—and life in general—that matters.

Some discussions of poetic inspiration encourage us to cultivate a source for our poems by keeping a journal or taking a walk in the countryside or by the sea (a motif left over from the Romantics). These strategies can be useful for some poets, and anyone who enjoys writing poetry will probably have tried some version of either or both. Keeping a journal or a commonplace book is a good way of making sure that you acquire material for your poems. Your journal can function as an incubator for ideas and perceptions in the same way that an artist's sketchbook can serve as a starting point for major paintings. Poets can still find inspiration in fields of daffodils, as did Wordsworth, but we can also run across some great concepts in the popular media and the daily news. Contemporary American poet Stephanie Lenox's poem about a reality TV show is good example.

After Uncle Fred Nearly Dies, We Send the Tape to
America's Funniest Home Videos
by Stephanie Lenox

It's clear we like our trampolines taut and ready
to dump our dumb asses into the nearest thorny hedge.

We like to watch ourselves mugging it up, big hams,
strutting our stuff, then falling down a flight of icy stairs.

We do it on purpose because we fear
we might grow too proud without the occasional crotch shot.

So consumed with our antics, practical jokes, dopey dogs
chasing their own tails, we can barely hold the camera still.

The toddlers who molest our windows are darling.
They don't yet understand the transparency of glass.

Cats. We must have cats. Lots of them, defying nature
or gravity, falling or flying toward their unsuspecting prey.

We use each other as piñatas. We set our blushing brides
on fire. Even the minister can't contain himself.

It doesn't take a genius to know the hockey puck,
a 70 mph insult, will find its way to the softest spot.

It's so funny, or will be, the broken noses, jammed fingers,
swollen testicles—just give us money and time.

We can't imagine the world wouldn't love us,
our hilarious rears stuck in lawn chairs, our slow children

ramming their heads over and over into chain-link fences.
Look! Look at the small dog pissing on the big dog!

We want so much for it to be worth something.

WRITING FROM MEMORIES

The philosopher Susanne Langer refers to fiction as "virtual memory";[2] poems
built around a narrative core resemble works of fiction to some extent, and they
too create the illusion of memory. Our memories of childhood and adolescence
can be an important source of material for poems. The child's perspective,
especially, is well suited to poetry, as it provides a fresh and innocent view of
the world. As they may lack logical and scientific explanations for the things
and events they encounter, children interpret their sense impressions in original
ways. A child's-eye view can resemble that of the makers of myths, who wove
stories around their perception of phenomena for which they had no rational
explanation. Casting your mind back to your childhood and narrating an
incident or describing a moment of perception from the perspective of your
child-self can be a useful starting point for a new poem.

---

2 Susanne Langer, "Virtual Memory," in *Feeling and Form* (New York: Charles
Scribner's Sons, 1953), 258–79.

WRITING FROM RESEARCH

In a more romantic age, poets might compose lyrics or longer poems about the gods and goddesses of ancient Greek or other mythologies. Such a topic would usually be handled with a touch of irony these days, though myth remains a durable source of ideas and imagery for poets. Every poet should be familiar with the mythology of at least one culture, ideally more than one. Myths explain the world through metaphors and symbolic narratives; the mythmaker's mind is essentially that of a poet. Although we usually think of mythology as a system of narratives that comes to us from ancient times and primitive societies, people still construct mythologies around the events and personalities of their own time and place.

Learning about history can provide great material for poetry. Some important long poems have been constructed around the life of an historical figure, and portrait or persona poems can channel an iconic figure as a source of material. Historical incidents can also be made into good poems. Local history is often a particularly useful source of inspiration.

REACTING TO ANOTHER WORK OF ART

One common source of inspiration for poets is the work of painters and musicians. That's not surprising, as poetry is related to both those art forms: poems are both painterly in their emphasis on concrete imagery and musical in their foregrounding of the sounds of language. **Ekphrastic poems**—poems that respond to visual art—are fairly common, and quite a few poems have paid homage to musical compositions, sometimes by attempting to echo the musical arrangement in the phrasing and lineation of the poem. The following poem refers to a famous work by American artist Edmonia Lewis (1844–1907). Lewis, who was of African and Native American descent, achieved great success in Rome in the 1860s and 1870s. The sculpture depicts a figure from the Old Testament.

Hagar in the Wilderness
by Tyehimba Jess

Carved Marble. Edmonia Lewis, 1875

My God is the living God,
God of the impertinent exile.
An outcast who carved me
into an outcast carved
by sheer and stony will
to wander the desert

in search of deliverance
the way a mother hunts
for her wayward child.
God of each eye fixed to heaven,
God of the fallen water jug,
of all the hope a vessel holds
before spilling to barren sand.
God of flesh hewn from earth
and hammered beneath a will
immaculate with the power
to bear life from the lifeless
like a well in a wasteland.
I'm made in the image of a God
that knows flight but stays me
rock still to tell a story ancient as
slavery, old as the first time
hands clasped together for mercy
and parted to find only their own
salty blessing of sweat.
I have been touched by my God
in my creation, I've known her caress
of anointing callus across my face.
I know the lyric of her pulse
across these lips . . . and yes,
I've kissed the fingertips
of my dark and mortal God.
She has shown me the truth
behind each chiseled blow
that's carved me into this life,
the weight any woman might bear
to stretch her mouth toward her
one true God, her own
beaten, marble song.

WRITING IN A FIXED FORM

Writing in a fixed form can solve some of the problems associated with poetic composition. The demands of the form can provide us with a mould into which we can pour whatever subject happens to be on our minds. Fixed forms come with a history, of course, and attempting to write a sonnet may invite us to explore one of the themes employed in sonnets that we've read. We'll discuss a range of such forms in a later chapter.

RE-IMAGINING TRADITIONAL SUBJECTS AND THEMES

As well as working in traditional fixed forms, poets often choose to address traditional themes. Tackling a traditional theme can be one way of finding material for your poetry; the worst-case scenario is that you'll have an opportunity to practise your craft, writing as an exercise being preferable to not writing at all, and there's always the possibility that the traditional theme will strike a chord in your mind and blossom into a "keeper."

- An **aubade** is a poem about the parting of lovers at dawn or sometimes simply a poem about dawn. In the troubadour tradition, a poem on this theme was called an "alba."

    Aubade with Foxes
    by Cecily Parks

    All night foxes ranged over the snow crust
    barking raggedly. This morning

    a warm rain softens the snow and dumbly
    I watch my love sweep it off the windshield

    and drive away. I'm in the road in little more
    than underwear, suspended in the edgy bliss

    of exhaust with two flights of stairs to climb.
    In dens nearby the coiled foxes lick

    their teeth in sleep and cover their eyes
    with bushy, white-tipped tails. When I go

    inside, my bare feet leave curved wet-marks
    on the stairway's metal treads. A fox

    will arc along a wall knowing the stone
    won't hold her scent. When a fox runs in leaves

    her sound is a rustle of leaves. No one is looking
    or listening for me. Nearby a bell hits its notes.

Which version of heaven will feed me
until my love comes home? In one, I understand

what the foxes say. In the other, the foxes
find what they want and are quiet with it.

- A **blason** praises the various parts of the lover's body by finding
a metaphor for each. The theme can lend itself to sensual love
poems, but it also invites imaginative and even surreal flights into
metaphor. Shakespeare's "Sonnet CXXX" is an ironic take on
this theme.

  Sonnet CXXX
  by William Shakespeare (1564–1616)

  My mistress' eyes are nothing like the sun;
  Coral is far more red than her lips' red;
  If snow be white, why then her breasts are dun;
  If hairs be wires, black wires grow on her head.
  I have seen roses damasked, red and white,
  But no such roses see I in her cheeks;
  And in some perfumes is there more delight
  Than in the breath that from my mistress reeks.
  I love to hear her speak, yet well I know
  That music hath a far more pleasing sound;
  I grant I never saw a goddess go;
  My mistress when she walks treads on the ground.
      And yet, by heaven, I think my love as rare
      As any she belied with false compare.

- A **carpe diem** (from the Latin, meaning, "seize the day!") addresses
the theme of the brevity of life and the urgency of action. Robert
Herrick's "To the Virgins, to Make Much of Time" begins with a
famous line that encapsulates the "carpe diem" motif:

  To the Virgins, to Make Much of Time
  by Robert Herrick (1591–1674)

  Gather ye rose-buds while ye may,
      Old Time is still a-flying;

And this same flower that smiles today
   Tomorrow will be dying.

The glorious lamp of heaven, the sun,
   The higher he's a-getting;
The sooner will his race be run,
   And nearer he's to setting.

That age is best which is the first,
   When youth and blood are warmer;
But being spent, the worse, and worst
   Times still succeed the former.
Then be not coy, but use your time,
   And while ye may, go marry;
For having lost but once your prime,
   You may forever tarry.

- An **elegy** is a poem lamenting someone's death. Famous examples include Thomas Gray's "Elegy Written in a Country Churchyard" (1751) and W.H. Auden's "In Memory of W.B. Yeats" (1940). Ben Jonson's poem about the loss of his young son is one of the most touching elegies in the language.

   On My First Son
   by Ben Jonson (1572–1637)

Farewell, thou child of my right hand, and joy;
   My sin was too much hope of thee, loved boy.
Seven years thou wert lent to me, and I thee pay,
   Exacted by thy fate, on the just day.
O, could I lose all father now! For why
   Will man lament the state he should envy?
To have so soon 'scaped world's and flesh's rage,
   And, if no other misery, yet age?
Rest in soft peace, and, asked, say here doth lie
   Ben Jonson his best piece of poetry;
For whose sake, henceforth, all his vows be such,
   As what he loves may never like too much.

- An **epistle** is, essentially, a letter written in verse. It may be directed to a specific person or to an imaginary ideal. As we move from a scribal and print culture to a digital future, the epistle can be re-imagined for email, Facebook chat, Twitter, Skype, and all the other emerging alternatives to ordinary "snail mail."

Letter to the Gnome Who Stole My Firstborn
by Shelley Puhak

Can I bring you a better bird,
perhaps a talking hawk?
A golden stew-pot? Might we still
negotiate?

My dear *rumpled-sheets,*
house-on-stilts, donkey-skin:
I would have written sooner,
had I the flour and fat

to make the words. Yesterday
it rained the primordial
roux, the A C G U proteins,
base of the mother sauce,

two consonants, two vowels—
tin and gut, metal
and mineral in the volcanic
vent of mouth. Yesterday

we met at that dressing room
entrance. I was seeking
a shirt for his funeral and you
were smirking at my deflated

belly: *you're pregnant!*
You caught me with a handful
of maternity shirts
struggling to find something

that would fit: *no, not*
pregnant. What is the name
for what I am now—full
of the vast gaps

between the smallest
spaces, the pinky's width
between two slabs
of granite meeting up

at the sea? Remember
how we met
at that animal sanctuary, among
caged rabbits, kenneled dogs?

You were minding falcons,
dwarfed by their tall
netted towers. My offering—
a fledgling, found half-hairless

and fly-swarmed.
Yet it lived.
My dear rock-spawn, rootresident,
underground-ether—

did you want more
than an ordinary starling?

- An **epithalamium** is written on the occasion of a wedding with the
intention of honouring the bride and bridegroom. Writing a poem
for the occasion of a royal wedding is one responsibility of the Poet
Laureate of the United Kingdom; writing a poem for a friend's
marriage might be a good project for any poet.

- A **pastoral** is a poem about the countryside and country living.
Traditionally, it focused on the tranquillity of forests and farmland.
Jennifer Chang's modern version puts a new spin on the old theme.

Pastoral
by Jennifer Chang

Something in the field is
working away. Root-noise.
Twig-noise. Plant
of weak chlorophyll, no
name for it. Something

in the field has mastered
distance by living too close
to fences. Yellow fruit, has it
pit or seeds? Stalk of wither. Grass-
noise fighting weed-noise. Dirt
and chant. Something in the
field. Coreopsis. I did not mean
to say that. Yellow petal, has it
wither-gift? Has it gorgeous
rash? Leaf-loss and worried
sprout, its bursting art. Something in the. Field fallowed and
cicada. I did not mean to
say. Has it roar and bloom?
Has it road and follow? A thistle
prick, fraught burrs, such
easy attachment. Stem-
and stamen-noise. Can I lime-
flower? Can I chamomile?
Something in the field cannot.

- An **ars poetica** poem is about the art of poetry or poetics. It seems
inevitable that poets embody their thoughts about the nature
of poetry in poems. The Latin term ars poetica—literally "the
art of poetry"—comes to us from the Roman lyric poet Horace
(65 BCE–8 BCE), whose treatise on the subject was written about
20 BCE. Ars poetica poems can be quite oblique in their treatment
of the subject, offering a metaphor for poetic creation or craft
rather than an argument or discussion.

Elements of Style
by Pauline Uchmanowicz

What if poets had to pick? The ocean or the stars.
A reputation in truth telling or a prize in diplomacy?

Seabed or zodiac. Water or fire. Density or infinity.
There's travel by Chinese junk with shipwreck

Or space capsule disaster. Commerce or exploration.
Marine biologist or aeronautic engineer.

Dictating rhyme, form and meter it's either
Waves as repetition or constellations as pattern,

Tide and undertow or equinox and quasar.
Cardinal points and horizons stay in joint custody

And every bard gets clarinets, trees and the rigadoon.
Also Spanish butterflies, mountains and Dutch windmills.

USING FORCED-INSPIRATION EXERCISES

Workshop leaders often like to begin a course with some forced-inspiration
exercises. Free writing, journaling, and composing "scratch" poems in class
are also popular workshop activities. Each chapter of this book contains at
least one forced-inspiration exercise. These exercises are intended to allow us
to practice writing poems and to conquer the phantom disease of writer's block.
Surprisingly often, forced-inspiration exercises can evolve to complete and
satisfying poems, just as practising scales can suggest an interesting melody
to a songwriter or composer.

BORROWING NON-LITERARY FORMS:
THE "HERMIT-CRAB POEM"

Hermit crabs are the seagoing equivalent of urban squatters. They're marine
animals that occupy the empty shells of deceased snails and use them as rent-
free accommodation. You'll see their little crab claws poking out of shells as
they scuttle along the sea-floor.

Like hermit crabs squatting in the shells of other creatures, poets borrow
structures from documents that aren't even remotely related to poetry. You
could, for example, write a "**hermit-crab poem**" by borrowing the structure of
a restaurant menu, with your stanzas grouped under headings such as "appe-
tizers," "entrées," and "desserts." Directions for assembling an appliance or
a guide to the levels of a video game might also work well. Have a browse
around the guidebooks and manuals in a used book store and see what you
can come up with. Modify headings to suit the subject of your poem, and
borrow the overall structure as an organizational principle for your stanzas
and cantos. The hermit-crab method can be inspiring, and it can also be fun
for you and your readers.

We've all responded to multiple-choice quizzes in school; in "First Love:
A Quiz," that structure makes a surprisingly effective stanza form—and a
strikingly original way of retelling the classical myth of Persephone and Hades.

First Love: A Quiz
by A.E. Stallings

He came up to me:
    a. in his souped-up Camaro
    b. to talk to my skinny best friend
    c. and bumped my glass of wine so I wore the ferrous stain
       on my sleeve
    d. from the ground, in a lead chariot drawn by a team of
       stallions black as crude oil and breathing sulfur; at his
       heart, he sported a tiny golden arrow.

He offered me:
    a. a ride
    b. dinner and a movie, with a wink at the cliché
    c. an excuse not to go back alone to the apartment with its
       sink of dirty knives
    d. a narcissus with a hundred dazzling petals that breathed a
       sweetness as cloying as decay.

I went with him because:
    a. even his friends told me to beware
    b. I had nothing to lose except my virginity
    c. he placed his hand in the small of my back and I felt the
       tread of honeybees
    d. he was my uncle, the one who lived in the half-finished
       basement, and he took me by the hair

The place he took me to:
    a. was dark as my shut eyes
    b. and where I ate bitter seed and became ripe
    c. and from which my mother would never take me wholly
       back, though she wept and walked the earth and made
       the bearded ears of barley wither on their stalks and the
       blasted flowers drop from their sepals
    d. is called by some men hell and others love
    e. all of the above

EXERCISES

Exercise 1/1: Rhetorical-Question Poem

Poems written in this form begin with a rhetorical question. The question may be anywhere from self-reflective and serious ("What right do I have to say this?") to surrealistic and absurd ("What show tunes are the penguins remembering?"). Sometimes, a rhetorical-question poem will consist entirely of a list of rhetorical questions. Start your poem with an interesting rhetorical question, and then build an argument around an attempt to answer the question.

Exercise 1/2: "Hermit-Crab Poem"

Make a poem using the format of a document that's not considered "literary": a restaurant menu, for example, or an advertising brochure, instruction sheet, technical manual, or form letter.

Exercise 1/3: Epistle

An epistle is a poem in the form of a message sent from one person to another. Think of the poem as a letter (or a telegram or an email message). You could begin this exercise by writing a thoughtful (or funny) letter to a friend. You might also consider writing to someone whom you don't know—a public figure, perhaps, or a deceased relative or a fictional character. Begin your poem with a salutation and work your way to a variation on a standard letter closing. When you've roughed out your poem, try to adapt it to an electronic format such as email or Facebook chat.

Exercise 1/4: Ekphrastic Poem

Write a poem that describes a work of visual art such as a painting, photograph, piece of sculpture, or even a display ad. If the visual art depicts a person (or even an animal or mythological creature), you might consider writing a persona poem from the point of view of the figure in the picture.

Exercise 1/5: "The Exquisite Corpse"

"The **Exquisite Corpse**" was one of a number of forced-inspiration exercises invented by the French surrealist poets in the 1920s. Influenced by the writing of Sigmund Freud and C.G. Jung, the surrealists were passionately interesting in exploring the unconscious mind. The mind, they believed, could be divided into the conscious and unconscious, and the creative impulses came from the depths of the unconscious, which was irrational, elemental, and (perhaps) universal. These impulses had to make their way "through" the barrier of the conscious mind, which was thought to be logical, rationalistic, and limited. To encourage this process, they devised several games that were intended to provide them with the means for bypassing the conscious mind and working directly from the unconscious. These games often involved the introduction of an element of chance into the creative process. Visual artists, for example, would spray or throw paint onto canvas, while composers would allow their musicians to improvise or would introduce the random noise of industrial machinery into their music. Poets experimented with automatic writing (a technique formerly associated with trance mediums), cutting up poems and reassembling their language at random, and writing poems in groups. The Exquisite Corpse is a group poem, a collaborative exercise. Here's how it works:

1. One member of the group writes two lines of poetry on a sheet of paper. The lines might, for example, tell us something about the weather at that moment. Or they might reveal a secret. Or they might tell us something the poet loves or hates.
2. Having written his or her two lines, the first poet folds the page so that only one line is visible. Then he or she hands the poem to the second group member. This second poet writes two more lines, folds the page so only the last line written is visible, and passes it on again.
3. Poet 3 does the same as Poet 2, and so on. When the poem has been around the table, so to speak, it is unfolded and read.

The name for this exercise came from the first example the surrealists produced, by the way: when they unfolded the page, the first two lines were (roughly translated from the French), "The exquisite corpse drank the young wine."

"The Exquisite Corpse" lends itself well to electronic collaborations: write your two lines, then send the second line by texting or messaging to the next poet. Poet 2 should then add two lines and send only his or her second line to Poet 3. When all the poets have contributed as often as the group wishes, you can all distribute *all* the lines or post them and collate the final poem.

TAKEAWAY

- Practising poets can't waste time waiting for inspiration. They have to go out and find the material for their poems.
- Ideas and images for poems can come from memory, research, reading, or other creative arts (e.g., music, photographs, sculptures, or paintings).
- Restricting your sources of subject matter to your own perceptions and emotions can be limiting: it's hard to keep mining your own psyche for material. Becoming a productive poet often involves becoming a skilled and dedicated researcher.
- Reinventing traditional themes can provide inspiration for new poems.
- Forced-inspiration exercises can be a useful way of getting the creative juices flowing.

TERMS TO REMEMBER

- ars poetica
- aubade
- blason
- carpe diem
- ekphrastic poems
- elegy

- epistle
- epithalamium (or epithalamion)
- "Exquisite Corpse"
- "hermit-crab poem"
- pastoral

CHAPTER TWO

Genre, Form, and Structure

*A poem is a verbal artifact which must be as skillfully
and solidly constructed as a table or a motorcycle.*[1]
—W.H. Auden

In order to participate in a poetry workshop or to exchange ideas with editors, we need a common vocabulary and a shared set of basic concepts. Learning the common types of poetry is a good way to start building that lexicon. First, poetry has been divided into subgenres according to various rationales, some more useful than others. We'll begin this chapter by looking at the most basic "big" categories. Second, poems are often classified according to their form. Third, every poem embodies at least one rhetorical mode; understanding that concept can be surprisingly useful in helping us to clarify the structure of our poems.

THE GENRES OF POETRY

Traditionally, poems have been classified in terms of three broad categories: the lyric, the epic, and the dramatic. A lyric was originally a short songlike poem on a personal subject. An epic concerned large historical events, often the deeds of a culture's hero or heroine. A dramatic poem, as the name implies, was spoken by one or more characters or personae and might dramatize historical events or episodes from everyday life. The lyric embodied the intimate, private voice while the epic focused on the public voice, the historical perspective of a community. The dramatic poem combined the two by presenting the personal voice in public space, the interactions of individuals immersed in society and history.

Knowing which genre suits your material and your vision can save you a great deal of frustration: trying to cram a political speech or a complicated story into a lyric poem probably wouldn't be an enjoyable experience. Most poets begin their work in the genre by writing lyrics, and it's the lyric form that we'll be spending most of our time on here.

---

1 W.H. Auden, "The Poetry of Andrei Voznesensky," *The New York Review of Books*, April 14, 1966, http://www.nybooks.com/articles/1966/04/14/the-poetry-of-andrei -voznesensky/.

Lyric

The tradition of **lyric poetry** dates from the seventh century BCE and (in the Western tradition at least) originated in the Greek islands. The lyric has been adapted to various fixed forms, including the sonnet, villanelle, and canzone, though modern lyrics are usually written in free verse.

Originally, lyric poems may have been intended to be sung or recited to music. We can imagine the lyric poets of ancient Greece playing or being accompanied by a musician playing the cithara or lyre, a stringed instrument that's one of the ancestors of the guitar. The term "lyric" is commonly used today to refer to the words of a song, but for our purposes, it refers to any short poem—say about fifty lines or fewer, which is roughly what a conventionally designed book or magazine might accommodate on a page or two.

Lyric poets of ancient Greece such as Sappho, Alcaeus, and Anacreon were monodists (solo singers): their poems represent one person's voice speaking to a silent or offstage auditor or to an audience of anonymous listeners. Other poets of the time wrote choral lyrics, in which two or more voices intertwine within the poem. The poetry of Sappho, Alcaeus, and Anacreon seems to have been composed for friends, associates, or patrons and generally centres on topics of interest to all or most people—love, friendship, family, religion and mythology, the conflicts and issues of their time and place. Their poems deal with the personal and everyday, though they could also address the newsworthy events of the moment from a personal perspective. Most modern lyrics, whether written in traditional verse or free verse, also focus on the personal and private rather than attempting to represent the voice of the public or a broad historical perspective. That said, the lyric mode embraces many ways of speaking and occasions for speech. A lyric may be an apostrophe, a **prayer**, a **chant** or **litany**, a **confession**, an **ode**, a satire, an **elegy**, and even a dialogue or conversation. More exotic applications of the lyric include the spell, the curse, the riddle, and the joke.

The lyric, then, is a flexible genre that can accomplish many different tasks. What the lyric *can't* do is address large metaphysical or historical themes in a direct narrative or expository manner. Such themes require a roomier form such as the verse drama or the epic (or, of course, the novel). There are, predictably, exceptions to this rule: W.B. Yeats's "The Second Coming" addresses a theme—the cycles of history—that would be hard to manage even in an epic, but Yeats pulls it off in fourteen lines. Such examples are very, very rare, however, and most poets would be wise to limit their lyric writing to more manageable subjects. The essence of the lyric is that it reveals the universal through the particular, and consequently most lyric poems foreground the specific details of our lives, our dreams, and our environment.

The flexibility of the lyric form is difficult to overestimate. The subject matter can be realistic, drawn from everyday events, but it can just as easily be surreal or imaginary. As they're often personal in terms of subject matter, lyric poems frequently make use of an informal, conversational voice. They usually employ conversational language, though some of the better lyric poets are adept at varying lexical registers within a poem. This preference for the "language of the street" echoes, however distantly, the language choices of Sappho, Alcaeus, Anacreon, and other early lyric poets, who wrote in their own dialect—Aeolian Greek in the cases of Sappho and Alcaeus.

Modern lyric poets usually prefer the concrete to the abstract and emphasize image rather than rhetoric—"No ideas but in things," as William Carlos Williams put it.[2] The lyric, then, is a form that suits meditation, confession, seduction, or simple observation, but that doesn't suit epic ambitions, political rants, complex debates, or complicated narratives. If you're trying to accomplish one of the tasks on that list, you might be wise to consider a different form and genre.

Epic

The traditional epic originated in preliterate cultures and featured some technical requirements that served as aids to memory. Epics began with an invocation to the Muse or some other embodiment of poetic inspiration. They often included epithets (stock phrases such as Homer's famous "rosy-fingered dawn") and grand catalogues such as the list of ships in the *Iliad*. **Epic poetry** has largely been replaced by the novel, and most contemporary long poems are lyric suites or collages rather than epics. We'll explore that genre in a later chapter.

Dramatic

Although Sappho and her contemporaries were monodists, the choral tradition existed in classical Greek literature and has also survived into modern times. Matthew Arnold's "Empedocles on Etna" is representative of the nineteenth-century vogue for **dramatic poetry**. It includes speeches by various characters and combines the attributes and mechanics of a poem and stage play. The poem begins with a prose description of the setting and then leads into a dialogue. The following brief excerpt should give you a sense of the general format. Note that the format of the poem closely resembles that of a stage play, with each character's speeches tagged with his or her name.

---

2 William Carlos Williams, *Paterson*, revised ed. (New York: New Directions Books, 1992), 6.

Excerpt from *"Empedocles on Etna"*
by Matthew Arnold

SCENE II
Noon. A Glen on the highest skirts
of the woody region of Etna
EMPEDOCLES — PAUSANIAS

PAUSANIAS

The noon is hot; when we have crossed the stream,
We shall have left the woody tract, and come
Upon the open shoulder of the hill.
See how the giant spires of yellow bloom
Of the sun-loving gentian, in the heat,
Are shining on those naked slopes like flame!
Let us rest here; and now, Empedocles,
Pantheia's history.
[A harp-note below is heard.

EMPEDOCLES

Hark! what sound was that
Rose from below? If it were possible,
And we were not so far from human haunt,
I should have said that some one touched a harp.
Hark! there again!

PAUSANIAS

'Tis the boy Callicles,
The sweetest harp-player in Cantana,
He is for ever coming on these hills,
In summer, to all country-festivals,
With a gay revelling band; he breaks from them
Sometimes, and wanders far among the glens.
But heed him not, he will not mount to us;
I spoke with him this morning. Once more, therefore,
Instruct me of Pantheia's story, Master,
As I have prayed thee.

Although the lyric, epic, and dramatic are the major genres of poetry, there are also a few categories that refer more to subject than to form and structure. **Fantasy poetry** is popular with readers of the various subgenres of fantasy or magic realist fiction; fantasy poems are often composed in fixed forms or ballad stanzas and sometimes mimic the style of the nineteenth-century Romantics or Pre-Raphaelites. **Cowboy poetry** resurrects the narrative ballad and—as the name suggests—attempts to evoke the atmosphere of the Old West. **Light verse** is just that: poetry that tries to entertain, often with epigrammatic and witty turns of phrase. Poems that address topical subjects—the "hot button" newspaper stories of the moment—are termed **occasional verse**. Both light verse and occasional verse are (perhaps sadly) out of favour these days, as most lyric poets focus on the personal and private experience and don't see themselves as entertainers or editorialists. A **devotional poem** grows out of the poet's sense of the spiritual and may take the form of a meditation or prayer.

The most durable and widely read subgenre of contemporary poetry is, of course, **children's verse**. Kids delight in the music of language and like to play with words. Some toddlers will happily sing or shout the same syllables over and over again, to the chagrin of any adults within earshot. Poems written for children foreground the sounds of words, using puns, wild alliteration, tongue-twisters, and so on. Children's verse often rhymes and is frequently cast in ballad stanzas or couplets. Free-verse poems are common enough in the genre, although they tend to be song like or to emphasize repetition, alliteration, and occasional rhyme. Obviously, any poem for kids has to be appropriate for its audience in terms of diction and syntax: children learn phrasing and pick up vocabulary from the poems they're read. Writing children's verse can be a useful sideline (or even specialty) for poets, as a successful book of poems for kids may find a larger audience than a poetry book for adults.

There are any number of minor subgenres within the wider world of poetry publishing, some as exotic as the scifiku (aka "SciFaiku"), which is poem about a science-fiction-related topic written in an approximation of the traditional haiku form.

FORM

Basic Principles: Rhetorical Strategy, Formal Envelope, Internal Design

Poems are built around a rhetorical strategy or mode of discourse, they're defined by their formal envelope, and they have an internal design. These principles are the "guts" of the poem, and we can enhance the clarity and unity of our poems by becoming more aware of them.

Poems have a formal envelope, a structural principle that defines and describes the overall form of the poem. There are, in terms of form, five types of poetry:

- traditional verse (rhymed metric verse)
- blank verse
- syllabic verse
- free verse
- prose poems

Note that the first four of these possibilities are types of verse poetry; they're written in lines as opposed to prose paragraphs. The vast majority of poems written in English fall into one of the first four categories.

Traditional verse (also known as "**metric verse**" or "formalist poetry") can be loosely defined as verse that has a pattern of end-rhyme and a set metre. Between the late Middle Ages and the twentieth century, most English-language poetry was built around a regular metre and a rhyme scheme. Traditional verse often makes use of fixed forms such as the sonnet or the villanelle.

Blank verse has a regular metre—iambic pentameter—but does not rely on end-rhyme as a patterning principle. While blank verse refers only to unrhymed iambic pentameter, it's useful to think of unrhymed verse in any set metre as a category that's distinct from either rhymed metric verse or free verse. It's surprising how often our "free-verse" poems are actually unrhymed iambic or anapaestic tetrameter or trimeter, and becoming aware of that possibility can give us an insight into how we could refine and develop the poems.

In **syllabic verse**, each line is allotted a set number of syllables, and that constraint, however arbitrary, structures the poem. Traditional Asian verse forms are often syllabic. Syllabic forms work against the importance of stress to English speech patterns and thus tend to "flatten" the natural rhythm of the language. Poets who want to get away from the singsong quality of metric verse are sometimes drawn to the syllabic alternative. Structuring a poem around a syllabic grid doesn't necessarily preclude organizing stresses or even maintaining a strict metre—an eight-syllable line could, for example, consist of four iambs.

You can invent your own syllabic form simply by stipulating a specific number of syllables for each line of a stanza or of the poem as a whole. Writing syllabic poems is an interesting challenge and may present an appealing alternative to traditional stress-related metre or prose rhythm for some poets.

Free verse doesn't rely on either metre or a regular rhyme scheme to determine its form. The important question—and one that's often ignored—is this: How is a free-verse poem structured? That's a complicated issue, and we'll discuss it in detail in a later chapter.

Part of building a successful poem is deciding which form suits the poem best. (It's possible, though less common, to reverse this logic: if we want to write in a particular form, we need to consider what sort of material might fit that form.) Either way, the relationship between content and form should be an important consideration.

We may start the process of composition with a formal strategy already in mind. If we've set out to write in a fixed form such as a haiku or a sonnet, we already know a lot about the structure of the poem. There will, inevitably, be quite a few things we probably *won't* know right away: a sonnet might consist of end-stopped lines, or it might employ enjambment. If we're smart, we'll also recognize that our preconceptions about the shape and form of the poem we're writing may have to be rethought before we can make the poem work as well as it might. Ideally, we should address the process of composition with some useful ideas about how we might write the poem, but we should also keep an open mind and be sensitive to the poem's potential. Perhaps our formal sonnet will evolve into a free-verse lyric or even a prose poem. It's always useful to think of the process of writing poetry as a dialogue between poet and poem and to listen carefully to whatever our emerging poem is telling us.

STRUCTURE

Although poetry is a strikingly diverse art form, a relatively small number of structural principles apply to a great many poems. Poems begin with the voice, but they also have a shape and form, in the same way that a building or a musical composition has a shape and form. To the artist, a painting—even an abstract painting—is highly formal. Finding the right proportions is as important as choosing the subject, and, in an abstract work, structure may *be* the subject. As soon as we begin to compose our new poem, decisions about form become important, and those decisions shape and define the poem. Looking for potential patterns and developing them into more or less symmetrical structural elements is an important part of the writing process.

There is a difference between form and **significant form**. Any sonnet, obviously, is constructed around a poetic form, but a poem that uses the sonnet structure to develop its theme is employing the form as a means of communication, as a way of signifying: in that poem, the form is significant. Similarly, a free-verse poem in which lines are broken within grammatical units (phrase, clause, sentence) communicates a sense of tension and hesitation, while one in which the lines end when the sentences or phrases end communicates the opposite feeling—a sense of emotional conviction and plain speech. Again, the form of the poem is used to communicate the theme. Some poems are even more obvious in their use of form as meaning: a centre-justified poem communicates a sense of harmony and balance through its symmetrical visual design. (Quite a few beginners make the mistake of centre-justifying every poem they write, whether that symmetrical presentation suits the theme or not.)

Basic Principles: Unity, Symmetry, and Circularity

A lyric poem should have as its central principle unity: one field of imagery, one argument or narrative line, one governing metaphor, one theme. (If we've wandered from that guideline, we're probably working in a more discursive form than the lyric.) Often, our first drafts don't conform well to this principle: we include too much information, too many images that jostle around and don't complement each other, too many ideas. In short, we try to do too much in the draft because we aren't very clear about the purpose or intention of the poem.

It's perfectly normal for a first draft (or even a fourth or fifth draft) to be unsure of its intentions. As long as we're prepared for that eventuality, we can come back to the poem with fresh eyes and look for its core idea and root metaphor. Poets get in trouble by clinging to the first draft: we have to be willing to develop, shape, and polish the part of the poem that actually works and to discard the rest, even if it contains good ideas and interesting moments. The old cliché about "killing your darlings" is often very good advice.

The lack of unity in an early draft isn't always dramatic: sometimes the poem shifts from narrative to descriptive or changes the tone of voice in a way that's awkward or confusing, but doesn't really deviate from its focus on a limited subject. That sort of wobbling around can be an indication that a poem needs to be extended and organized rather than simply pruned down and streamlined. Instead of seeing the poem as a single lyric, then, we may need to be open to the poem's potential for being developed into something longer and more complex. Perhaps we can improve the poem by reconceptualizing it as a lyric suite consisting of several cantos, each of which is focused on a single idea and field of imagery. Too often, beginning poets have a hard time seeing that potential; their concept of a poem doesn't go beyond the lyric form.

Aesthetically successful art is characterized by overall symmetry and balance leavened with a touch of the asymmetrical. The symmetry communicates a sense of order and purpose, while the asymmetrical elements keep the art work from becoming too predictable and lacking in tension and energy.

Most poems are to some degree symmetrical. Some display a high degree of symmetry: a poem written in iambic pentameter quatrains is symmetrical both in terms of stanza form and metre. If the same poem includes a line or phrase that's repeated in each stanza or at the beginning and end of the poem, it's more symmetrical still. Some free-verse poems aren't symmetrical in any obvious way. The stanzas may be irregular, and there might not be any regular metre. There may, however, be some repetition of lines or phrases, or at least of grammatical structures. There may be repeated images. The poem may end with the same image, rhythm, grammatical structure, or idea with which it began. Even a prose poem will often repeat a certain word or phrasing. Relatively few poems, even the most "traditional," are completely symmetrical. Equally few poems, even the most "experimental," are absolutely lacking in symmetry.

Symmetry is an important tool in creating lyric poems, but too much symmetry implies a lack of tension and invention: nothing is more mind-dulling than a cut-and-dried verse structure or a phrasing that repeats absolutely predictably throughout a poem. We need to establish a balance between the symmetrical and the asymmetrical: there is beauty in perfection, but there is more beauty in perfection with a touch of the paradoxical and contradictory.

Thinking about symmetry can help you to build your rough draft into a complete and successful poem. Look for hints of symmetry and consider developing those possibilities more broadly throughout the poem. Work toward a balance of symmetry and asymmetry.

Quite a few successful poems are *circular*: they end where they began. The villanelle, the pantoum, and the sonnet crown are traditional forms that lend themselves to this approach. The folk song or pop song is another form that is often circular, ending with the repetition of a chorus or refrain. One way of finding an effective resolution for your poem is to consider how the poem began. Ending the poem where it began may provide a natural sense of completion and resolution. Circularity doesn't have to be limited to simple repetition; the end of the poem can recast the ideas or phrasing of the beginning in a way that's ironic or revelatory—that note of asymmetry within the symmetrical is often the key to an effective resolution. Jericho Brown's memorial poem "Tradition" begins and ends with a list.

The Tradition
by Jericho Brown

Aster. Nasturtium. Delphinium. We thought
Fingers in dirt meant it was our dirt, learning
Names in heat, in elements classical
Philosophers said could change us. *Star Gazer.*
Foxglove. Summer seemed to bloom against the will
Of the sun, which news reports claimed flamed hotter
On this planet than when our dead fathers

Wiped sweat from their necks. *Cosmos. Baby's Breath.*
Men like me and my brothers filmed what we
Planted for proof we existed before
Too late, sped the video to see blossoms
Brought in seconds, colors you expect in poems
Where the world ends, everything cut down.
John Crawford. Eric Garner. Mike Brown.

When you're writing or revising the end of the poem, go back and consider what you did in the first few lines: you may discover that the poem has wandered from its original premise or that you haven't resolved the narrative or argument that you set out to develop. You may also notice possibilities for repeating or inverting the opening in the resolution. It's always worth a try.

RHETORICAL MODES

Most poems are structured around a particular mode of discourse: rhetoric, narrative, or description, though many poems take us from one of those modes to another in a carefully orchestrated manner.

Rhetoric is argument or explanation: the poet states a theory and then tries to demonstrate or "prove" its validity and truth. We're all familiar with that strategy from writing essays: the structure of an expository essay takes us from thesis to proof, and a poem can accomplish the same task. One common way to structure a poem is to begin with exposition, stating a problem or theory, and then to conclude with a resolution that offers a proof of the thesis or a solution to the conundrum. The Petrarchan (Italian) sonnet, for example, presents a problem or theory in the octave and a resolution in the sestet, while the English sonnet presents the problem or theory at the beginning and wraps up the resolution in a final epigrammatic couplet. Shakespeare's "Sonnet LV" achieves this effect by starting with a clear statement of a theory—that the poem, his "powerful rhyme," will outlast marble and the "the gilded monuments / Of princes." In the subsequent lines, he elaborates on that idea by suggesting that his auditor will achieve immortality through having been the subject of the poem. The sonnet ends with a kicker in the final couplet, affirming the auditor's immortality through art. Until the Judgment Day (a Christian concept referring to the judgment of humankind by God), the subject will live on in the poem ("in this"): "So, till the judgment that yourself arise, / You live in this, and dwell in lovers' eyes." It's a neat little essay in verse, an argument effectively backed up with poetic imagery rather than scholarly research.

Sonnet LV
by William Shakespeare (1564–1616)

Not marble, nor the gilded monuments
Of princes, shall outlive this powerful rhyme;
But you shall shine more bright in these contents
Than unswept stone, besmeared with sluttish time.
When wasteful war shall statues overturn,
And broils root out the work of masonry,
Nor Mars his sword, nor war's quick fire, shall burn
The living record of your memory:
'Gainst death, and all oblivious enmity,
Shall you pace forth; your praise shall still find room
Even in the eyes of all posterity
That wear this world out to the ending doom.
So, till the judgement that yourself arise,
You live in this, and dwell in lovers' eyes.

Some modern free-verse lyrics are also structured around an argument. We
have to remember, though, that the "thesis" of a poem can be whimsical,
gnomic, or surreal, and the logical structure doesn't preclude an analogical
approach to the material. Here's a poem that starts with a theory—"It's hard to
improve on the poetry of a bus"—and uses that apparently whimsical statement
to explore an important aspect of poetics, the relation of content to form. Note
that the poem works its way to a resolution that restates the thesis—another
example of an essentially circular structure.

Busman's Honeymoon
by A.F. Moritz

It's hard to improve on the poetry of a bus,
a city bus—whether full of passengers,
friends and strangers, or with no one but the driver,
or empty, dead in the water of lot or barn:

a box with wheels and windows. Empty form
waiting for content. And yet, how form alone
makes a clear statement, although just what it says
is hard to say. Then the driver pulls it out,

it streaks through storm, now flashing Not In Service
from its radiant forehead, polluted and obscured
by splattered mud, till it can reach its station

and help to ease the overflow of us
waiting in anger. Then we all barge in
and improbably improve the poetry of the bus.

Narrative is storytelling. The structure of narrative is chronological; the events related in the story occur in time and can be arranged on a timeline. These events may not be related in the order in which they occur, but we could, if we wished to, relate them to a straightforward linear chronology.

Narrative poems have always been popular, though the topic and scope of the narratives we write and read are subject to the fashions of the day. The two traditional forms that rely most heavily on narrative are the epic and the ballad. Epic poems, as we've learned, are rare these days, but the ballad is a hardy perennial. In the nineteenth century, ballads were in vogue in the work of poets such as Wordsworth and Coleridge. Today, the ballad belongs for the most part to the world of popular song and enjoys a popularity that eludes most poetry for the page. As far as modern print verse is concerned, the most vital narrative form is the lyric poem constructed around the recounting of a brief and often personal occurrence. These lyrics are sometimes called new narrative poems. While the epic poem told us stories about public figures and historical events, the "new narrative" lyric focuses on events from ordinary lives. Quite a few contemporary lyric poets specialize in "new narrative," building short poems around brief stories, usually about everyday events. Lyrics are short and unified, so the story has to be a simple one in terms of the number of characters and events. Often, we're just told about a single character (the narrator, for example) performing some simple act or witnessing some ordinary event.

Henry James famously said, "Tell a dream, lose a reader," but he was offering advice to fiction writers, not to poets. **Dream narratives** are common in poetry. Dream narratives—sometimes called **metaphysical narratives**—depend heavily on (often surreal) imagery, and they invite us to interpret the imagery just as a Freudian or Jungian psychologist might interpret a dream. James Pollock's "The Museum of Death" has the dreamlike quality of a magic realist painting.

The Museum of Death
by James Pollock

In the Museum of Death the guests are eating lunch
made from a dead man's recipe.
They use knives and forks invented by the dead.

Everyone sits in a room
built by those who are no longer with us,
everyone speaking words the dead have made.

Everything is archaeological:
prayer, toilets, table manners, cash.
Even the air was once breathed by the dead.

Look how impatiently the curator taps
his fingers on his desk. It's getting late.
Very soon the guests will have to go.

Good poems almost invariably include interesting imagery. Any draft that
doesn't include some descriptive imagery should be eyed with suspicion. Unless
it's a brief epigram or a found poem, a poem without imagery is almost certainly
a mistake. Some poems may seem to be nothing but image; they're structured
around a **description**. The narration of a purely descriptive poem tends to be
third person, and the voice is objective, as if the narrator were a camera rather
than a thinking, evaluating subject.

While the structure of narrative is temporal, description is spatial. Like
musical compositions, narrative poems unfold in time; they are **diachronic**
(changing through time). Purely descriptive poems, conversely, tend to be
painterly, offering the reader a single motionless image; they are, like paintings, **synchronic** (existing at a single time). Even in the shortest descriptive
poem, however, there's a tension between the poet's desire to present a picture
and the reader's need to process language one word or phrase at a time. We
can see this tension in some haiku, in which the first two lines may present a
static image while the third line shifts into commentary or presents a slightly
different perspective.

Though lyric poems typically foreground one of the three modes, it's common for a poem to include more than one. Poets often shift modes near the
end of a poem in order to achieve a resolution. A "new narrative" poem might
end with a static image, or a descriptive poem might shift into rhetoric as the

poet comments on the subject of the description. Garret Hongo's "The Legend" moves through all three rhetorical modes: the poem begins with a description (stanza 1); then it moves into a brief narrative (stanzas 2 and 3); finally, it shifts into rhetoric as the narrator struggles to understand and come to terms with the events we've just witnessed. There's even a shift within that final stanza from the declarative ("I feel so distinct . . . I am ashamed") to the imperative ("Let the night sky cover him") as the poem resolves on a poetic prayer. Hongo's expert orchestration of modes draws us into the world of the poem, tells an important story within that world, and then expands the field of reference to include the poet-narrator's perceptions, finally bringing us to a thoughtful resolution. Notice, by the way, that he references a painter (Rembrandt) in the descriptive passage and a philosopher (Descartes) in the stanza that leans heavily on rhetoric.

The Legend
by Garrett Hongo

In Chicago, it is snowing softly
and a man has just done his wash for the week.
He steps into the twilight of early evening,
carrying a wrinkled shopping bag
full of neatly folded clothes,
and, for a moment, enjoys
the feel of warm laundry and crinkled paper,
flannellike against his gloveless hands.
There's a Rembrandt glow on his face,
a triangle of orange in the hollow of his cheek
as a last flash of sunset
blazes the storefronts and lit windows of the street.

He is Asian, Thai or Vietnamese,
and very skinny, dressed as one of the poor
in rumpled suit pants and a plaid mackinaw,
dingy and too large.
He negotiates the slick of ice
on the sidewalk by his car,
opens the Fairlane's back door,
leans to place the laundry in,
and turns, for an instant,
toward the flurry of footsteps
and cries of pedestrians

as a boy—that's all he was—
backs from the corner package store
shooting a pistol, firing it,
once, at the dumbfounded man
who falls forward,
grabbing at his chest.

A few sounds escape from his mouth,
a babbling no one understands
as people surround him
bewildered at his speech.
The noises he makes are nothing to them.
The boy has gone, lost
in the light array of foot traffic
dappling the snow with fresh prints.

Tonight, I read about Descartes'
grand courage to doubt everything
except his own miraculous existence
and I feel so distinct
from the wounded man lying on the concrete
I am ashamed

Let the night sky cover him as he dies.
Let the weaver girl cross the bridge of heaven
and take up his cold hands.

When you've written a draft of a new poem, ask yourself whether the central principle behind your poem is narrative, rhetoric, or description. Then ask yourself whether you've remained in that mode throughout the poem or shifted modes at some point. It's not a mistake to change modes, but you should do so for a reason, and you should consider how you could make the transitions between modes clear to your readers—often, as in "The Legend," a stanza break will do the job. Analyzing your draft poem in terms of its constituent rhetorical modes is one good way of gaining insights that can help you develop and improve the poem. You might, for example, note that your stichic (one long stanza) poem shifts from rhetoric to description and back, and that insight might suggest that the poem would work better if it were divided into stanzas or even separate cantos so that the reader could navigate the shifts in mode more easily. You might also consider whether a shift in mode—from narrative to description, perhaps—might be a good way of creating a resolution.

EXERCISES

Exercise 2/1: Simple Act Narrative

Write a brief passage of prose narrative, perhaps a paragraph or two, recounting some action and describing the scene in which the action unfolds (as much as you feel is necessary). The action should be brief and simple. Casting a fly rod, riding a horse or a bicycle, falling asleep, skydiving, walking through a forest, or cooking a meal might be examples of narratives you could write from a first-person point of view. Third-person narratives might include a child playing, salmon moving up a spawning stream, dancers performing, athletes playing a game, or an old person walking down a street. Remember, the action you describe doesn't have to be dramatic or obviously "poetic" in order to be made into a suitable subject for a poem: the poetry comes from the poet's perception, not from the nature of the scene. When you've written your prose piece, begin to rework the material into a poem. Keep in mind that there is more to poetry than words arranged in lines of verse. What needs to be done to make the piece a successful poem? Try moving from particular images to more general ideas, or structure your narrative around some central image or images that can give your poem a metaphoric or symbolic dimension. Keep in mind the basic principles of unity, symmetry, and circularity. You may decide to deviate from those guidelines, but thinking about them should give you an opportunity to reflect on the structure and theme of your poem.

Exercise 2/2: Theory and Resolution

Write a short poem that states a theory and then provides a resolution. Limit yourself to a set number of lines: a sonnet accomplishes the thesis to resolution arc in fourteen lines, and your poem shouldn't have to be much longer. You may have a theory in mind, but if not try one of these options:

1. Have you ever wondered why so many couples break up? If you have a theory about that conundrum, start your poem by stating your theory and develop it by offering evidence.

2. Quite a few poets have written a poem about the nature of poetry—the ars poetica poem. Consider what makes a good poem (or a good song, or a good dance routine, or a good friend, or a good lover) and expand on your theory in a poem.

3. Why is being young better than being old? Okay, maybe being old is better. Decide which side of the fence you're on, and write a poem that begins with a statement of your position on the issue.

Then offer some evidence *in concrete images* and bring your poem to a simple resolution.

4. Why do you write? Start your poem with an answer—serious or imaginative—to that question, or build the poem around a list of possible answers.

5. What's your favourite animal? What factors make that particular critter so fabulous? (You could substitute a particular breed of horse, brand of guitar or shoes or car or motorbike and explain why it's better than its competitors.)

Exercise 2/3: Q&A Poem

Write a short poem in question-and-answer format. Ask a question in stanza one, and then answer it in the next stanza. Continue the question-and-answer format throughout the poem. Consider whether headings for the speeches would be appropriate.

Exercise 2/4: Romantic Love Tweet

Write a love poem in less than 140 characters, suitable for tweeting through your Twitter account. Use abbreviations, numerals, Internet slang, pop-culture references, and Internet memes as required. Try to embrace the possibilities of the medium as well as cope with its inherent limitations—in fact, try to use the limitations as a stimulus to doing something cool and original.

Exercise 2/5: Headline Poem

Tabloid newspapers have provided civilization with some of the weirdest and most entertaining found poetry since Gutenberg was a paperboy. Scope out the headlines on a few of the tabs next time you're waiting in line at the supermarket, and see if you can find yourself a title for a poem. Don't be afraid to fudge on the truth—enhancing reality (or lying outright) is certainly in the fine old tradition of tabloid journalism. When you've hit on your title (and been thrown out of the supermarket for giggling uncontrollably), write a short lyric poem to go with it.

Alternate Strategy: Gamer Fantasy Poem

Write a lyric poem about (or from the point of view of) a favourite character or place from a video game. Tell a story about the character or simply paint a portrait.

TAKEAWAY

- Poems can be classified into three major genres: lyric, epic, or dramatic. As well, some poems fall into a subcategory that relates to their subject matter or intended audience.
- The form of a poem is significant; it communicates meaning.
- Poetry, like most art, is unified and focused.
- Poems usually display a high degree of formal symmetry.
- Poems are often circular.
- Poems are structured around one of five forms: metric verse, blank verse (or unrhymed verse in any regular metre), syllabic verse, free verse, or prose.
- Most poems are constructed around one of three rhetorical modes: argument (rhetoric), narrative, or description. Many poems combine two or more of these modes.
- Shifting between modes near the end of a poem is one effective way of creating a sense of resolution.

TERMS TO REMEMBER

- blank verse
- chant
- children's verse
- confession
- cowboy poetry
- description
- devotional poem
- diachronic
- dramatic poetry
- dream narratives
- elegy
- epic poetry
- fantasy poetry
- free verse
- light verse
- litany
- lyric poetry
- metaphysical narratives
- metric verse / traditional verse
- narrative
- new narrative
- occasional verse
- ode
- prayer
- rhetoric
- significant form
- syllabic verse
- synchronic

CHAPTER THREE

"Telling the Poem"—Some Options for Narration

THE MASK OF THE POET

A poem is a voice. The voice can be intimate, whispering secrets into our ear, or it can be public, the voice of an orator thundering from a podium. Poetry affords us the opportunity to speak in as many voices as there are human personalities, moods, relationships, and intentions. Think of all the occasions you have to speak to another person. Consider the role you adopt for each of those speech acts. You may be the sage advisor, the tempter, the mourner, the jilted lover, the witty raconteur, or the questioning child. Then imagine that you're an actor who is consciously performing a role, pretending to be someone you're not—a medieval peasant, perhaps, or an alchemist or a mythical beast or character from a cartoon or TV show.

The simplest narrative convention is the **first-person monologue**, in which the voice of the poem purports to be that of the poet. Poetry is a genre with roots in the preliterate (i.e., oral) past of the culture, and the idea of the poem being spoken and listened to rather than written and read is a natural one.[1]

For the poem to be spoken in the voice of the poet is both a time-honoured technique and a very modern one. Epics such as *Paradise Lost* often began with an invocation that, though it was addressed to the poet's Muse, was ostensibly spoken by the poet him- or herself:

> I thence
> Invoke thy aid to my adventrous Song
> That with no middle flight intends to soar
> Above th' *Aonian* Mount, while it pursues
> Things unattempted yet in Prose or Rhime.
> (*Paradise Lost*, bk. 1, lines 12–16)

---

1 Susanne Langer notes that "Speech in the first person [. . .] may be found in ballads, novels, and essays; but there it is a deviation from the usual pattern, and in the lyric it is normal." See Langer, *Feeling and Form* (New York: Charles Scribner's Sons, 1953), 258.

Here the voice of the poem seems to be that of the poet, John Milton. This is Milton in a formal role: he doubtless used a different tone when he was chatting with his neighbours in London, and in fact he varied his approach from poem to poem. For the invocation quoted above, he conjured up a voice that suited the occasion: the traditional epic required that the poet address the Muse, and you weren't expected to speak to the personification of poetic inspiration in quite the same voice that you used to ask for parsnips from your greengrocer. It's often—possibly *always*—a mistake to equate the voice of a poem with the personality of the poet. We poets are great liars, though we like to think that our falsehoods reveal a greater truth. Ultimately, the idea of the poet speaking to the reader through the poem is simply a literary convention; the voice that declaims the lines from some metaphoric hillside or whispers them softly in our ear is not really that of the poet but rather that of a fictional character, the mask of the poet that the real poet has chosen to wear for the occasion. Being aware that we need to *create* an appropriate voice can clarify the way we choose to narrate and structure our poem.

For traditional poets, the mask of the poet may be formal, a ceremonial robe in which the writer drapes him- or herself as a matter of course, choosing the colour and style of the robe in accordance with the form of the poem: one mask for the epic, another for the pastoral poem, still another for the love lyric, and so forth. For more modern writers, the poetic persona or mask may be chosen for one particular poem or set of poems and then discarded, but it may also be coextensive with the poet's career and the entire body of his or her work. One of the more interesting schools of modern poetry is the group of American writers sometimes known as the neo-metaphysical or "confessional" poets. The voice of the writer of a **confessional poem** is (or purports to be), as the sobriquet implies, that of the poet in emotional or spiritual *extremis*; even in this instance, however, it's important to understand that the voice is not simply that of the poet but rather that of a persona the poet has created—a modern "confessional" poet is no more likely to speak to his or her friends in the language he or she uses in a poem than Shakespeare was to have ordered his ale in iambic pentameter. That said, it's also true that some poets consciously develop a consistent poetic persona, and it is this persona that we come to associate with the poet's work. In commercial terms, that persona can function as an exercise in "branding," and it's often effective in helping to establish a poet's career. Other poets vary the voice from one poem to another, and some are "invisible" poets who speak through a variety of masks.

From creating a poetic persona or mask, it's a short step to putting on other masks, those of fictional or historical characters or of inanimate objects, concepts, or animals. Quite a few poems are "spoken" from the point of view of a specific "character" or a representative of a generic type or class. The speaker could be a god or a goddess or, for that matter, Godzilla. He or she could be a medieval princess, a serial killer, a carnival barker, a mythical hero, a movie star, the poet's left foot, an electric toaster, or Bugs Bunny.

Amy Gerstler's "Siren" is a contemporary **persona poem**. The narrator conjures up the voice of a figure from mythology and imagines what she might say if she were both archetypal and unmistakably modern. As Gerstler's poem demonstrates, writing a persona poem requires us to engage our imagination: we have to create the speaker, visualize his or her actions and environment, and also consider what the persona would want to communicate and to whom she or he might be speaking.

Siren
by Amy Gerstler

I have a fish's tail, so I'm not qualified to love you.
But I do. Pale as an August sky, pale as flour milled
a thousand times, pale as the icebergs I have never seen,
and twice as numb—my skin is such a contrast to the rough
rocks I lie on, that from far away it looks like I'm a baby
riding a dinosaur. The turn of centuries or the turn
of a page means the same to me, little or nothing.
I have teeth in places you'd never suspect. Come. Kiss me
and die soon. I slap my tail in the shallows—which is to say
I appreciate nature. You see my sisters and me perched
on rocks and tiny islands here and there for miles:
untangling our hair with our fingers, eating seaweed.

SPEAKER AND AUDITOR

As well as the "voice" who "speaks" the poem, there's another presence in a poem: the listener, the person to whom the poem is delivered. In some poems, the auditor is a specific figure—the confessor, the friend or the enemy, the rival, the beloved. He or she is usually "offstage," and his or her situation is similar to that of the recipient of a letter, text, or email. We may know that the poem is directed to a specific "real" person, but many love poems are simply iterations of a long-standing convention: the poet is working within a traditional genre, one that involves the lover-poet addressing a beloved. Literary scholars have argued for generations over the vexing question of whether the "Dark Lady" and the "Fair Young Man" addressed in Shakespeare's sonnets were real people or simply fictional characters, stock figures conjured up as convenient props for the poems. Most readers, of course, will enjoy the poems without caring if the characters existed in reality or not. The **auditor**, then, may be real or imagined from the poet's perspective, but he or she is a palpable presence in the poem and thus to the reader.

One of the most durable conventions in poetry is the love poem in which a speaker addresses his or her beloved. Elizabeth Barrett Browning's *Sonnets from the Portuguese* is a lengthy sequence of love lyrics; the example below is narrated in the first person (using "I" and "my") and addressed to an auditor identified simply as "Beloved."

> *Sonnets from the Portuguese 44: Beloved, thou hast brought me many flowers*
> by·Elizabeth Barrett Browning (1806–61)
>
> Beloved, thou hast brought me many flowers
> Plucked in the garden, all the summer through
> And winter, and it seemed as if they grew
> In this close room, nor missed the sun and showers,
> So, in the like name of that love of ours,
> Take back these thoughts which here unfolded too,
> And which on warm and cold days I withdrew
> From my heart's ground. Indeed, those beds and bowers
> Be overgrown with bitter weeds and rue,
> And wait thy weeding; yet here's eglantine,
> Here's ivy!—take them, as I used to do
> Thy flowers, and keep them where they shall not pine.
> Instruct thine eyes to keep their colours true,
> And tell thy soul, their roots are left in mine.

If we're familiar with Barrett Browning's biography, we may assume that the auditor of this poem is her husband, the poet Robert Browning, but we don't need to know about that background in order to understand and enjoy the poem. The situation—lover and beloved—is an archetypal one, and the "actors" in the poem are iterations of that archetype.

Sean Thomas Dougherty's "Dear Tiara," like Barrett Browning's sonnet, is a love lyric addressed to a particular auditor. Unlike the earlier poem, his modern lyric names the intended auditor in the title, but the "I" and "you" relationship of narrator and auditor remains the same.

> *Dear Tiara*
> by Sean Thomas Dougherty
>
> I dreamed I was a mannequin in the pawnshop window
>   of your conjectures.

I dreamed I was a chant in the mouth of a monk, saffron-robed
   syllables in the religion of You.

I dreamed I was a lament to hear the deep sorrow places
   of your lungs.

I dreamed I was your bad instincts.

I dreamed I was a hummingbird sipping from the tulip of your ear.

I dreamed I was your ex-boyfriend stored in the basement
   with your old baggage.

I dreamed I was a jukebox where every song sang your name.

I dreamed I was in an elevator, rising in the air shaft
   of your misgivings.

I dreamed I was a library fine, I've checked you out
   too long so many times.

I dreamed you were a lake and I was a little fish leaping
   through the thin reeds of your throaty humming.

I must've dreamed I was a nail, because I woke beside you still
   hammered.

I dreamed I was a tooth to fill the absences of your old age.

I dreamed I was a Christmas cactus, blooming in the desert
   of my stupidity.

I dreamed I was a saint's hair-shirt, sewn with the thread
   of your saliva.

I dreamed I was an All Night Movie Theater, showing the
   flickering black reel of my nights before I met you.

I must've dreamed I was gravity, I've fallen for you so damn hard.

A lyric suite by Edgar Lee Masters, *The Spoon River Anthology*, presents the voices of people who lived in a small town in America and who now lie in the town cemetery. In "Doctor Meyers," we hear the voice of a small-town physician:

> Doctor Meyers
> by Edgar Lee Masters (1868–1950)
>
> No other man, unless it was Doc Hill,
> Did more for people in this town than I.
> And all the weak, the halt, the improvident
> And those who could not pay flocked to me.
> I was good-hearted, easy Doctor Meyers.
> I was healthy, happy, in comfortable fortune,
> Blest with a congenial mate, my children raised,
> All wedded, doing well in the world.
> And then one night, Minerva, the poetess,
> Came to me in her trouble, crying.
> I tried to help her out—she died—
> They indicted me, the newspapers disgraced me,
> My wife perished of a broken heart.
> And pneumonia finished me.

Like Amy Gerstler's siren, the speaker of "Doctor Meyers" is an invented persona, though in his case a realistic character rather than a figure from mythology. Although the speakers in Barrett Browning's sonnet and Dougherty's litany address an individual, Lee Masters's narrator is speaking to anyone and everyone—the people of "this town"—and by extension anyone who can relate to the lives of small-town people. All three poems employ first-person narrators; it's the type of auditor that differs.

Although every poem may not be addressed to a specific auditor, real or imagined, every poem has an **implied auditor**. The implied auditor is the *type* of person whom the speaker of the poem is addressing. That category might include anyone who has been in love, perhaps, or anyone who has contemplated his or her own mortality or mourned the loss of a loved one, or anyone who dreams of travel and adventure—substantial constituencies in each case.

As well as an implied auditor each poem addresses an **implied reader**. As Paul Valery said, "Each poet necessarily relies, in his [or her] work, on some ideal reader. . . ."[2] Some poems are directed toward readers who want an

---

2 Paul Valéry, *The Art of Poetry*, trans. Denise Folliot (New York: Vintage, 1961), 162.

"easy read"; others imply a sophisticated audience that's willing to track down allusions and that delights in complexity and technical virtuosity. Some poems speak to the romantic in us; others to the realist or even the cynic. Every poem assumes an ideal reader, and being aware of our expectations of that mythical personage can help us to "dial in" the voice of our poem.

The various "players" in the poem form a continuum: poet, implied poet, poetic persona, auditor, implied auditor or ideal reader, and finally the actual reader. Poet and reader interact in virtual time through this complex hall of mirrors: the poet imagines the person or people he or she wishes to address; the reader imagines the personality, mood, and intentions of the poet. We may even visualize these people as we write or read.

Table 3.1: Communications Model for Poetry

	Implied poet	Persona or "mask"	Auditor	Implied auditor/ reader	
P O E T	The personality we assume from the tone and lexicon of the poem; this personality may not be identical to the poet him- or herself.	The poet speaks through a character whom the poet invents or uses in some poems.	A specific person addressed by the poet or persona. The auditor can be a named "character" or simply an "offstage" presence.	The *type* of person the poem seems to address; this might be any reader of poetry, but it could also be someone of a specific gender, age group, or interest group, or simply someone who enjoys a certain type of poetry.	**R E A D E R**

Apostrophe and Imperative

An **apostrophe** is a poem in which the speaker addresses an object (a Grecian urn, for example) or an idea ("Ode to Duty") or, for that matter, an animal ("Ode to a Skylark"). We're not supposed to believe that the object, animal, or idea is the intended audience. The poet is, in some sense, speaking to him- or herself. His or her situation is like that of a character in a drama who is giving

voice to a **soliloquy**. We, the readers, are like the audience at a play: we're
not part of the illusory world of the drama, but we can "overhear" the speech,
which is really intended for us. In the sonnet below, John Keats addresses an
aspect of nature.

>*Bright Star*
>by John Keats (1795–1821)
>
>Bright star, would I were steadfast as thou art —
>   Not in lone splendour hung aloft the night
>And watching, with eternal lids apart,
>   Like nature's patient, sleepless Eremite,
>The moving waters at their priestlike task
>   Of pure ablution round earth's human shores,
>Or gazing on the new soft fallen mask
>   Of snow upon the mountains and the moors —
>No — yet still steadfast, still unchangeable,
>   Pillow'd upon my fair love's ripening breast,
>To feel for ever its soft fall and swell,
>   Awake for ever in a sweet unrest,
>Still, still to hear her tender-taken breath,
>And so live ever — or else swoon to death.

James Arthur's modern take on the Romantic ode addresses a book—the
encyclopedia he found so much interest in as a boy, an experience many poets
will recognize and remember.

>*Ode to an Encyclopedia*
>by James Arthur
>
>O hefty hardcover on the built-in shelf in my parents' living room,
>O authority stamped on linen paper, molted from your dust jacket,
>Questing Beast of blue and gold, you were my companion
>
>on beige afternoons that came slanting through the curtains
>behind the rough upholstered chair. You knew how to trim a sail
>and how the hornet builds a hive. You had a topographical map
>of the mountain ranges on the far side of the moon
>and could name the man who shot down the man
>who murdered Jesse James. At forty, I tell myself

that boyhood was all enchantment: hanging around the railway,
getting plastered on cartoons; I see my best friend's father
marinating in a lawn chair, smiling benignly at his son and me

from above a gin and tonic, or sitting astride his roof
with carpentry nails and hammer, going at some problem
that kept resisting all his mending. O my tome, my paper brother,

my narrative without an ending, you had a diagram of a cow
broken down into the major cuts of beef, and an image
of the Trevi Fountain. The boarding house,

the church on the corner: all that stuff is gone.
In winter in Toronto, people say, a man goes outside
and shovels snow mostly so that his neighbors know

just how much snow he is displacing. I'm writing this
in Baltimore. For such a long time, the boy wants
to grow up and be at large, but posture becomes bearing;

bearing becomes shape. A man can make a choice
between two countries, believing all the while
that he will never have to choose.

Another use of the second-person narrative mode in poetry is the **imperative construction**, a grammatical structure in which the second-person subject can be either explicit or implied. Consider how the narrator of John Donne's "Song" addresses an implied auditor, giving him directions to follow:

Song ("Go and catch a falling star")
by John Donne (1572–1631)

Go, and catch a falling star,
    Get with child a mandrake root,
Tell me, where all past years are,
    Or who cleft the Devil's foot,
Teach me to hear mermaids singing,
Or to keep off envy's stinging,
        And find
        What wind
Serves to advance an honest mind.

If thou be'st born to strange sights,
    Things invisible to see,
Ride ten thousand days and nights,
    Till age snow white hairs on thee,
Thou, when thou return'st, wilt tell me,
All strange wonders that befell thee,
      And swear,
      No where
Lives a woman true, and fair.

If thou find'st one, let me know,
    Such a pilgrimage were sweet;
Yet do not, I would not go,
    Though at next door we might meet;
Though she were true, when you met her,
And last, till you write your letter,
      Yet she
      Will be
False, ere I come, to two, or three.

Imperative-construction poems are sometimes called "ritual poems" because they invite (or, in fact, command) the reader to perform a kind of ritual. Think of the **ritual poem** as a "how-to" lesson, a recipe, or a set of directions to a particular place. Ritual poems are often organized something like a chant, with some lines beginning with a verb—"Take a sprig of rosemary, twine it around. . . ." They're addressed to the reader, and consequently they use second-person narration. Remember, you're directing someone to do something, so there should be some result at the end of the process: make that result the resolution of your poem.

    A **spell poem** is a version of a ritual poem. It differs from a ritual poem in that it may include an invocation and address some spirit or force and ask that spirit to perform some task.

    Prayers are—in a sense—apostrophes, but they're usually addressed to a divine being. There's no reason, however, why one couldn't address a prayer to the weather forecasters or the Golf Gods or the car you wish would start. The prayer is a popular poetic form, whether in its original, sacred context or as a secular reshaping of the traditional form. Robert Herrick wrote this witty take on the prayer, addressing his imaginary "household gods" on the occasion of his eviction from his home in Devonshire, England.

To His Household Gods
by Robert Herrick (1591–1674)

Rise, household gods, and let us go;
But whither I myself not know.
First, let us dwell on rudest seas;
Next, with severest savages;
Last, let us make our best abode
Where human foot as yet ne'er trod:
Search worlds of ice, and rather there
Dwell, than in loathed Devonshire.

The Communal Voice: First-Person Plural

Some poems may be narrated in the first person, but in the first-person plural, as if the speakers were members of a specific community or simply everyone. The effect of this technique is to create a kind of Greek chorus, the voice of both reader and writer.

Sci-Fi
by Tracy K. Smith

There will be no edges, but curves.
Clean lines pointing only forward.

History, with its hard spine & dog-eared
Corners, will be replaced with nuance,

Just like the dinosaurs gave way
To mounds and mounds of ice.

Women will still be women, but
The distinction will be empty. Sex,

Having outlived every threat, will gratify
Only the mind, which is where it will exist.

For kicks, we'll dance for ourselves
Before mirrors studded with golden bulbs.

The oldest among us will recognize that glow—
But the word sun will have been re-assigned

To a Standard Uranium-Neutralizing device
Found in households and nursing homes.

And yes, we'll live to be much older, thanks
To popular consensus. Weightless, unhinged,

Eons from even our own moon, we'll drift
In the haze of space, which will be, once

And for all, scrutable and safe.

Dialogic and Choral Poems

A **dialogue poem** is just what the title implies: two characters carry on a conversation. The characters may be symbolic—as in W.B. Yeats's "A Dialogue of Self and Soul"—or they may be the sort of characters you'd encounter in a realistic story. As we've seen, dialogue poems can be presented in the format of a dramatic script, with the name of the character presented before his or her speeches. A **choral poem** expands on the idea of the dialogue by presenting a number of speakers in the same poem.

The Objective Narrator

Not all poems are narrated in the first or second person; some aspire to objective presentation of events or perceptions. The quintessential modern technique is the lack of a narrative persona, the poem that aspires to the directness and simplicity of a painting or a photograph. This trend in modern poetry is associated with the early modernists, and in particular from the group of poets who called themselves "imagists"—Pound, H. D., Eliot, Amy Lowell, and Richard Aldington. The imagists believed in the "direct presentation of the thing," and their legacy includes such image-based poems as W.C. Williams's "The Red Wheelbarrow," in which the narrator has been completely effaced. The easiest way to create that sense of objective observation is to narrate the poem in the third person. A third-person narrator gives a poem a sense of objectivity; the "narrator" is an eye, a camera recording sense impressions without interpretation. This poem, by early Canadian poet E. Pauline Johnson, is a painterly evocation of a landscape:

Marshlands
by E. Pauline Johnson (Tekahionwake; 1861–1913)

A thin wet sky, that yellows at the rim,
And meets with sun-lost lip the marsh's brim.

The pools low lying, dank with moss and mould,
Glint through their mildews like large cups of gold.

Among the wild rice in the still lagoon,
In monotone the lizard shrills his tune.

The wild goose, homing, seeks a sheltering,
Where rushes grow, and oozing lichens cling.

Late cranes with heavy wing, and lazy flight,
Sail up the silence with the nearing night.

And like a spirit, swathed in some soft veil,
Steals twilight and its shadows o'er the swale.

Hushed lie the sedges, and the vapours creep,
Thick, grey and humid, while the marshes sleep.

Purely descriptive poems are usually relatively short: it's difficult to build a longer poem without a narrative or argument to serve as a "spine." It's also surprisingly rare to run into a descriptive poem that doesn't include any commentary; keeping our interpretive urges out of our poems requires a considerable act of will.

The Questioning Narrator

Although the objective narrator speaks from a position of relative omniscience, in some poems the speaker is trying to understand the world that he or she perceives. That questioning stance brings the reader into the world of the poem and into the narrator's perspective. The narrator of Tami Haaland's "Little Girl" poses epistemological questions—"Who did she ever want to please?" and "Why won't they let her go?"—and invites the implied auditor, and by extension the reader, to join in the quest for meaning.

Little Girl
by Tami Haaland

She's with Grandma in front
of Grandma's house, backed
by a willow tree, gladiola and roses.

Who did she ever want
to please? But Grandma
seems half-pleased and annoyed.

No doubt Mother frowns
behind the lens, wants
to straighten this sassy face.

Maybe laughs, too.
Little girl with her mouth wide,
tongue out, yelling

at the camera. See her little
white purse full of treasure,
her white sandals?

She has things to do,
you can tell. Places to explore
beyond the frame,

and these women picking flowers
and taking pictures.
Why won't they let her go?

DEVELOPING AND REFINING THE VOICE OF THE POEM

First, consider the identity of the speaker of your poem. The answer may seem obvious—the speaker is you, the poet. We've already discussed the fact that each of us has a wide range of moods and personae that we draw on consciously or unconsciously when we're speaking to others. Selecting a voice that suits the material is essential and may require some "tuning in" to get the right tone. That process involves choosing a lexical level (see Chapter 6), deciding how much emphasis you wish to place on communicating the narrator's personality, and deciding whether the poem should be spoken to a specific auditor or to any reader who happens to be "listening in." Keeping the voice consistent can be surprisingly challenging, as the poem exists within a limited lexical field: some choices of diction are appropriate to the speaker; others may not be. Similarly, the tone can only vary within reasonable limits: a speaker could progress from an elegiac mood to a tone of righteous indignation or optimism, perhaps, but a speaker who shifts suddenly from despair to levity may seem implausible.

Second, consider your options. Some concepts arrive in our minds with a "built-in" sense of voice. The narrative mode and tone are so essential to the act of communication that it's very difficult to imagine the poem being told in any other way. If that's the case, then it is probably wise to stick with the original game plan. If the voice lacks force and conviction or wanders between one mode of narration and another, then it's a good idea to try recasting the poem in a different mode. Here is a sign that the poet may need to reconsider the narrative mode: a first-person voice appears late in a poem or starts to speak the poem and then disappears—a very common phenomenon.

Settling on one consistent mode of narration and refining the voice to make it consistent and convincing is one way of developing a poem. It's possible, though, that a poem may *need* to be somewhat fragmented in terms of its narration. For instance, a first-person narrator may address an auditor or implied auditor while intermittently thinking about something related to the subject of the speech. Similarly, some poems juxtapose the narrator's voice with snippets of song, ambient voices from passers-by or media, advertising slogans, or voices drifting up from memories. (If you've read T.S. Eliot's *The Wasteland* or *The Hollow Men*, you'll be familiar with this technique.) If varying the narration is a vital part of your strategy, do your readers a favour and signal shifts in mode through the graphic design of the poem. Put one voice or tone in plain type and another in italics, or indent one voice and keep the other flush left. Verse poetry offers us opportunities for communicating through visual design that prose genres generally don't, so remember to consider those possibilities and to make them part of your technical repertoire.

Third, if you're speaking through the mask of a persona, think carefully about the language that the persona would use. Putting contemporary language into the mouth of an historical figure is as bad a mistake as filling your own mouth with antiquated "poetic" clichés—unless, of course, you're attempting to be ironic or making a point about the commonalities between past and present. Again, research is the key to making your persona convincing.

Last, try to make the voice of the poem accessible enough for your target audience: remember that poetry is communication. A poem should not be used as an opportunity to show off your intellectual or moral superiority; it's an opportunity to speak to people who may enjoy what you have to say and how you say it. Think of your readers' needs rather than worrying too much about your own. Think of your readers as guests at a party; they don't want to be stuck with a pedant or a bore any more than you would. One of the most useful skills a poet can possess is the ability to speak in a voice that's engaging and interesting; cultivating that sort of persona and voice is always a good idea.

EXERCISES

Exercise 3/1: Tarot Poem

As the psychologist C.G. Jung noted, some cultural artefacts represent the archetypes of the human unconscious. Jung found archetypal imagery in alchemical symbols, in dreams, in shamanic legends, and in certain occult symbols such as the pictures represented on the tarot cards used by fortune-tellers.

Tarot cards were originally used as playing cards but are now more commonly used in fortune-telling. There are variously designed tarot decks, some quite famous. Each deck includes seventy-eight cards divided into two sets, the minor arcana and the major arcana. The minor arcana consists of fifty-six cards divided into four suits with ten numbered "pip" cards and four "face" cards in each suit; the suits may vary from one region to another, but the most common suits are swords, wands, coins, and cups. The major arcana includes twenty-two cards depicting such allegorical figures as the Emperor, the Empress, the High Priestess, the Lovers, the Hanged Man, and Strength.

- Pick a card from a tarot deck at random, or, if you prefer, select one that intrigues you. If you belong to a writers' group or workshop, pass the deck of tarot cards around the room so that each group member can take a card from the deck. Each poet will then consider what the figure depicted on his or her card might have to say if it could speak.
- Begin by jotting down some notes or writing a prose paragraph. Imagine that you are the person (or one of the people) represented on the card you have been dealt. Try to evoke the voice of the figure on the card. First, try to answer the following questions: Who are you? What are you doing? What has happened or is about to happen? Then, note the details of the scene and describe them in precise, evocative language.
- Convert your notes into a verse poem by arranging the language into lines and adding or deleting lines as required. Work toward a suitable rhythm. Try to create a voice that embodies the characteristics that you see in the figure on the card.

- Remember to give your poem a title. You can always use the name of the card; a simple title of that sort would give your readers an immediate sense of the context of the poem.
- Read your poem to your workshop or to your friends.

Exercise 3/2: Postcard Poem

Imagine that you're sending a postcard to someone you know (or know of). First, find a postcard with a picture that you find interesting, or just print up an image in postcard size. Try to imagine why you might be sending this particular image to that particular person. Before beginning to write, ask yourself a few questions:

- Who are you?
- Where are you?
- Why are you sending this card?
- Why did you choose this particular image?
- Who is the receiver?

Now write the poem. You might begin by writing a short letter, just as if you were actually writing on the back of a postcard. Then convert your letter into a poem by using line and stanza breaks and making the language denser and more interesting. Give your poem a title, and try to make the poem independent of the image: we shouldn't have to see the image to understand the poem. This poem should be a *free-verse lyric* in first-person or second-person narration.

Exercise 3/3: Apostrophe

Write a lyric poem addressing an inanimate object or abstract concept. Be original in your choice of auditor—you might, for example, address a McDonald's hamburger or your phone bill or your boyfriend's new hipster beard or the robot voice on your iPhone.

Exercise 3/4: "Persona" Poem

A poetic persona is a mask that the poet wears in order to compose the poem: in other words, the poet assumes the voice (persona) of some other person, idea, or thing and narrates the poem from that assumed point of view. The persona poem should speak to the reader directly, as if confiding the essence of the character. The trick here is to take on the mask of the new persona genuinely: consider what a particular historical or mythical figure might have to say about her- or himself. If you choose to use the mask of an historical figure, you could research your poem and use the historical figure's own words as the "raw material" for your poem; in the case of a figure from mythology, consider elements of the stories connected with that figure for inclusion in your poem. Try to use a conversational tone in your narration; don't be too self-consciously "poetic."

Your poem should be narrated in the *first person*. Your narrator may address a general audience or an individual auditor, implied or specified. Try to make your language appropriate to your character's time, place, and personality.

Here are some suggestions for selecting a persona: 1) an historical figure; 2) a figure from myth; 3) a pop-culture "icon"; 4) a character from fiction, film, television, cartoons, comic books, or video games; 5) a generic figure such as a refugee, gangster, mill worker, prison guard, or fast-food clerk.

Exercise 3/5: Ritual Poem (Imperative Construction)

A ritual poem *commands* the listener to do something or tells the listener how something can be done. Think of the ritual poem as a "how-to" lesson, a recipe, or a set of directions. A typical recipe includes a list of commands, each of which begins with an action verb: *Cut* acorn squash into quarters. *Discard* seeds and pulp. *Place* pieces on a foil baking sheet. *Bake* for 30 minutes in an oven at 400 degrees. *Remove* from oven. *Set aside* to cool. Remember, you're directing someone to do something, so there should be some result at the end of the process—make that result the resolution of your poem.

Some possible topics might be

- how to write a poem,
- how to grieve for someone or something you've lost,
- how to celebrate the end of exam week,
- how to make dinner for a visiting Martian,
- how to cook your favourite dinner,
- how to cook a poem,
- how to fall in love,
- how to fall out of love,
- how to get to the house you lived in when you were three years old,
- how to get to the house you will live in seventy years from now,
- how to get to the past, or
- how to cure insomnia (or anything else you can imagine).

Alternate Possibility: Spell Poem

A spell poem is a version of a ritual poem. It differs from a ritual poem in that it may include an invocation and address some spirit or force and ask that spirit to perform some task. It may also, of course, be addressed to the person on whom the spell is supposed to work.

TAKEAWAY

- A poem embodies a human voice. That voice may be public or private.
- The voice of the poem may be that of an individual, a group, or an omniscient third-person narrator.
- The speaker of a poem is never simply the author: each poem implies a specific narrator, and each poem also implies an auditor, who may be a specific person to whom the poem is addressed or a type of person. Poems aren't just spoken by someone; they're also intended to be heard by someone. That implied auditor can be a figure "inside" the poem, but it's always an audience of readers and listeners who are "eavesdropping" on the act of communication that forms the poem.
- The voice of a poem may imply omniscience, but it may also embody a questing consciousness that's trying to explore and understand its world.

TERMS TO REMEMBER

- apostrophe
- auditor
- choral poem
- confessional poem
- dialogue poem
- first-person monologue
- imperative construction

- implied auditor
- implied reader
- persona poem
- prayers
- ritual poem
- soliloquy
- spell poem

CHAPTER FOUR

Developing Imagery

Poetry has to be something more than a conception of the mind.
It has to be a revelation of nature. Conceptions are artificial.
Perceptions are essential.[1]
—Wallace Stevens

THINKING IN IMAGES

You can't write an enjoyable poem simply by summarizing a story or arguing a theory in abstract language—the only exceptions to that rule are epigrams and the occasional comic or experimental poem. Poetry engages the senses; it works by representing ideas and emotions with concrete images. Those images can be objects, plants, animals, atmospheric conditions, landscapes, bodies of water, celestial bodies, and people—anything you can perceive with your senses. Although the word "image" may suggest a visual bias, images can evoke tactile, olfactory, auditory, and gustatory sensations. Scenes aren't simply pictures; they contain sounds, smells, textures, awareness of heat and cold, possibly even tastes. When you're drafting a poem, try to engage at least one—and preferably more than one—of the reader's senses.

The emphasis on imagery as opposed to rhetoric is to some degree a modern bias and specifically an article of faith among the modernist poets of the early twentieth century. Nineteenth-century poets tended to lean heavily on narrative, and their eighteenth-century counterparts often wrote poems that were essentially arguments or "essays." Though the poems we associate with those premodern poets were more discursive than the high-modernist works of Ezra Pound, Marianne Moore, T.S. Eliot, H. D., Mina Loy, and W.C. Williams, they still relied on imagery for their impact. Aside from the relatively rare exceptions already mentioned, a poem without imagery is a bird without wings.

---

1 Wallace Stevens, *Opus Posthumous*, ed. Milton J. Bates, revised, enlarged, and corrected edition (New York: Vintage Books, 1990), 191.

TECHNIQUES FOR DESCRIPTION

Engaging the Senses

The primary technique for engaging the reader's senses is the use of concrete, specific diction. Casual readers may think that poems should consist of philosophical language, but, in fact, poets generally shy away from "big" concept words. "Go in fear of abstractions" is an old and still-useful injunction. Telling our readers that we're "happy" or "sad" or "content" or "afraid" doesn't accomplish much. The concept or emotion remains within the consciousness of the poet (or the voice that's telling the poem, at least); it's opaque to the reader. In order to make the reader understand the idea we want to communicate, we have to give him or her images that he or she can perceive and react to on a visceral level. The conviction that representing is more effective than explaining cuts across the various literary genres: "show; don't tell" is the prime directive of fiction workshops, and that concept applies equally well to writing poetry.

Suzanne Buffam's poem (below) begins with rhetoric: "I was ready for a new experience." The key words "new" and "experience" are both **abstractions**. Notice how she moves quickly from abstract to concrete by "backing up" her rhetoric with concrete images. Experiences are "burned out." That's a common locution; we speak of being "burned out" if we no longer bring any enthusiasm to an undertaking. Buffam continues that "burning" metaphor, envisioning the abstract experiences as "little ashy heaps" and using related words such as "smoke" and "smouldering." Notice, as well, that she returns to rhetoric for the resolution, which appears in stanzas 9 and 10 ("nothing worth doing is worth doing / For the sake of experience alone") and then circles back to the first image—"burned out"—for that witty reference to the sun.

The New Experience
by Suzanne Buffam

I was ready for a new experience.
All the old ones had burned out.

They lay in little ashy heaps along the roadside
And blew in drifts across the fairgrounds and fields.

From a distance some appeared to be smouldering
But when I approached with my hat in my hands

They let out small puffs of smoke and expired.
Through the windows of houses I saw lives lit up

With the otherworldly glow of TV
And these were smoking a little bit too.

I flew to Rome. I flew to Greece.
I sat on a rock in the shade of the Acropolis

And conjured dusky columns in the clouds.
I watched waves lap the crumbling coast.

I heard wind strip the woods.
I saw the last living snow leopard

Pacing in the dirt. Experience taught me
That nothing worth doing is worth doing

For the sake of experience alone.
I bit into an apple that tasted sweetly of time.

The sun came out. It was the old sun
With only a few billion years left to shine.

Like a good photographer, the poet choses details from the natural world and its inhabitants to represent ideas and emotions, frames aspects of the scene, crops anything irrelevant, and tries to see clearly and with as little "noise" and "grain" as possible. That **analogy,** of course, is inadequate: the photographer represents the visual world, but the poet must also cultivate an awareness of the information that flows into the mind and the heart through the other senses—smells, tastes, textures and temperatures, balance and disequilibrium, the universe of sounds and silences, the movement of everything growing and crumbling and trembling with the vibrancy of life as it passes through time.

The images that well up from the imagination aren't necessarily metaphors, unless we subject them to some Freudian or Jungian analysis and insist on seeing them as the symptoms of some pathology or the symbols of the collective unconscious. Within the logic of the poem, they're as palpable as perceptions of the empirical world. The poet's mind connects each image to the other images in the poem. A poem is a composition, not just in terms of its phonological dimension, its music, but also in terms of its representative dimension, its imagery.

The poem that follows began with the observation of a simple act: a toddler encountering a book, remembering perhaps that books could be fun, and pretending to eat the delicious words and pictures on the pages. The volume in question was an illustrated collection of fairy tales, so the folk-tale imagery suggested itself readily. Selecting *which* tales to glean images from took a little more thought: the idea of eating the words of a book mandated a bias towards gustatory images—tastes such as "salt," "ice," "candies," "berries," or the sensation of holding a stone on your tongue. Rumpelstiltskin's trick of weaving gold from straw seemed to suit the theme of transformation, words to edibles, and so did the idea of animals becoming human—the "half-transformed foxes." Then there are some standard folk-tale motifs such as smiling wolves, a wicked queen, a wood-chopper, and so on. Some snow bears even make a guest appearance, drifting in from Hans Christian Andersen.

Language Arts
by Stephen Guppy

My daughter, who is 20 months,
is lying on the living-room floor,
plucking words from her brother's story-book
as if they were Cheerios
or berries from the garden plot
and eating them like candies.

Each time she believes
she's caught a word, she places the tips
of her stubby fingers up to her mouth,
makes a sucking noise, just as if she were pulping
the memory of each luscious sound
she's ever heard or dreamed of,
and giggles as she reaches for
the next word of the fable.

Curious, I lie down on the carpet
next to my little girl and, reaching
past her busy hands,
pretend to take a couple of words
from the illustrated story. She giggles again
and grins at me as I pluck my words
like windfalls from the virtual shade
of the fairy-tale forest
and touch them to my lips. She's right: they're good;

they taste like night, like the smiles
of wolves; you can hold them in your mouth,
cup them on your tongue like stones
worn smooth by the pads of snow bears.

They taste like salt, like the skin of your hand
when you lick it after hours of work
weaving straws of gold from golden straw
in the blunt crayon sunlight of August.

They taste like the ice
in the Wicked Queen's heart,
so cold that your bones burn like x-rays
and your teeth are the strokes of the wood-chopper's axe
in the bodies of half-transformed foxes.

"Daddy eat!" my little daughter says, and I do
just what she tells me: pick
the bitter, inky fruit from trees
and spiky bushes bright as blood;
crush them on my tongue and taste
the winter hush before my birth,
the chrysalis, the blind brown seed,

primaeval forest shade between
the winding paths of stories.

Eliminating the Observer

Verse can work as a kind of shorthand; we can often eliminate the words and
phrases that explain or background our perception of the image and just give
the reader the image itself. In the example below, the first-person narrator
explains that he or she is perceiving a butterfly.

Example 1: I see a butterfly that resembles a swatch of calico.

The "I see" probably isn't essential to our appreciation of the image of the
butterfly. We don't need to be told that someone sees it; what's important is
that we, the readers, see it for ourselves. Telling us that the butterfly "resembles"
the cloth is also redundant: just put one term of the comparison next to the
other, and we'll process the connection between them. So instead of the wordy

and cumbersome Example 1, we have the more efficient Example 2. In that version of the description, we've used a line break to arrange the two terms of the comparison in visual space; the visual juxtaposition does the same job as the phrase "that resembles." The emphasis, you'll notice, has moved from the narrator to the reader.

> *Example 2:* a butterfly
> a swatch of calico.

Between the first example and the second, we've gone from the wordiness of prose to the efficiency of verse, and we've focused the reader's attention on the concrete image. When we read Example 1, we're being told about someone else's experience; when we read Example 2, we're experiencing a perception of our own.

Using Synaesthesia

Synaesthesia is, in literary terms, the mixing of senses in an image. (It's also a psychological condition, but that's another story.) When a decorator recommends painting a room in "warm colours," he or she is using synaesthesia as a descriptive tool by assigning a tactile sensation (warmth) to a visual image (colour). The same thing happens when we complain about our uncle's "loud" Hawaiian shirt or say that our new Fender Stratocaster has a "bright" tone. Poets employ that blending of senses as a strategy for engaging readers on a sensory level. John Keats mixes the auditory sense with the visual when he speaks of a "melodious plot / Of beechen green" ("Ode to a Nightingale") and then blends vision and sound with taste in the next stanza:

> O for a draught of vintage! that hath been
> Cool'd a long age in the deep-delved earth,
> Tasting of Flora and the country green,
> Dance, and Provençal song, and sunburnt mirth!

You may have noticed a moment of synaesthesia in "Language Arts" (above): "taste like night."

Keeping Images "In Key"

When you're writing a poem, it's usually a good idea to keep all the images within the same general frame of reference. They shouldn't be scattered or incoherent; they should work together to create a unified impression. Some poems revolve around organic imagery, others around images of machines or clockwork, still others around water or fire or the seasons. You can think of this as keeping the images in the same "key," to use a metaphor from music. Think of your images as notes in a musical composition and make them resonate with each other; if you wander from one context to another, make sure that the transition is constructive and adds to the impact of the poem in the same way that changing keys might add to the impact of a song.

Don McKay's "Astonished" is built around a geological motif; the imagery elaborates that motif and doesn't deviate from it, even portraying the auditor's face as a "crater" and relating the auditor's persona and situation to the accumulation of sediments and the dissolution of minerals in the sea.

> *Astonished* —
> by Don McKay
>
>   astounded, astonied, astunned, stopped short
>   and turned toward stone, the moment
>   filling with its slow
>   stratified time. Standing there, your face
>   cratered by its gawk,
>   you might be the symbol signifying eon.
>   What are you, empty or pregnant? Somewhere
>   sediments accumulate on seabeds, seabeds
>   rear up into mountains, ammonites
>   fossilize into gems. Are you thinking
>   or being thought? Cities
>   as sand dunes, epics
>   as e-mail. Astonished
>   you are famous and anonymous, the border
>   washed out by so soft a thing as weather. Someone
>   inside you steps from the forest and across the beach
>   toward the nameless all-dissolving ocean.

Although most lyric poems can gain strength and coherence from the elaboration of one field of imagery, there are exceptions to that guideline. In a poem that's surreal or whimsical, it can be effective to offer a few different metaphors for the subject of a description. Surrealist poems often feature a "scattergun" approach to imagery that reflects the genre's emphasis on the irrational. It's also most effective if the kaleidoscopic quality of the images reflects the theme of the poem. Consider the two short poems below: each develops varied metaphors in the context of a poem in which the subject undergoes a kind of metamorphosis.

When You Wear Clothes
by Nelly Kazenbroot

I'll miss seeing you naked
Your skin soft and seamless
Like Emmenthal sliced straight
Pink cigars unrolling at
Your neck, the crease between
Your buttocks pressed flat
In that blind male gap
Below the little jointless finger
Of your sex. When you wear clothes
That shadow you in indigo
And silver studs decorate the
Replica of your grandfather's nose
I'll acquire tunnel vision
From my blue eyes through yours
To where your tattooed skin peels back
And your lazy bones shrink
Waxy and bird-white bright
To fit the naked baby-doll
That jittered slug toes
Upon my lap.

In the Airport
by Eleni Sikelianos

A man called Dad walks by
then another one does. Dad, you say
and he turns, forever turning, forever
being called. Dad, he turns, and looks
at you, bewildered, his face a moving
wreck of skin, a gravity-bound question
mark, a fruit ripped in two, an animal
that can't escape the field.

Conducting an "Image Inventory"

Ask yourself whether you've followed your images through the poem from beginning to end. Too often, poets create an exciting image in the first stanza of a poem and then forget all about it. The images in a lyric poem should support each other and work together to create a unified impression. It's often useful to inventory the images you've included in a draft of the poem you're working on (see Exercise 4/3).

POETIC MYTHOLOGY

In his introduction to *The Penguin Book of Irish Verse*, Brendan Kennelly wrote, "A poet without a myth is a man confronting famine. Like the body, the imagination gets tired and hungry: myth is a food, a sustaining structure outside the poet that nourishes his inner life and helps him express it."[2]

Learning to write poems well isn't just a matter of learning tricks and techniques; it's also important to learn how to *think like a poet*. Poets are masters of language, but they're also adept at communicating in higher-order symbolic language. In "Yeats and the Language of Symbolism," Northrop Frye wrote that "just as the words of a language are a set of verbal conventions, so the imagery of poetry is a set of symbolic conventions."[3] Just as mathematicians, physicists, and computer scientists must assimilate the abstract signs used in their disciplines, poets have to learn the symbolic language of poetry, which is a language of things and the relationships between things. In the poet's mind, objects, plants, and animals have meaning: all the elements of our world are meaningful. This lexicon of meaningful things is sometimes called "stock symbolism," though the term "stock" implies the rote invocation of familiar and potentially stale analogies, and poets are always capable of spinning the old correspondences in fresh and inventive ways.

The most common analogies used by poets would have been familiar to our earliest forebears. In ancient times, people's lives were governed by the cycle of day and night and the larger cycle of the seasons. The profound influence of the transition from day to night and of the circular movement from one season to another has been reflected in the imagery chosen by poets throughout the history of literature.

Seasonal Symbolism

The most important symbol for poets has always been the wheel of the seasons. That cycle governed our ability to hunt and gather our food; to plant, tend, and harvest our crops; and to prepare appropriate clothing and shelter.

---

2 Brendan Kennelly, "Introduction," in *The Penguin Book of Irish Verse*, ed. Brendan Kennelly (London: Penguin, 1970), 26.
3 Northrop Frye, "Yeats and the Language of Symbolism," in *Fables of Identity: Studies in Poetic Mythology*, 218–38 (New York: Harcourt, Brace & World, 1963), 218.

It wasn't so long ago that everyone thought in terms of the importance of the time of year to agriculture, hunting, and such everyday concerns as getting from place to place and keeping warm; we're all affected by the change of seasons to some extent even today, though for most modern people living in cities the issue is less a matter of life and death than it was for our ancestors. Still, the change from spring to summer to autumn and finally to winter has associations to which we can all relate. Spring is the time of birth, childhood, innocence, hope, and the joy of first love. Summer brings the full heat of vigorous youth. Autumn may provide the prosperity and sense of achievement and fulfilment symbolized by the harvest, but it also signals the fading of our dreams and the lengthening shadows of old age, infirmity, and loss. Winter, finally, brings us to the end of our life cycle, and we enter the stillness and frigidity of death, though we gain the clarity of vision that comes with experience and age.

Seasonal imagery is best understood as a language, a simple but resonant set of signs: each season corresponds to a phase of our life cycle and of the life cycles of all of the myriad aspects of the natural world. If we're writing about the advent of new life and new love, then it makes sense to use the imagery of springtime in our poem. If, conversely, we're writing an elegy about a friend or public figure, then autumn, the season of loss, is perhaps the best source of imagery. Autumn provides a ready symbol for the loss of youth, love, and happiness. Elizabeth Barrett Browning encapsulated that idea in the following lines from "To Autumn":

> Youth fades; and then, the joys of youth,
>   Which once refresh'd our mind,
> Shall come—as, on those sighing woods,
>   The chilling autumn wind.

While it's standard practice to match the season to the subject, sometimes poets contrast imagery and theme: an elegy or a poem of lost love might normally be set in autumn but by setting it against the freshness and hopefulness of spring, we could create an effective sense of irony. There's something particularly painful about someone dying or a love affair ending in the spring: suffering loss in that season seems to go against Nature. Shakespeare expresses that feeling when, in "Sonnet XCVII," he writes,

> From you have I been absent in the spring,
> When proud pied April, dressed in all his trim,
> Hath put a spirit of youth in everything.

If spring is the time of budding romance, then summer equates to marriage and the consummation of a relationship. Beyond summer lies the decline into autumn and winter—the pages of the calendar have turned, and the book of life is closing. Deborah Landau draws on those associations in her meditation on the inevitability of aging.

I Don't Have a Pill for That
by Deborah Landau

It scares me to watch
a woman hobble along
the sidewalk, hunched adagio

leaning on—
there's so much fear
I could draw you a diagram

of the great reduction
all of us will soon
be way-back-when.

The wedding is over.
Summer is over.
Life please explain.

This book is nearly halfway read.
I don't have a pill for that,
the doctor said.

Diurnal and Nocturnal Symbolism

Daylight brought our ancestors the ability to work and explore and communicate, and light became associated with both rational thought and spiritual revelation. Night was a dangerous time for our hunter-and-gatherer forbears, and they populated those hours with evil spirits and taboos, but they also saw in them the fluidity and magic of dreams and the intimacy of shelter and community.

Like the wheel of the seasons, the cycle of day and night is traditionally associated with our own life cycle: dawn brings rebirth; morning corresponds with the vitality of youth; noon sees us in the power of our prime; afternoon shifts our thoughts to the contemplative and elegiac, and we consider the fall of the mighty or the loss of our own vitality; in the evening, we confront the eternal and consider the lessons our lives have taught us; finally, night brings the end of life—but it also gives us entrance to the underworld of dreams and magic and reunites us with the spirits of those we have lost.

P.B. Shelley mines the connection between night and death in his "To Night," which, as the title implies, is an apostrophe addressed to darkness and death.

To Night
by Percy Bysshe Shelley (1792–1822)

1

Swiftly walk o'er the western wave,
    Spirit of Night!
Out of the misty eastern cave,
Where, all the long and lone daylight,
Thou wovest dreams of joy and fear,
Which make thee terrible and dear,—
    Swift be thy flight!

2

Wrap thy form in a mantle gray,
    Star-inwrought!
Blind with thine hair the eyes of Day;
Kiss her until she be wearied out,
Then wander o'er city, and sea, and land,
Touching all with thine opiate wand—
    Come, long-sought!

3

When I arose and saw the dawn,
    I sighed for thee;
When light rode high, and the dew was gone,
And noon lay heavy on flower and tree,
And the weary Day turned to his rest,
Lingering like an unloved guest.
    I sighed for thee.

4

Thy brother Death came, and cried,
    Wouldst thou me?

Thy sweet child Sleep, thy filmy-eyed,
Murmured like a noontide bee,
Shall I nestle near thy side?
Wouldst thou me?—And I replied,
        No, not thee!

            5
Death will come when thou art dead,
        Soon, too soon—
Sleep will come when thou art fled;
Of neither would I ask the boon
I ask of thee, beloved Night—
Swift be thine approaching flight,
        Come soon, soon!

Other Popular Motifs

Closely related to the symbolism of day and night is the association of celestial bodies with states of mind. For our ancestors, stars symbolized the eternal and planets the cyclical; the sun was the source of power, fertility, inspiration, and wisdom, but it could also be blinding and lethal. The moon, conversely, seemed hauntingly close to the earth, and its association with the tides suggested an almost magical power over the elements. We saw beauty and romance in moonlight, but the face of the moon seemed pale as death.

Emily Brontë explores the connotations of moonlight and summer in the rhymed quatrains below. The imagery of the poem evokes a typical "romantic landscape" from a Victorian painting.

XVIII: 'Tis Moonlight, Summer Moonlight
by Emily Brontë (1818–48)

'Tis moonlight, summer moonlight,
All soft and still and fair
The solemn hours of midnight
Breathes sweet thoughts everywhere

But most where trees are sending
Their breezy boughs on high,
Or stooping low are lending
A shelter from the sky.

> And there in those wild bowers
> A lovely form is laid
> Green grass and dew-steeped flowers
> Wave gently round her head

The landscape around us, whether mountain, forest, or prairie, suggested its own lexicon of meaningful images, and so did our own bodies and those of the animals with which we shared our world. Processes such as cooking, carving, gathering, trapping, and butchering could all be seen as metaphors for various states of mind and emotions. As we entered the age of relatively advanced technology, we naturally reached for analogies in the new crafts of clockwork, metallurgy, steam power, internal combustion, and other aspects of the mechanical. Read a novel or memoir from the 1840s, and you may notice that the author draws on images of assembly lines, railroads, steamships, and so on. Twentieth-century writers reference electricity and electronics, and poets of the twenty-first century are assimilating the "mythology" of a global Internet. Whatever we behold, we turn into imagery.

Any aspect of our world could conceivably serve as a field of imagery in a poem; here's a brief list of some of the more popular motifs:

- *Celestial*: images of stars, planets, galaxies
- *Climatic*: clouds, rain, sunlight, wind
- *Topographical*: mountains, plains, cliffs, hillsides, riverbeds, estuaries
- *Mechanical*: gears, pulleys, wheels, pistons and connecting rods, engines
- *Electrical*: sparks, lightning, wiring, dynamo, light bulbs
- *Pastoral*: fields, forests, lakes, groves, trails, wildflowers, rivers and creeks
- *Nautical*: ship, compass, oar, sail, waves, seaweed, barnacles, docks and jetties
- *Urban/architectural*: buildings, paved roads, freeway overpasses, sidewalks, signage
- *Physiological*: any part or process of the human body
- *Organic*: roots, leaves, gardens vegetables, soil, fruit, mulch, compost
- *Culinary*: stoves, pots and pans, charring and simmering, boiling water

BUILDING WITH IMAGERY

When you've completed a draft to your satisfaction, take a close look at your imagery and see if you can build on what you've written. First, make sure that your poem isn't limited to rhetoric: every poem (with the exceptions we've noted) should contain some interesting, clearly perceived concrete imagery. Second, do a quick "inventory" of the images in the poem. Third, consider whether you've "followed" your imagery by linking your strongest images to a consistent motif—be suspicious of imagery that appears early in the poem and then vanishes or of strong images that don't show up until the end of the game. As well, ask yourself whether your images are all "in key"; if they're not, perhaps there's some potential for dividing the poem into cantos or orchestrating the shifts in motif through the visual design. Finally, make sure that your images convey the theme of the poem. Whether you're describing an object, person, animal, or scene, the question in poetry is not just "what does it look like?" but also "what does it *mean?*"

Not all images in poetry, it must be said, function as signs, existing in a Platonic relationship with ideas, emotions, themes, and so on. Sometimes, as Sigmund Freud reputedly said, a cigar is just a cigar, and a red wheelbarrow is just that—a simple farm implement standing there glazed with rainwater beside some stubbornly non-symbolic, non-Platonic chickens. In some instances, it's enough that readers perceive the object with the same clarity as the poet.

EXERCISES

Exercise 4/1: Imagining Concrete Images

Imagine that you're a potter, and you're preparing to make a ceramic pot. First, you have to force the air out of the clay by dropping it forcefully against a tabletop or some other surface, a process called "wedging." What sound does the ball of wet clay make when it hits the table? Think of at least three good words. Then imagine that you're pushing your fingers into the wet clay. What does that feel like? Think of three precise, interesting words to describe the sensation. Now imagine that you're spinning the clay on a potter's wheel. Can you hear anything? What does the clay feel like in your hands as it rotates between your palms? Does the clay have a smell? What does it smell like? Does the process of wheel throwing make a sound? Imagine that sound and describe it. Finally, put your sensation words together into a brief poem about throwing a pot.

Exercise 4/2: Developing Descriptive Imagery and Exploring Metaphors

1. Describe a small, particular object from the landscape. Pick a twig, a blade of grass, a fallen leaf, a pinecone, or some other similarly sized object.
2. List at least five characteristics of the object.
3. Write a brief paragraph describing the object. Use literal language and try to make your description precise and detailed. Limit yourself to no more than 50 words.
4. If you're in a discussion group or workshop, organize yourselves into groups of three or four, then read each other's paragraphs and point out the best descriptive details. Cross out any abstractions.
5. Revise your paragraph based on the suggestions you've received from the other members of your group.
6. Create metaphors that link some aspect of the object to a *different* object or being. Make your metaphors concrete and original.
7. Consider what field of imagery you've created. Identify the field of imagery (see the list above) and be prepared to discuss it.
8. Organize your description into lines of verse or a brief prose poem.
9. Consider what your object (as you've described it) should *mean* to your readers and be prepared to discuss.

Exercise 4/3: Image Inventory

When you're revising your lyric poem, make a list of the images you've used. Remember to distinguish between abstract language and concrete imagery. If there aren't any concrete images, your poem is almost certainly incomplete. Try to imagine concrete things that could represent the ideas and emotions you want to communicate. If you're having trouble making that distinction, read ahead to the discussion of abstract and concrete language in Chapter 6.

Classify the images on your list according to their subject. Have you included, for example, images of the sea or the stars? These marine and celestial images might work well together—it's easy enough to imagine a seascape at night, with a sky full of stars. It's also possible, however, that you're trying to mix two different fields of imagery; if that's the case, ask yourself whether the images complement each other or perhaps create a "scattergun" effect that's appropriate to the theme of the poem.

Have you followed your images through the poem from beginning to end? If you've got a strong image in the draft of your poem, consider elaborating that image or adding more images from the same field of reference. You might even be able to develop that striking image into a governing metaphor.

Exercise 4/4: Portrait Poem

Write a free-verse lyric poem describing a person. The subject of the poem can be someone you know, yourself, a celebrity or an historical or mythical figure, or the image in a photograph or painting. Describe your subject carefully, using precise diction and avoiding abstractions and the overuse of modifiers. Write your poem using second-person or third-person narration—try to avoid using the pronoun "I" and interposing the narrator's interpretations between the reader and the subject you're describing.

Exercise 4/5: Mythic Analogue Poem

Write a poem that narrates or describes something familiar from your own experience but that compares that experience to a specific myth. You may have to do some research into mythologies in order to begin this exercise. Remember that every culture has a rich mythology; the fact that you're writing in English shouldn't necessarily tie you to European myths.

TAKEAWAY

- As a general rule, poets try to avoid using abstract language. If you use an abstract term, "back it up" with a suitable image, one that uses concrete language and that communicates the abstract idea by evoking the appropriate emotion.
- Try to engage all the reader's senses. Scenes aren't simply pictures; they contain sounds, smells, textures, tastes, and so on.
- Limit your field of imagery. Keep the images in your poem "in key"—or at least ask yourself why they aren't in the same field of reference.
- Remember the old rule about "showing" as opposed to "telling." Build your description around the reportage of sensations. Avoid evaluations such as "the old city is a depressing place."
- Avoid authorial intrusions such as "I SEE," "I HEAR," "I SMELL," or the like. Just report the sensation itself. "The field is lush and green" rather than "I notice that the field is lush and green."
- Use synaesthesia, but use it judiciously, making sure that your readers can follow the connections between impressions from different senses.
- Be aware of the language of poetic symbolism.

TERMS TO REMEMBER

- abstractions
- analogy
- concrete images
- diurnal
- nocturnal
- symbolism
- synaesthesia

CHAPTER FIVE

Using Figurative Language

Usually, we want our words to mean what they say: "She dives into the swimming pool" means that some female person leapt into a pool, nothing more. This is a **literal** use of the word "dives." Sometimes, however, we use language in more imaginative ways. "She dives into her homework" is not intended to be taken literally: she does *not* leap off a chair into a pile of textbooks. In that instance, "dives" is used figuratively; linking the concept of diving to the act of doing homework adds drama and emphasis to the action. She doesn't just start to do her homework; she propels herself into the task in the same way that a diver propels herself into the water. Perhaps the simplest definition of **figurative language** is that it defines or describes something by relating it to something else. Figurative language links disparate ideas in order to give us a fresh and precise perspective on familiar things.

Poets use both literal and figurative language. Literal language can be used to create **descriptive imagery**; figurative language takes us beyond the evidence of the senses and into the imagination. We describe by relating one thing (person, animal, event) to another or by identifying something or someone by its subset, part, aspect, or quality. Using figurative language effectively involves engaging (and stretching) your imagination. You can't create interesting and insightful metaphors and metonymies in a rote or clichéd manner; you have to be willing to "leap" from one perception to another. Poets are the acrobats of language: they jump chasms and find hidden alleys that no one else has seen. That's part of the fun of writing and reading poetry.

TROPES

A dictionary of literary terms will provide you with a list of the many types of figurative language (also called "tropes"). If you're studying literature from the perspective of a scholar or critic, knowing about the various **tropes** will be of interest to you. For working poets, it's really only necessary to think in terms of the major categories. Understanding the structure and use of metonymies, metaphors, and allusions of one sort or another can provide you with effective strategies for creating and building your poems.

Metonymy and Metaphor

Metonymy relates the thing or idea you're describing to one of its qualities or aspects; metonymies involve the substitution of one term for another with which it is commonly associated or closely related. Creating metonymies is a logical process: the general is broken down into particular subsets, the particular is related to the general, and factual connections are streamlined into figures of speech.

- Wall Street = New York's financial district and thus finance in general
- the White House = the presidency of the United States of America
- The Crown = the federal government of Australia, Canada, and the UK
- Downing Street = the residence of the prime minister of the United Kingdom and thus the government of that country
- Sussex Drive = the residence of the prime minister of Canada and thus the government of that country
- Detroit = the American auto industry
- the press = journalists, newspapers, the media in general
- Hollywood = the movie industry
- the suits = executives, management

A **synecdoche** (*si-nek-da-key*) is a special type of metonymy that substitutes the part for the whole: "all hands on deck" refers to the sailors, not just to their hands. A synecdoche is a sort of intellectual and linguistic shorthand. Calling a manual labourer a "hand" doesn't require a particularly fertile imagination: "manual" comes from the Latin *manus*, meaning "hand," and the meaning will be transparent to anyone who knows a little French (*main*) or Spanish (*mano*).

- the Smoke = London, England
- Cowtown = slang for Calgary
- the ear of the public = everyone's attention and interest
- bread = food in general, as in "daily bread" or "breadwinner" or, in the sixties, "money" to buy that bread
- wheels = car or truck
- head = cattle

A synecdoche can also substitute the whole for the part, so that "society" can sometimes refer to the upper class or social elite rather than to the society as a whole. Similarly, "Romania" might refer to the Romanian Olympic badminton team rather than to the country as a whole.

Metaphor is an **analogical** process. Metaphors link things, ideas, or events that may initially seem to have little in common. A fresh, insightful metaphor makes us see the world in a new and exciting way. When we studied poetry in school, we may have come away with the mistaken impression that metaphors are ornaments that can be attached to the language of a poem: in fact, metaphor is a mode of thought, a way of perceiving and understanding the world. Our distant ancestors understood their world through analogies by linking objects, animals, or phenomena with common colours, shapes, abilities, behaviours, and thoughts. That's a different process from logical analysis, through which we might arrange things and phenomena hierarchically rather than associating them laterally through a shared characteristic. We humans can think both logically and analogically, and writing poetry requires us to do both.

Aristotle said that the ability to create metaphors cannot be taught, but it's difficult to imagine how one could speak and understand English (or many other languages) without being able to grasp any reasonably well-crafted metaphor. We use figurative language all the time in conversation and in most types of writing.[1] Our everyday conversations are full of them. Your child's messy bedroom isn't really a "disaster area"; you're using a metaphor to link an untidy room to the site of a hurricane or earthquake. In doing so, you're sacrificing scientific accuracy, but you're adding colour and humour and thus retaining your auditor's interest and keeping him or her and yourself from dying of boredom (another metaphor). Without metaphor, our conversations would resemble a dialogue between a Vulcan and a computer.

The capacity for understanding metaphor seems to be inherent in our species; a capacity for *creating* original and insightful metaphors may be considerably less common. We can all develop our ability to generate interesting metaphors by thinking about the mechanism at work in metaphor; reading poetry carefully and analyzing the metaphors we enjoy in other poets'

---

1 I.A. Richards addressed this issue in a series of lectures delivered at Bryn Mawr College in February and March of 1936. As Richards put it, "That metaphor is the omnipresent principle of language can be shown by mere observation" (I.A. Richards, *The Philosophy of Rhetoric* [New York: Oxford UP, 1950], 90). James Edward Mahon takes issue with Richards's assertion, noting that "Aristotle is not claiming that metaphors per se are exceptional. He is only claiming that new good metaphors that are coined by tragedians and epic poets are exceptional" ("Getting Your Sources Right: What Aristotle Didn't Say," in *Researching and Applying Metaphor*, ed. Lynne Cameron and Graham Low [Cambridge, UK: Cambridge UP, 1999], 77).

work; and refusing to allow ourselves to get away with lacklustre, familiar, or "easy" analogies.

Let's consider how we generate metaphors. Imagine that you've woken up in an unfamiliar room. It's dawn, and there's a little light in the room but not enough to allow you to see anything clearly. There's a large object in the shadows across the room. It's an unusual shape, and you can't decide what it is. You're still sleepy, and you're reluctant to get out of bed and find out. Consider the process that you might undertake in order to satisfy your curiosity without having to put your warm bare feet on a cold floor. Probably, you'd try to relate what you're seeing to something you've already seen. What does this mysterious object resemble? An armoire, perhaps? A ceramic vase on top of a chest of drawers? An entertainment unit with oddly shaped speakers? A stray moose that's wandered inside looking for breakfast?

The process you're using to solve this simple riddle is one of the methods we typically use to understand our world and navigate our way through it. We flip through the collection of "file cards" that we've accumulated in the course of our lives in search of a set of sense perceptions that fits the new model. Most of the time, we'll be able to link the new experience to past experiences and thus to understand whatever it is that we've encountered. We may be surprised by unexpected correspondences: we may notice that dissimilar things or events have some similar elements or attributes. Nature is full of interesting similarities—the spiral of seeds on a sunflower and the spiral of stars in a galaxy, for example. The human imagination can bring to light correspondences that range from fanciful to insightful to shockingly revelatory.

Our example probably won't resolve into an interesting metaphor: the room will get lighter as the morning advances, and we'll ascertain that the object across the room is in fact just a dresser, though we may also learn that our host or hotel-keeper has questionable taste in furniture. If our objective isn't to orient ourselves in a new environment but rather to create an analogy that will illuminate the situation on a psychological or spiritual level, then we might reach for a more out-there correspondence than the literal-minded, shape-in-the-dark to ugly-dresser linkage.

Craig Raine's "A Martian Sends a Postcard Home" is written from an alien (space alien, in this case) perspective. That "outsider" point of view gives us a sense of how our world looks when seen with fresh eyes, and it's a perspective artists often employ. Here the Martian is trying to make sense of the Earthlings' strange customs, particularly as they relate to the details of domestic life—perhaps this interplanetary tourist was billeted with a family in the suburbs. "Caxton" refers to William Caxton (c. 1422–91), thought to be the first English printer.

A Martian Sends a Postcard Home
by Craig Raine

Caxtons are mechanical birds with many wings
and some are treasured for their markings –

they cause the eyes to melt
or the body to shriek without pain.

I have never seen one fly, but
sometimes they perch on the hand.

Mist is when the sky is tired of flight
and rests its soft machine on the ground:

then the world is dim and bookish
like engravings under tissue paper.

Rain is when the earth is television.
It has the property of making colours darker.

Model T is a room with the lock inside –
a key is turned to free the world

for movement, so quick there is a film
to watch for anything missed.

But time is tied to the wrist
or kept in a box, ticking with impatience.

In homes, a haunted apparatus sleeps,
that snores when you pick it up.

If the ghost cries, they carry it
to their lips and soothe it to sleep

with sounds. And yet, they wake it up
deliberately, by tickling with a finger.

Only the young are allowed to suffer
openly. Adults go to a punishment room

with water but nothing to eat.
They lock the door and suffer the noises

alone. No one is exempt
and everyone's pain has a different smell.

At night, when all the colours die,
they hide in pairs

and read about themselves –
in colour, with their eyelids shut.

Raine's Martian tourist is struggling to understand the utility of books (Caxton's "birds with many wings"), bathrooms ("a punishment room / with water but nothing to eat"), and various other aspects of the everyday world of Earthlings, and the alien is approaching the task through an analogical process. A telephone must be haunted because when you pick it up it snores, and you have to wake it up by tickling it with your finger. The *telephone = ghost* analogy is about as scientifically accurate as the *mushrooms in a circle = ring where fairies danced* analogy that gave birth to folk legends or the idea that making a medicine out of red woodpecker feathers and red berries would cure measles. Poetry isn't science and neither is religion: in those fields, analogical thought can lead us to insights that might elude the rationalistic thought processes of the scientist.

In order for a metaphor to "work," it has to relate two ideas (things, phenomena, events) that are clearly different from each other but that have some property in common. The object (or whatever) that we're trying to describe is called the tenor of the metaphor while the object (or whatever) that we use as an analogue is called the vehicle. Robert Burns's famous simile "Oh my Luve's like a red, red rose" relates a flower (the rose) to a person (his love). If we think of both tenor and vehicle as sets, we can illustrate the mechanism of the metaphor using a simple Venn diagram:

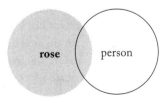

The set of all the characteristics of the rose and the set of all the characteristics of the person overlap: they are both beautiful.

The set of all characteristics of the rose and the set of all attributes of the person are distinct, but they overlap. What do tenor and vehicle have in common? They're both beautiful, to the speaker at least. The area of the diagram that the two sets have in common represents "beauty." Both the flower and the person are beautiful, though the beauty is of a particular kind: the person has the same sort of beauty as a rose that's "newly sprung in June." Using a metaphor allows the poet to represent an abstract idea with a concrete image. Why should we prefer the concrete to the abstract, the image to the idea? Because the abstract word—"beauty"—doesn't represent the same concept to everyone, and because it doesn't engage our senses.

A good metaphor is exciting: it challenges readers to make the connection between tenor and vehicle. It's also thoughtful and insightful: a successful metaphor opens the world to the reader and is never merely irrational or arbitrary. Imagine an electrical diagram with a power source at the base and two long wires extending vertically from the box. If the wires are sufficiently close to each other, a spark should pass between them, completing the circuit. If the wires are *very* close together, the spark will always jump the gap, but the spark will be small, its size and brilliance limited by the narrow gap. Push the wires further apart, and the spark will be larger—you'll get a bigger bang. Push them too far apart, and the current won't be able to jump the gap between the wires. The diagram I've just described is, of course, itself a metaphor—a metaphor for metaphor. The two wires represent the tenor and vehicle of a metaphor. Place them too close together, and there's very little spark: saying that someone's eyes are as brown as a hazelnut doesn't require much imagination, and understanding that simple metaphor doesn't strain our powers of comprehension or offer us any new insight. Saying that a tuna sandwich is a Buick Roadmaster fails even more dramatically: we've placed the wires too far apart, and the analogy doesn't make sense.

That said, it's true that some poets delight in pushing the metaphorical wires as far apart as they dare. The poets of the surrealist group, established in Paris in the early 1920s, liked to combine widely disparate images into startling but sometimes obscure metaphors. While Robert Burns compared the object of his affections to a rose—a simple and easily comprehended analogy—surrealist poet Benjamin Péret compared his lover to a "black forest filled with blue and green postage stamps" and a "kite over a vacant lot where children are fighting."[2]

Some wit once remarked that the first person to say "My love is like a red, red rose" was a genius, and the second person to say it was an idiot. That's a little harsh, but it does point out the necessity of freshness and originality in

---

2 Benjamin Péret, "Wink," trans. Keith Hollaman, *Surrealism-Plays*, http://www.surrealism-plays.com/surrealistpoems.html.

the creation of metaphors. You've all heard stock similes such as "he's as strong as an ox" or "her voice is as sweet as sugar" or "your hands are as cold as ice." These analogies may have been interesting at one time, but we now consider them **dead metaphors**. They've lost their "spark," and they no longer engage us on an intellectual and sensory level. Our conversations are full of dead metaphors: make sure that they don't show up in your poems.

You're no doubt familiar with the standard definition of a **simile**: "a comparison using 'like' or 'as.'" A simile is a type of metaphor (or an alternate way of stating a metaphor). We can turn the list of similes in the previous paragraph into full-on metaphors easily with a little rephrasing: "he's an ox"; "her voice is sugar"; "your hands are ice." Deleting the word "like" and thus transforming a simile into a metaphor is an easy way of making your poems more efficient: you do, however, have to think carefully about the rhythm of the line before you make that deletion.

An **extended metaphor** links a series of images to one analogy. "The whiskey burned his thoughts; his memories were ashes and the room turned to smoke." Here the extended metaphor consists of "fire" imagery. A **governing metaphor** links all the major images in a lyric poem into one analogy that represents the theme of the poem. A lot of successful lyric poems are built around a governing metaphor. Looking for strong metaphors in the early drafts of your poems and extending them throughout the poem so that they form a governing metaphor is a reliable technique for building a draft into a complete poem.

Alexandra Teague connects the image of a storm to her narrator's memory of a personal relationship and sustains that analogy throughout the poem.

Hurricane Season
by Alexandra Teague

When I become accustomed at last to lying in bed alone,
    sheets finely wrinkled as curtains blown across the windows

of dreams, and the crane-necked streetlight fills the room
    with its electric-nerved, luminous vision, what I had

seen for my future (the restless flowering of his arms in sleep
    around my shoulder, the soiled pillows in their matching cases

where our faces, breaths apart, turned toward and away) recedes
    like the hurricane that never hit land the night we met,

when the beach was evacuated, the buildings shuttered in plywood,
    and the news crews stood dry amid the whipping palms,

in the margins of their own story. Later, we saw a photograph shot
    high in the clouds: the storm's eye turning above the ocean,

as we swam at midnight in the pool naked, waiting to be swept up
    in a chlorine shudder, a geyser of winds, into the rapture

of our lives. And though we almost bought it together, we didn't.
    Somewhere, framed in its calm bay of glass, that storm is hanging—

on the gallery's wall at the pinpoint end of this land, or in a room
    like the one where even now he is lying beside her, sleep's

aperture narrowing around them, and all the years when we almost
    loved each other forever, at last, blown far off the shore of this life.

A **prepositional metaphor** puts the vehicle first and the tenor in a prepositional phrase that follows the noun or vehicle: "tarnished plate of evening." Too many prepositional metaphors in a short poem or in a single passage of a long poem can become tedious, and of course a prepositional metaphor is relatively wordy.

A **mixed metaphor** is the result of using two or more metaphors from different fields of reference in the same construction. The politician who promises to "set sail on a new course and get the train back on the tracks" is mixing metaphors. We'd avoid that sort of howler in our poems, but we should also give some thought to keeping our metaphors, like our descriptive imagery, in the same "key." As we noted in the previous chapter, some poems—surrealist poems and "beat" poetry in particular—feature metaphors from various fields of reference, but usually this "scattergun" technique is used in service of a theme that makes the chaotic nature of the imagery seem appropriate.

Kennings and Circumlocutions

Beginning poets sometimes confuse **circumlocution** with metaphor. A circumlocution is a roundabout, wordy way of saying something. The term derives from two Latin words, *circum*, meaning "round about" and *loquor* or *locūtus*, meaning "to speak." Saying "the person who has been trained to care for people who are sick and infirm" instead of saying "the nurse" is a circumlocution; so is saying "an absence of all sounds" instead of "silence." Circumlocution—also known as **periphrasis**—can be used for comic effect in satirical verse, but it's difficult to justify wordiness in most poems.

A kenning is a type of circumlocution traditionally associated with Anglo-Saxon or Norse poetry. The word comes from the Saxon word "ken," meaning (roughly) "to know or to be acquainted with," and it's still in use among speakers of the Scots dialect as well as some other dialect groups in the north of England. Saxon poets disseminated their poems orally, through recitation, and kennings were a useful aid to memory: a familiar stock phrase could be inserted into a recitation as required. Kennings usually replace a single noun or verb with a phrase or a compound word consisting of two or more words, sometimes linked by hyphens. The sea, then, became the "whale-road," a ship was the "sea's steed," a battle was a "sword-storm," blood became "slaughter-dew" or "battle-sweat," the sun was the "sky-candle," to kill was "to feed the eagle," and so on. Fans of fantasy fiction and fantasy poetry will recognize the use of kennings in medieval and dark-ages fantasies, and some poets have adapted the technique to modern poetry: Gerard Manley Hopkins invented highly original compound words that resemble Old English or Norse kennings, and his technique has influenced generations of more recent poets.

BUILDING IMAGERY WITH METONYMY AND METAPHOR

One way of building a poem—that is, taking a poem from the idea stage to the completed work—is to construct "webs" of metonyms and metaphors around the key words in your first draft. If, for example, you wanted to write a poem about an owl, you might begin by surrounding the word "owl" with metonymies and synecdoches. Ask yourself about the owl. What are its parts (beak, feathers, talons)? What are its abilities or attributes (flight, silence, hooting calls, the ability to revolve its head 360 degrees, hunting prowess, nocturnal and solitary habits)? To what class does it belong (birds, predators, night hunters, arctic fauna)?

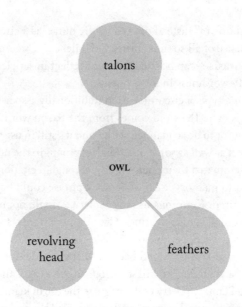

Then begin to build metaphors onto some of the metonymies. What does the owl's face look like? A radar dish, perhaps? With what could you compare its talons? Do they resemble knives, perhaps, or crescent moons or thorns? When you've taken the poem through this process of web building, you should have a complex of ideas (and, more important, a collection of images, thoughts, and interesting diction) that will help you push the poem toward completion.

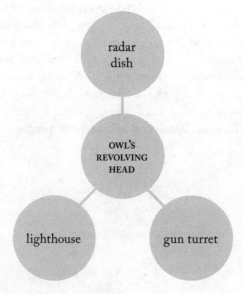

Stretching your imagination is the key to developing the sequence further: take some risks with metaphor so that the ideas presented in the poem are backed up with striking images. Ultimately, there may be limits to what can be *explained*, but there are few limits to what can be *shown*: that's one of the keys to understanding how to write poetry.

Aislinn Hunter conjures up a list of kennings in her poem about the Voyager 1 and Voyager 2 spacecraft, addressing the vehicles as "Purse of greetings, aperture of hope, carrier of bird song." The poem is rich with metaphors, yet it imagines "the absence of comparison" at the "end of what's known." St. Brendan, who is mentioned in the poem, is also known as "the Voyager" or "the Navigator" and is the subject of a ninth-century manuscript describing his legendary journey to the Isle of the Blessed.

Fare Forward, Voyagers
by Aislinn Hunter

Voyager 1 and Voyager 2 continue their current mission to study the region in space where the Sun's influence ends and the dark recesses of interstellar space begin.
—NASA, http://voyager.jpl.nasa.gov, 2003

Beyond the blue gate, beyond the river,
       You are farther away than anything we've touched.
Purse of greetings, aperture of hope, carrier of bird song.
A blinking eye reeling through space,
Acorn, bellwether.
       And like Brendan on his voyage —
Antennas for oars — you push into the wake storm.
And we are the ghosts that follow, a necklace of stars
Yes, *fare forward, voyagers,*
       The end of known space could be anything:
A desert stretched between galaxies,
Darkness dusted, pearls of sand. A lighthouse.
Or the absence of comparison,
       so purely itself it can't be framed.
Or, maybe the end of what's known is a kind of humming.
The echo of everything we've said and done,
Have yet to do,
       out there,
drifting between shores.

Personification

Poets live in an **animistic** world—animals and things can be humanized, endowed with spirits and personalities, and possessed of will and character. Sue Goyette's "Eight" is one of a suite of poems about the ocean.

> *Eight* (from *Ocean*)
> by Sue Goyette
>
> The trick to building houses was making sure
> they didn't taste good. The ocean's culinary taste
>
> was growing more sophisticated and occasionally
> its appetite was unwieldy. It ate boats and children,
>
> the occasional shoe. Pants. A diamond ring.
> Hammers. It ate promises and rants. It snatched up
>
> names like peanuts. We had a squadron of cooks
> specifically catering to its needs. They stirred vats
>
> of sandals and sunglasses. They peppered their soups
> with pebbles and house keys. Quarts of bottled song
>
> were used to sweeten the brew. Discussions between
> preschool children and the poets were added
>
> for nutritional value. These cooks took turns pulling
> the cart to the mouth of the harbour. It would take four
>
> of them to shoulder the vat over, tipping the peeled
> promises, the baked dreams into its mouth.
>
> And then the ocean would be calm. It would sleep. Our mistake
> was thinking we were making it happy.

Allusion and Allegory

Allusion and allegory repeat, on a somewhat grander scale, the analogical thought process we encountered in metaphor. An **allusion** is a reference—often a veiled reference—to something outside the poem, typically to another work of literature but potentially also to historical events, religious mythology, or people from history, for example. Poets recognize that no poem is an island: the history of English literature is a gigantic echo chamber, one that, although it may foreground the English canon in the minds of some poets and readers, also includes translations of texts and transcripts from other languages and cultures. One of the many efficiencies that poetry offers is the ability to reference that vast storehouse of literary and mythic narratives, arguments, epigrams, songs, and images quickly and easily through quotation or parody.

Kim Addonizio's "The First Line is the Deepest" is a collage of allusions. A reasonably well-read reader will recognize parodies of lines from a couple of Robert Frost's poems, Eliot's *The Wasteland*, Allen Ginsberg's *Howl*, and Lord Tennyson's "The Charge of the Light Brigade." Pop music fans will be familiar with the much-covered Cat Stevens song that's parodied in the title, and older readers (or young fans of retro television) may remember the theme song to the sixties sitcom *The Beverly Hillbillies*. There's also a reference to Halliburton Oil, which was commonly associated with President George W. Bush and America's involvement in the Second Gulf War—again, one can allude to history as well as to literature or myth.

The First Line is the Deepest
by Kim Addonizio

I have been one acquainted with the spatula,
the slotted, scuffed, Teflon-coated spatula

that lifts a solitary hamburger from pan to plate,
acquainted with the vibrator known as the Pocket Rocket

and the dildo that goes by Tex,
and I have gone out, a drunken bitch,

in order to ruin
what love I was given,

and also I have measured out
my life in little pills—Zoloft,

Restoril, Celexa,
Xanax.

      For I am a poet. It is my job, my duty
      to know wherein lies the beauty

      of this degraded body,
      or maybe

      it's the degradation in the beautiful body,
      the ugly me

      groping back to my desk to piss
      on perfection, to lay my kiss

      of mortal confusion
      upon the mouth of infinite wisdom.

      My kiss says razors and pain, my kiss says
      America is charged with the madness

      of God. Sundays, too,
      the soldiers get up early, and put on their fatigues in the blue-

      black day. Black milk. Black gold. Texas tea.
      Into the valley of Halliburton rides the infantry—

      Why does one month have to be the cruelest,
      can't they all be equally cruel? I have seen the best

      gamers of your generation, joysticking their M1 tanks through
      the sewage-filled streets. Whose

      world this is I think I know.

An **allegory** is essentially an extended metaphor. The high modernists—notably Pound, Eliot, H. D., and David Jones in poetry and novelists such as James Joyce and Malcolm Lowry—wrote major works that use existing narratives as templates for their plot structure. Eliot called that technique "two-plane writing"; his epic poem *The Wasteland* (1922) is a suite of cantos in varied styles and forms that parallels the myth of the Fisher King from Arthurian mythology.

    Although we may associate allegory with works that parallel earlier narratives, the term can also refer to the creation of plots and situations that dramatize historical trends and events. Priscila Uppal's "Sorry, I Forgot to Clean Up

After Myself" allegorizes the rhetoric of apologists for the detrimental effects of technological progress. The first-person narrator speaks to us in the voice of a huckster or carnival barker, and the auditor—the "you" of the poem—is the huckster's potential mark. As with all essentially allegorical works, getting the message involves reading *through* the poem to a secondary level of meaning.

> *Sorry, I Forgot to Clean Up After Myself*
> by Priscila Uppal
>
> Sorry, Sirs and Madams, I forgot to clean up after myself
> after the unfortunate incidents of the previous century.
>
> How embarrassing; my apologies. I wouldn't advise you
> to stroll around here without safety goggles, and I must insist
> that you enter at your own risk. You may, however, leave
> your umbrella at the door. Just keep your ticket.
>
> We expected, of course, to have this all cleared away by the time
> you arrived. The goal was to present you
> with blue and green screens, whitewashed counters.
>
> Unforeseen expenses.
> Red tape.
> So hard to find good help these days.
>
> But, alas, excuses. Perhaps you will appreciate
> the difficulties I've faced in providing you a clean slate.
> If you step into a hole, Sirs and Madams, accept the loss
> of a shoe or two. Stay the course.
>
> Progress is the mother of invention. Here: take my hand.
> Yes, that's right. You can return it on the way back.

EXERCISES

Exercise 5/1: Metonymy or Metaphor map

Pick an image from one of your poetry drafts and, following the method described in "Building Imagery with Metonymy and Metaphor" (above), think of at least ten metonymies or synecdoches relevant to that image. Put each of these words or phrases in a "thought bubble" surrounding your image. Then choose five of the metonymies and link a metaphor to each one. Select the best metaphors for your poem and work them into your revision.

If you're participating in a writers' group or workshop, try doing this exercise in pairs or groups of three.

Exercise 5/2: Keeping Metaphors "In Key"

Create (at least) three metaphors, pick one, and then develop at least two more in the same key. If you're looking for ideas, use the list of common motifs in the previous chapter.

Exercise 5/3: Kenning Poem

A kenning is a metaphorical word or phrase used primarily in Anglo-Saxon poetry. The kenning is a figure of speech in which we name something not denotatively but by "defining" it with an image. Anglo-Saxon poets used stock kennings frequently, as for example when they called the sea the "whale-road."

Here's a poem that attempts to "define" a simple object, in this case an ordinary silver-coloured, rectangular, tin cigar box. This poem is composed entirely of kennings: in other words, the poem is a list of possible metaphors for a single object—the tin box "looks like" or "is like" the imaginary objects in the list.

Tin Box
by Stephen Guppy

○   A clam designed by bureaucrats

○   A brief hymn to arithmetic, performed
     on pewter bird bones

○   The heart, grown weary of chaos

○   A roomful of empty mirrors.
     (The Wicked Queen is sleeping)

○   A womb, giving birth to a concept

○   A coffin for the general's tongue

○   The case from the geometer's cello

Choose a familiar object from your home and then try to describe it by saying that it's something else. Do this at least three more times, using different analogies each time and trying to make your analogies as imaginative and original as possible. Collate your kennings into a list poem.

Exercise 5/4: Palmistry Poem

Consider your hand. This may seem like a rather strange request, but the word "hand" brings with it a wealth of connotations and associations in addition to its denotative meaning; some of these associations will be etymological (that is, built into the history and structure of the word), while others may be much more subjective. Whatever the source of the associations that cluster around the word "hand," they may also be the source of poetry.

Focus on one or two specific associations (the appearance, for example, of your own hand, or that of an elderly person or a child, or the traditional association of hands with personal identity and Fate), and try to write a brief poem based on those associations. A little research into the physiology of the hand and the arcane practice of palmistry might yield some useful ideas. You might begin by free writing a prose passage or by "mind mapping" or by simply listing associations. Again, work on finding the appropriate form (e.g., line or breath) and diction for your subject.

Exercise 5/5: Bestiary Poem

In the Middle Ages, the bestiary or "book of beasts" was a popular form of literature. Medieval writers believed that animals had been put on earth to instruct us: various animals were associated with various types of behaviour: for example, nesting birds might be considered examples of proper child rearing. The beasts depicted in these texts were sometimes real animals such as bears or lions, but they could also be mythical creatures. Some fiction writers create their own bestiary of imaginary beasts.

Write a free-verse lyric poem describing a real or mythical animal. Use precise, concrete descriptive language, and try to employ a governing metaphor. Your poem can be a third-person description, or it can be narrated from the point of view of the animal. Make your poem colourful and interesting.

TAKEAWAY

- Language can be literal or figurative.
- Metonymy and metaphor are the most commonly used types of figurative language.
- Synecdoche is a particular form of metonymy. A synecdoche identifies the whole by the part (a worker is a "hand") or the part by the whole (The Toronto Maple Leafs are "Toronto").
- A simile is a particular form of metaphor.
- One way of building the imagery in a poem is constructing metonymies by listing some of the more interesting parts or qualities of the thing or person or idea that you want to describe. Having done that, you can then create metaphors for each of the metonymic subsets.

TERMS TO REMEMBER

- allegory
- allusion
- analogical
- animistic
- circumlocution
- dead metaphors
- descriptive imagery
- extended metaphor
- figurative language
- governing metaphor
- kenning
- literal
- metaphor
- metonymy
- mixed metaphor
- periphrasis
- personification
- prepositional metaphor
- simile
- synecdoche
- tenor
- tropes
- vehicle

CHAPTER SIX

Choosing the Best Words

A poet is, before anything else, a person who is
passionately in love with language.[1]
—W.H. Auden

Language is to humans what water is to fish; we live inside it, and we don't necessarily think much about its qualities and characteristics. Poetry, however, foregrounds the materiality of language: when we read a poem, we're as aware of the words themselves as we are of the subject and theme of the poem. One of the hallmarks of a poet is the urge to play with language. Poets think about words in the same way that potters approach clay: they dig around in it and get their hands dirty, feel the textures and hear the unique snap and crackle of each word and phrase. As a poet, you imagine what you can build with words and what opportunities a particular cluster of sound and meaning offers you. You go through the immense junk drawer of the English language looking for bits and pieces that will complement what you already have. You scrape away any verbiage that isn't absolutely necessary and sculpt what you have left into a beautiful and useful final product.

Poets are also adept at framing complex and subtle ideas that other folk have difficulty putting into words. The most depressing phrase a poet can write is this one: "more than words can express." That phrase is an admission of abject poetic incompetence. If you believe that there are things you can't express in language, you're in the wrong game.

You can improve almost any poem by replacing weak diction with more interesting and accurate language. When you've finished drafting a new poem, look carefully at the words you've used and ask yourself whether you've opted for the obvious and "easy" choice or used a word that's trite or inaccurate. Highlight or underline any words that look suspect and then get out the thesaurus, use your online thesaurus, do some research, or just engage your linguistic imagination, and "bump up" the diction in your poem.

Words used in a poem should be a) precise, b) concrete and sensual, c) phonologically interesting, d) allusive, and e) original.

---

1 W.H. Auden, "Squares and Oblongs," in *Poets at Work*, ed. Charles D. Abbott (New York: Harcourt, Brace, 1948), 170.

Precision is important because poets try to create sense impressions: when we describe a tree, we don't want our readers to imagine just any tree; we want them to see the exact, specific tree we have in our minds. In order to achieve that goal, we need to use concrete language. As we noted in our discussion of imagery, poets look for the most specific and concrete words. Not "tree" but "screw pine," "locust," "ginkgo," or "silver maple."

Language is sound as well as graphic signs, and a poem is, among other things, a musical composition. A poem should always be interesting on a phonological level: we'll discuss that important idea in other chapters, so we won't dwell on it here.

A poem doesn't exist in a vacuum; the language existed before the poem was written, and so did a great many other poems and documents from other genres. Poets recognize that the whole of language and literature is an echo chamber and that the words we choose bring with them echoes of other texts. Some words are inherently allusive: I've used the word "echo" twice in the sentence that precedes this one, and it's a word with some interesting associations. In the myth of Echo and Narcissus, Echo is a nymph who tries to trick the goddess Hera and is punished by being limited to endlessly repeating the last words she spoke—hence the connection between the myth and the modern meaning of the word. If we've read some poetry, we might be aware that the story of Echo comes from Ovid's *Metamorphoses*, and if we've read even more poetry, we might know that Samuel Beckett wrote a poem and titled a collection of poems *Echo's Bones*. And so on. . . . It's not always necessary to factor these allusions (these, ah, *echoes* . . .) into the meaning of a poem, but if we're writing for a sophisticated audience, then the allusions may provide us with an additional level of signification that we can exploit.

Art should refresh our senses and make us perceive the world anew. To accomplish that objective, poets have to find new and original ways of communicating their perceptions and insights to their readers. To do this, poets must explore all the resources of language; they must often, in fact, *extend* the resources of language by "bending the rules" and treating the English language as raw material from which to forge new and unforeseen possibilities.

DENOTATION AND CONNOTATION

The **denotation** is the literal meaning of the word. **Connotations** are the ideas we associate with the word. A mule is a quadruped mammal, but the word "mule" also has connotations of stubbornness. A chicken is a bird, but to be "chicken" is to be cowardly. "Slim," "scrawny," and "svelte" all have roughly the same meaning—being thin—but the connotations are strikingly different.

Finding a sufficiently specific noun, adjective, or verb can be challenging; finding the word with just the right connotations is even trickier. When we're writing a poem, we have to be clear about the denotative meaning of each word we use, but we also have to consider the word's connotations. Often, we can pick between a few words that have similar or identical meanings but very different connotations.

English includes a wide range of synonyms; each has specific connotations, but there are usually at least a couple of good options for inclusion in your poem. A thesaurus has always been a useful tool for poets, and most poets have access to an online thesaurus, which is a handy and user-friendly option. Highlight a word that seems slack or too familiar and get your thesaurus app to offer some synonyms (in MS Word, that's Shift–F7). Choose an interesting alternative and substitute it for the word you started out with. Keep repeating that action, and you should be able to locate a word with some sizzle and spark.

Consider the following sets of broadly synonymous words and phrases. Read each row horizontally from left to right. Highlight or underline any words that aren't familiar to you, and then look them up in your dictionary or by searching online. *Which word in each row has the most positive connotations? Which word has the most negative?* When you've done that, select ten words that seem to you to belong together and that would create a consistent tone if they appeared in the same poem.

Table 6.1: Evaluating Connotations

house	mansion	hut	residence
mauve	violet	lavender	plum
bum	beggar	cadger	mendicant
fat	plump	chunky	heavy
prototypical	original	primitive	rudimentary
wise	enlightened	discerning	sharp
gruff	throaty	grouchy	husky
guts	innards	internal organs	viscera
headstrong	stubborn	resolute	pigheaded
small	petite	diminutive	runty

VERB-BASED AND NOUN-BASED POETRY

The core of any English sentence is the combination of a noun (subject) and a verb (predicate). Nouns allow us to create concrete images or express abstractions. Verbs express motion, action, or simply existence. Poems sometimes don't consist of complete sentences, so it's possible that a poem will use nouns and verbs independently, rather than using them in subject-verb pairs.

The subject of a sentence is a noun or noun phrase (a group of words acting as a noun) or a pronoun (a word that takes the place of a noun—such as "it," "she," or "they"). For a poem, we're likely to choose the first of these options. A pronoun is, in a sense, an "empty" marker word; pronouns don't carry any sensory punch. The verb or verb phrase is the "engine" of the sentence: it supplies the action or denotes the state of being. When we're writing a poem, we'd probably choose a single-word verb over a verb phrase, and we'd also try to eliminate a verb that simply expresses a state of being.

You can write an imagistic poem (of a sort) just by stacking up nouns:

> swallows
> forsythia
>
> April

As this embryonic poemlet demonstrates, a noun-only poem is necessarily static and descriptive. It might be possible to imply narrative, particularly if you gave yourself some latitude with the title, but the exclusion of verbs would make it difficult to tell a story or even to argue a point.

Unlike nouns, verbs alone don't always carry a concrete and specific image. Consequently, strings of verb forms tend to create a vague and transitory impression on the reader, rather than confronting him or her with an image. Too often, beginning poets are content to throw verbs around rather than putting together a coherent narrative or sequence of images. The result of this tendency is often something like this:

> Running
> falling
> singing
> staring
> at the wonder
> of the day

The following excerpt from Robert Southey's "The Cataract of Lodore" (1820) should serve as an illustration of the perils of getting too carried away with strings of verbals. This is only a modest slice of the poem as a whole, by the way. Difficult as it may be to believe, there's more (and more and more) of this obsessive verbo-mania to follow.

The cataract strong
    Then plunges along,
    Striking and raging
    As if a war waging
Its caverns and rocks among;
      Rising and leaping
     Sinking and creeping,
     Swelling and sweeping,
     Showering and springing,
   Flying and flinging,
   Writhing and ringing,
   Eddying and whisking,
   Spouting and frisking,
    Turning and twisting
Around and around
    With endless rebound!
Smiting and fighting,
A sight to delight in;
   Confounding, astounding,
Dizzying and deafening the ear with its sound.

     Collecting, projecting,
     Receding and speeding,
    And shocking and rocking,
    And darting and parting,
    And threading and spreading,
    And whizzing and hissing,
    And dripping and skipping,
    And hitting and splitting,
    And shining and twining,
    And rattling and battling,
    And shaking and quaking,
    And pouring and roaring, . . .

The modernists and those poets influenced by modernist aesthetics—which is practically everyone from the mid-twentieth century to the millennium—tended to lean toward noun-based poetry rather than the verb-based alternative as a symptom of their preference for the painterly over the narrative. Contemporary poets have returned to narrative to some degree, usually in the form of "new narrative" or "metaphysical narrative" lyrics, and those genres require a balance between the noun-based and verb-based options. Leaning too hard on the nouns can make a poem seem *too* static and slightly precious—an affliction that plagues some writers of haiku and other types of short, imagistic poems—while getting carried away with verb strings can put poets in the same boat as Mr. Southey, and that's a vessel that's clearly heading over a cataract.

"Nouns on Wheels" and Nominalization

English is a flexible language. Words can be used in various ways. A "play" is a noun, to "play" darts is a verb, and to be "playful" is an adjective. A poet might use one of those "flexible" words in any or all of those contexts, and he or she might also push less obliging words beyond their normal usage by converting them from verb to noun or from noun to verb. The conversion of verb to noun is called **nominalization**. Nouns that are used as if they were verbs are sometimes referred to as "**nouns on wheels**."

We're all familiar with a long list of nouns made into verbs that have evolved out of popular culture and that we use every day. Anyone who grew up in the late twentieth or early twenty-first centuries has adapted to the emergence of a "tech-speak" lexicon that has evolved to deal with an avalanche of hi-tech gadgets, software programs, communications media, and so on. There's nothing odd to us about using verbs such as "to Google," "to fax," "to message," "to friend," or "to unfriend," "to gift" (and, if you're a fan of the TV sitcom *Seinfeld*, to "re-gift"), "to globalize," or "to internationalize." Academics sometimes bemoan this conversion of nouns to verbs—right before they go "conferencing" to see what's "trending" in their discipline. The opposite process, verbs becoming nouns, is also common: an enjoyable book is a "good read."

The flexibility of English provides poets with opportunities for using language in creative ways. In Paul Tyler's "Manitoba Maples," a noun, "python," becomes a verb: "their roots python." Consider the conventional alternatives to that choice of diction: the poet could have used a verb such as "twist," for example, or "curl" or "spiral." None of those options offers the striking image of the coils of a big snake's body. Because he engaged his imagination and visualized a snake, and not just any snake but specifically a python, we're presented with a precise and concrete image that's embedded in the verb choice. The noun "bean" is similarly reincarnated as a verb—"beaning"—in the opening line, and the familiar abbreviated noun "condo" becomes the startling coinage "condoized." The diction in Tyler's poem is consistently inventive and lively: the "nouns on wheels" trick is just one of several techniques he's used to provide the poem with interesting textures and echoes. There are also Hopkinsesque compound words ("fund-pinched" and "lawn-squid"), wildly unusual choices

of adjectives ("bouffant heavies" and "hemophilic spilling"), and nominaliz-
ations ("winter heaves").

Manitoba Maples
by Paul Tyler

Beaning from pavement moss, eyelets in walls, green-quivered
delicates spiked into asphalt morass, helpless, twig-legged.
Until their roots python, bulge into sewer-veins, Godzilla-limbs
arching over rooftops. Opportunistic cuckoo trees, seeding
fund-pinched, zoned-to-be-condoized intersections, unnoticed
in the dumpster-moist dark and sprayed brick lairs, sprouting.
These halloween decorations gone feral loiter in disused lots
plotting chaos. Megalomaniac weeds, bug havens, bird bramble,
messed-up, misshapen bouffant heavies, more given names
than a nineteenth century Austrian countess. No one just says:
tree. Laid-back neighbours suddenly insist on shredders, buy
mid-life crisis chainsaws. One maple, rumoured to have dropped
a branch on a widow's head, waited years for the right angle.
Another slipped a muddy claw inside a basement duct, opened
the house right up in a hemophilic spilling of oil and heartache.
Near a stumbling Manitoba town I saw some last-century hutch
stabbed up the middle by a young maple, pronged out windows,
deciduous mess of dust bowl bankruptcy. Could be your life next—
the neighbour points, eyeing up the grand trunk's indifference
to fence lines—could cause wires to snap, flatten your roses, a cat,
bring down satellite beams, screw with calls to old world aunts,
nest in the driveway's winter heaves, spring through the Camaro
convalescent on blocks, stripping it to its chassis. See that crack?
Your foundation might be next. It'll creep inside while you sleep,
drop pods in your dreams, this shambling mound of uncompostable
leaves, this pollen puffing lawn-squid; it has nothing better to do.

ABSTRACT AND CONCRETE

Nouns and adjectives can be classified as either abstract or concrete. A concrete
noun denotes something (or someone) that we can perceive with our senses (or
with technological extensions of our senses—a planet seen through a telescope
is still concrete). An abstract noun denotes something we *can't* perceive: an
idea or emotion.

Concrete nouns such as *ribbon, book, clay, paper, elm, water, frost, lips,* or *strawberry* denote things we can perceive with our senses. We can see each of those things, and we could, if we wished, touch, smell, or taste them. If we dropped a book, we could presumably hear it land on the floor. We could feel the ribbon if we passed it through our fingers. We could crumple a sheet of paper. The water would be cool or warm if we splashed our faces with it, and it might taste anything from refreshing to brackish or sour.

Abstract nouns such as *happiness, courage, fear, confusion, anger, fatigue, loneliness, inspiration, patriotism,* and *memory* don't correspond to specific sense impressions. We can't touch *happiness* or smell it or taste it. We can taste a chocolate truffle, and if we like chocolate the taste might make us happy, but notice that we have to imagine a specific concrete thing before we can relate the idea of happiness to our senses. We might be able to perceive the results of fear—someone screaming or running away—but we can't smell or touch or taste the concept *fear*; that concept resides in the mind and not in the world of the senses. Poets generally shy away from using abstractions, at least unless they've "backed up" the abstract word with a concrete image that illustrates the concept.

The same approach applies to adjectives as to nouns: poets (and all professional writers) try to avoid adjectives that are abstract and general—*happy, brave, big, good, splendid, magnificent, fabulous.*

The Abstraction Ladder

Although nouns and adjectives can be classified as either abstract or concrete, there are differing levels of abstraction, at least in the sense that we can visualize a hierarchy from the most concrete and particular words to the most abstract and general; that continuum is called the "**abstraction ladder.**"

Imagine that you've just opened a clothing shop in a suburban mall. You've researched the market and stocked your store with the latest fashion items. You have *shirts, sweaters, dresses, pants, jackets,* and *suits.* It's your Grand Opening, and you wait, breathless with excitement, as your first customer walks into your store and says, "I would like a buy a *garment.*"

Now you have a dilemma. Which type of garment does he want—a shirt, perhaps? A sweater? A snazzy pair of pants? You ask the customer to clarify his request, but he refuses to do so and just keeps repeating that he wants a "garment." You finally give up in despair.

You're so frustrated by your experience with your first customer that you close your store and get a job in the big department store at the end of the mall.

Now you're covered. You have garments. You have furniture. You have major appliances and minor appliances. You even have housewares and notions. It's your first day on the job, and you're wandering around with your "Assistant Manager" tag pinned proudly to your jacket, when in walks the same customer who drove you out of your previous business. "I would like," he says, "to buy some *merchandise*." Once again, he refuses to be more specific.

Completely disheartened, you quit your job and retire to a tiny island in the South Seas. One sunny day, you're lying on the beach taking life easy when the phone on the nearest palm tree rings. It's your fabulously wealthy Aunt Agatha. She's the President and CEO of AgathaCorp, a diversified global conglomerate. "Quit lying around wasting your time!" your aunt commands you. "Come back here, and I'll give you a job." Agatha's a very scary sort of aunt, and you've always done whatever she asks, so you hop on the first passing banana boat and relocate to Manhattan's financial district, where you take up a position as a senior executive in AgathaCorp's central office. Now you're *really* covered. You have merchandise. You have livestock. You have transportation systems. You have currencies from various countries. You have natural resources. What could possibly go wrong?

Your first day on the job, you're sitting in your private office on the 47th floor of the AgathaTower behind a desk the size of Montana. The doors of your private elevator open, and out walks the same customer who made you close down your retail outlet and quit your job with the department store. "I would like to buy," he says, "some of your *assets*." As you fall forty-seven floors toward the pavement below, having thrown yourself out the window in despair, it comes to you that you have been climbing a kind of intellectual ladder, one that took you from the most *concrete and particular* (sweaters, dresses, shirts) to the most *abstract and general* (assets).

We can arrange nouns into a hierarchy in which specific and precise words are gathered into larger categories denoted by general terms. The nouns that denote those categories are more abstract than the relatively concrete nouns within that category. The philosopher S.I. Hayakawa coined the term "abstraction ladder" in his book *Language in Action* (1939), and it's an idea that rings a bell with writers and with poets in particular.

Here's the little hierarchy you encountered in your adventures in business:

The Abstraction Ladder

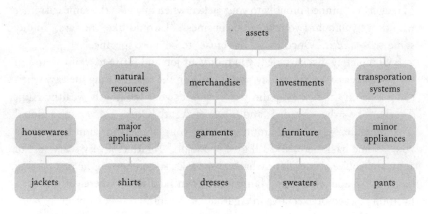

Note, by the way, that even the lowest "rung" of our ladder doesn't take us to the most specific possible words. The term "sweater" is less specific than the words for the various types of sweater: e.g., cardigan, pullover, or V-neck. ("Sweater" is also a North American dialect word not commonly used in England or in some other English-speaking communities.) Shirts, similarly, could be classified into dress shirts, tuxedo shirts, T-shirts, sweatshirts, or various other types.

When do we reach the bottom of the abstraction ladder? When we've arrived at a noun that denotes a unique individual—a proper noun as opposed to a common noun. "Poet" is a general term that includes various types of poet: formalists, free-verse poets, narrative poets, aleatoric and experimental poets, spoken-word performers, sound poets, and so on. Those categories are more particular than the larger category of "poet," but they're still category words and thus still relatively general. We won't get to the bottom of the ladder until we name individual poets. When we're discussing Robert Lowell or Mina Loy or Edna St. Vincent Millay, we're down to the bottom of the ladder, though we might also be near the top of the hierarchy of poets!

Poets recognize that a concrete noun is more effective than an abstract one because concrete nouns affect our senses while abstractions only engage the intellect, and then often in a vague and general manner. Poets try to go "down" the abstraction ladder by choosing the most concrete and specific words. Never say "tree" when you mean "elm."

In order to write from the bottom of the abstraction ladder, you'll probably need to do some research. If you want to use a more specific concrete noun than "flower," you'll need to know something about the different species of flower. The poet and novelist Thomas Hardy reputedly considered himself an expert on the various types of wildflower in his region; he needed to know a lot about wildflowers in order to enrich his pastoral poems with specific and accurate terms. Dictionaries and encyclopaedias can be useful when you're looking for the right word, and fortunately there are dictionaries for various fields available online. Again, if you want to write poetry well, be prepared to do some research.

THE DNA OF VOICE: WHERE DOES OUR LEXICON COME FROM?

As we discovered in Chapter 3, the voice of a poem can closely resemble your own voice, but it can also be a voice you've conjured up for the occasion. Each different voice implies a distinct lexicon, and defining the parameters of that lexicon is an important part of writing the poem. Analyzing some of the characteristics of your own voice is a good place to start. Your voice is shaped by various pressures: where you grew up; your level and type of education; whether you were brought up by English speakers and, if so, what dialect of English they spoke; what type of slang you encountered as an adolescent; and what jargon and technical language you assimilated in your education and profession. Consider how these factors may have influenced your sense of voice. Each of these categories should also present you with some options for widening and focusing your lexicon.

Dialect Words

The English language isn't fixed and monolithic: there are, in a manner of speaking, several different English languages, and there's really no "standard English" that prescribes every English speaker's vocabulary, usage, pronunciation, and even orthography. Jamaican English is not the same as Australian or Nigerian or Canadian or American English, yet each is functional and "correct" within its own regional context and for its own community of speakers. Within these forms of English are smaller regional dialects; consider, for example, the difference between the American English spoken in Boston and in Dallas. Even the home country, England, is still divided between dialects: Yorkshire English includes words that aren't commonly used in Dorset or Essex. A person from Yorkshire might use dialect words such as "owt" and "nowt" instead of saying "anything" and "nothing" or say "anyroad" instead of "anything." The differences between the English spoken in England and that spoken in North America are even more striking: in Canada and the United States babies wear "diapers" and travel in a "buggy" or "carriage" or "stroller" while in England they wear "nappies" and go about town in a "pram."

Some poets foreground their own regional dialects in their poems. Here's an excerpt from a poem by William Barnes, who lived in the west of England in the nineteenth century and who often wrote in the Dorsetshire dialect. A "clote," by the way, is a lily.

The Clote
by William Barnes (1801–86)

O zummer clote, when the brook's a-slidèn
So slow an' smooth down his zedgy bed,
Upon thy broad leaves so siafe a-ridèn
The water's top wi' thy yoller head,
By black-rin'd allers
An' weedy shallers,
Thou then dost float, goolden zummer clote.

The grey-bough'd withy's a leänèn lowly
Above the water thy leaves do hide;
The bendèn bulrush, a-swâyèn slowly,
Da skirt in zummer thy river's zide;
An' perch in shoals, O,
Do vill the holes, O;
Where thee dost float, goolden zummer clote.

O when thy brook-drinkèn flow'r's a-blowèn,
The burnèn zummer's a-zettèn in;
The time o' greenness, the time o' mowèn,
When in the hây-viel', wi' zunburnt skin,
The vo'ke da drink, O,
Upon the brink, O,
Where thou dost float, goolden zummer clote!

Even in Barker's time, Dorsetshire was only a few hours' train ride from London, but the regional dialects of those places were, as this poem illustrates, strikingly different. Ask yourself which regional dialect you speak, and then ask yourself whether you want to make that dialect a feature of your poetry. Even a few dialect words can help to give a poem an interesting texture and to "locate" it in relation to a place and culture.

Slang and Jargon

Slang is informal language that belongs to a particular social circle. Slang is usually generated by young people, typically teenagers, and is often specific to a subculture—kids who identify as Goths or gamers or skater punks or jocks or hipsters, for example. A typical high school probably plays host to a few different slang cultures, and using the slang of a group implies membership in that subculture. Slang is generational—most slang words age quickly, and you can sometimes date a person by listening to the slang he or she uses. It's a social faux pas to use the slang of another generation: there's nothing more pathetic (and unintentionally funny) than an older person trying to use the slang of a younger generation.

Jargon is language that relates to a particular trade, profession, craft, or interest group. When we join a profession or trade or become part of an organization, we'll probably have to assimilate and use some new jargon; the military and law enforcement are obvious examples of organizations with their own complex jargon, but restaurant servers and construction workers and most other professionals also have their own ever-evolving set of terms. Think about the jargon you've had to learn in the jobs you've had and ask yourself whether you might be able to build a poem around that specialized lexicon.

Technical and Scientific Language

It's a cliché to say that modern universities educate people in either the sciences or the humanities and that relatively few students acquire expertise in both. Cliché or not, the "two cultures" paradigm remains true. One consequence of this great divide is that some contemporary poets live in a world of advanced technology but lack the vocabulary to communicate that experience in any but the most subjective terms. Poets can extend and enrich their working vocabulary by researching the language used in other disciplines. Taking an interest in the patois of biologists, computer scientists, technicians, economists, herbalists, meteorologists, astronomers, and specialists in other fields of expertise can help you build a repertoire of interesting words to use in your poems. That sort of research might also help you to discover rich veins of imagery and perhaps even themes and subjects for your poems.

August Kleinzahler draws words from a wide array of sources in his "The Strange Hours Travelers Keep." The lexicon of philosophers mingles with the jargon of business, finance, astronomy, astrology, anatomy, and technology. The juxtaposition of words from all those lexicons is ironic and witty, but it's also realistic: the lingo of business, hi-tech, and modern science floats around on the Internet and news media and is a part of our cultural surround, whether we fully understand it or not.

> *The Strange Hours Travelers Keep*
> by August Kleinzahler
>
> The markets never rest
> Always they are somewhere in agitation
> Pork bellies, titanium, winter wheat
> Electromagnetic ether peppered with photons
> Treasure spewing from Unisys A-15 J mainframes
> Across the firmament
> Soundlessly among the thunderheads and passenger jets
> As they make their nightlong journeys
> Across the oceans and steppes
>
> Nebulae, incandescent frog-spawn of information
> Trembling in the claw of Scorpio
> Not an instant, then shooting away
> Like an enormous cloud of starlings
>
> Garbage scows move slowly down the estuary
> The lights of the airport pulse in morning darkness
> Food trucks, propane, tortured hearts
> The reticent epistemologist parks
> Gets out, checks the curb, reparks
> Thunder of jets
> Peristalsis of great capitals
>
> How pretty in her tartan scarf
> Her ruminative frown
> Ambiguity and Reason
> Locked in a slow, ferocious tango
> Of *if not, why not*

Ancestral Echoes

English differs from one region to another; it also changes through time. A language is not a machine, though it may be convenient to look at sentences as if they were as predictable as mechanical contraptions. A language is actually more like an organism than a mechanism. Like a plant or animal, a word has a history. A word is the product of an evolutionary process: it appeared in the language at a particular time in response to particular conditions and needs, and it evolved as the language as a whole changed due to migrations, invasions, trade, technological innovation, or the intermarriage of different dialect or language groups.

English is formed from a variety of sources; it's a hybrid language, composed of Latin and Anglo-Saxon (Old English) root words; it has since been further enriched by the additional of a sizable repertoire of "loan words" from other languages. The hybrid nature of the language gives it a special richness; we can often choose between a Latinate word or phrase and a word or phrase that is Germanic (Old English) in origin. Thus, one can choose between deciding to "think" (from the Old High German *denken*) or to "ratiocinate" (from the Latin *ratiocinatus*, to reckon). Given this built-in richness, writers working in English can generally count on having a spectrum of synonyms or near synonyms to choose from.

If we wish to use language precisely and accurately in our poems, we need to think about the origins and history of words. Take, for example, the word "chronological," meaning "in the order of time." A good dictionary will tell us that the word came to us from the ancient Greek and that it is a combination of two shorter words: "khrónos," meaning time, and "logos," meaning sense or logic. An etymological dictionary will also tell us that the word "chronological" was first used in print in English in 1593. Further research might lead us to the origins of the two root words. "Khrónos" (aka Chronus) was a god from ancient Greek mythology who helped order the universe and became associated with the concept of time, as well as with the Titan named Cronus, who was descended from the marriage of Earth and Sky and gave birth to Zeus. "Logos" has a few different connotations, including the association of the word with order and reason and, in Christian theology, with Jesus as the incarnate Word. That's a lot of baggage for one word!

Knowing the background of words can be a source of inspiration. If we refer to a calliope (the musical instrument) in a poem, we should be aware that we are also referring to the Muse of epic poetry, Calliope, and that as ordinary a word as "cereal" contains the name of the Roman goddess of agriculture, Ceres. Other English words come from other cultural backgrounds, and many bring with them intriguing histories that we can incorporate into our poems. At the very least, we should be sufficiently aware of the etymology of our words that we can control the echoes that they generate.

Loan Words

English contains a great many "**loan words**" from other languages; new ones can usefully be brought into the language of poetry. Exploring your own cultural background or your travels may suggest some useful possibilities for bringing foreign words into your poems. In Chapter 15, we'll discuss some protocols for using foreign-language words in poetry.

Neologisms

In their search for precise and musical language, poets occasionally coin new words or join two words into a compound word. Such words as "Pandemonium" (Milton), "twindle" (Hopkins), and "chortle" (Lewis Carroll) were invented by writers. Consider these compound words from Gerard Manley Hopkins (1844–89):

Table 6.2: Compounds from Hopkins

couple-colour	fawn-froth	fell-frowning	fresh-firecoal
dapple-dawn-drawn	heathpacks	rollrock	chestnut-falls
windpuff-bonnet	beadbonny	rose-moles	fathers-forth

Hopkins was marvellously inventive with his diction, and he also took extraordinary risks with the order of words in phrases and sentences. He seems, at times, to have approached the English language with few rigid preconceptions regarding grammar, syntax, or lexical choice. It's not surprising that his creative approach to language has been influential.

LEXICAL REGISTER

The literary theorist Northrop Frye makes a distinction between the **hieratic** style, which is self-consciously literary and formal, and the **demotic** style, which is modelled on the language of everyday speech. In some premodern poetry, the high or "hieratic" style was used extensively, and the language of poetry was often ornate and self-consciously "poetic." The eighteenth-century poet Thomas Gray remarked that "the language of the age is never the language of poetry."[2] Most poets of the modern era would have little sympathy for the attitude expressed in Gray's statement; for them, "the language of the age" is *always* the language of poetry. Poets, in modern times, generally write in the language of their time and their place. There are, however, some poets who have made a conscious choice to employ the "high" style in their work, against the grain of the times, as it were. Consider the diction employed in the two poems that follow, the first by Canadian poet Ralph Gustafson and the second by his contemporary, Al Purdy.

Biography
by Ralph Gustafson (1909–95)

What time the wily robin tuggeth worm,
Dragging my grandsire from reluctant dust,
Did I, through fatal lips of unction thrust,
Lunge headmost lidded from Cassandra's womb:
Puberal, still with bended bow did shoot
Heroic arrows tipped at the fabulous sky,
Whose silver barbed the snow. To testify
The cryptic acorn plus the accurate root,
I, fool, with words of paper, scissors, paste,
Mailed awkward anagrams to Love and Death,
And lagged and loosed the ravelling threads that baste
This bone to cerements of flesh. Beneath
The purchase of my present jaw, I taste
The apple twixt the tombstones of my teeth.

My '48 Pontiac
by Al Purdy (1918–2000)

All winter long it wouldn't start
standing in the yard covered with snow
I'd go out at 10 below zero and coax
and say
        "Where's your pride?"
and kick it disgustedly
Finally snow covered everything

---

2 Quoted in *The Cambridge History of Literary Criticism: Volume 4, The Eighteenth Century*, ed. H.B. Nisbet and Claude Rawson (Cambridge, UK: Cambridge UP, 2005), 140.

but television aerials and the world was
a place nobody came to
so white it couldn't be looked at
before nothing was something
But the old Pontiac lay there
affirming its identity
like some prehistoric vegetarian
stupidly unaware of snow
waiting for Tyrannosaurus Rex
to come along and bite off its fenders
"You no good American Pontiac you
(I'd say)
you're a disgrace to General Motors"
then go out and hitch up the dog team
When June hurried by it still wouldn't start
only stop
and the wreckers hauled it away

If we were to generalize about the diction employed in the two poems, we might say that Purdy belongs to the **vernacular** tradition in modern poetry, while Gustafson evokes a more formal and Latinate sense of language. Interesting effects can be achieved by mixing the hieratic and demotic in a single poem, as in the following example.

Money
by Carmine Starnino

Coin Exhibit, British Museum.

Their misshapenness strikes the table in tiny splashes,
like still-cooling splatters of silver. Stater and shekel,
mina and obol. Persia's bullion had a lion and bull.

Athens an owl, Messana a hare, a jar for Terone, Melos
a pomegranate. Call it museum money, written off
and not expected back—some Ozymandian loose change,

or a bit of dodo boodle, bygone swag, has-been loot,
history's tithe to itself. And God knows after all this
gazing at glass maybe even you mull the quaintness

of things kept too long. But not so fast. This old currency
returns us to first principles, to a time when poverty
had heft, when debt was assigned its correct weight,

spilled metal coldcocking its solid clink against metal,
when taxes, rents and sundry dues were made real
by the real coins that paid for them, knurled and oblong,

dented and pinched, coins that called out your cost
when spoken on scales and so relentlessly palpable
they held their ground as outlaw selves of your reflective tact,

giving the middle finger to poetic truth. They belong
to days before dollars dipped, when it was futile to speculate
on the facts; ingots were unillusionary, would mean

what you spent, and prosperity, like perdition, properly
shouldered its burden, like those last Roman senators
forced to carry their assets in carts. Know what truth was?

Truth was the unapproximating mix of gold and silver
smelted and cast into bars, the alloy hammered flat,
blanks cut with shears, stacked, then hammered again

into circular shape. Now that's genuine, that's proof.
The heat and hiss, the loud crack of tools. When what you earned
was itself evidence of a life lived in labor, the stubble-

to-beard truth of busting your butt—a few, of course,
added bronze to phony the weight, but being neither metaphor
nor symbol, its quality could be checked by a chisel cut.

Starnino is intentionally ratcheting back and forth between lexical levels here.
Street-level slang terms such as "coldcocking" and "busting your butt" contrast
with Latinate diction ("relentlessly palpable," "reflective tact," and "unillusionary"), and there's a literary allusion ("Ozymandian"), a coined term ("dodo
boodle"), and some archaic diction ("knurled," "tithe," and "swag") thrown
into the mix. This juxtaposition of contrasting lexical levels is a sophisticated
technique, but it's one we can all learn from. An important part of the appeal
of poetry is the linguistic high-wire act that poets can perform by using the

various resources of the language. In order to play the game at that level, we first have to cultivate a lively curiosity about the language and a willingness to research and explore and invent and take risks.

DICTION CLUNKERS: PROBLEMS TO AVOID

Vague and General Diction

Here's a descriptive sentence that's full of polysyllabic, Latinate diction. How effective would it be as a line in a poem?

"The panoramic splendour of the majestic mountains was breathtaking."

Consider the language in that sentence. A panorama is simply a wide-angle (180 degree) view. "Splendour," "majestic," and "breathtaking" report the speaker's emotions, but they don't describe the scene that provoked those reactions, and they do nothing to create those reactions (or any reactions, except possibly boredom) in the reader. Every reader may have a different sense of the majestic and the splendid, and there's no reason for the reader to feel that his or her breath has been taken away just because you, the poet, had that feeling.

When writing a description, you have two tasks to perform: 1) Make the reader see (and perhaps hear, smell, feel, and taste) the subject of the description; 2) Make the reader react emotionally and intellectually to the scene you've described. To accomplish these goals, you'll need precise, concrete, interesting, original diction. Remember, it's the reader's experience that matters, not yours.

Archaic and Pretentiously "Poetic" Diction

One of the most common mistakes that beginning poets make is to assume that the language of poetry is removed from the language they actually speak. Instead of listening to the language of their own time and place, they take the poetry of the eighteenth or nineteenth centuries as their model. The result is often an awkward hybrid of modern and archaic diction: words such as "eldritch," "gossamer," and "azure" begin to crop up in their poems, often in conjunction with modern slang and jargon, with unfortunate results. These stanzas from Coleridge's "The Rime of the Ancient Mariner" contain words such as "stoppeth," "may'st," and "eftsoons" that weren't contemporary diction in 1834, when this version of the poem was published, and that certainly aren't now.

It is an ancient Mariner,
And he stoppeth one of three.
"By thy long grey beard and glittering eye,
Now wherefore stopp'st thou me?

"The Bridegroom's doors are opened wide,
And I am next of kin;
The guests are met, the feast is set:
May'st hear the merry din."

He holds him with his skinny hand,
"There was a ship," quoth he.
"Hold off! unhand me, grey-beard loon!"
Eftsoons his hand dropt he.

Coleridge was consciously employing an archaic lexicon in order to distance the narrative at the core of the poem from contemporary experience—the ancient mariner who tells the tale to the wedding guest isn't the average person you'd bump into on the street, and his story is intended to have the tone and feel of myth.

Fashions in diction change just like fashions in hats or shoes. The following poem by late-Victorian poet Ernest Dowson was popular in its day and deservedly so; in many ways, it's an enjoyable poem, though Dowson's choice of words may seem overblown to the modern ear. The use of archaic pronoun forms ("thy" and "thee" and "mine arms" instead of "my arms") seems a self-conscious attempt to make verse appear "poetic," and there are a few more modifiers than a contemporary poet would be comfortable with. That said, Dowson's poem is both musical and memorable, and he possessed an ability to conjure up phrases that stick in the mind: "gone with the wind" became the title of both a best-selling novel and one of the most famous Hollywood movies.

Non Sum Qualis Eram Bonae Sub Regno Cynarae
by Ernest Dowson (1867–1900)

Last night, ah, yesternight, betwixt her lips and mine
There fell thy shadow, Cynara! thy breath was shed
Upon my soul between the kisses and the wine;
And I was desolate and sick of an old passion,
    Yea, I was desolate and bowed my head:
I have been faithful to thee, Cynara! in my fashion.

All night upon mine heart I felt her warm heart beat,
Night-long within mine arms in love and sleep she lay;
Surely the kisses of her bought red mouth were sweet;
But I was desolate and sick of an old passion,
    When I awoke and found the dawn was gray:
I have been faithful to thee, Cynara! in my fashion.

I have forgot much, Cynara! gone with the wind,
Flung roses, roses riotously with the throng,
Dancing, to put thy pale, lost lilies out of mind;
But I was desolate and sick of an old passion,
    Yea, all the time, because the dance was long:
I have been faithful to thee, Cynara! in my fashion.

I cried for madder music and for stronger wine,
But when the feast is finished and the lamps expire,
Then falls thy shadow, Cynara! the night is thine;
And I am desolate and sick of an old passion,
    Yea, hungry for the lips of my desire:
I have been faithful to thee, Cynara! in my fashion.

It's not invariably true that poets should write the way they speak, but using archaic diction is usually a mistake. Unless you're being ironic or writing a persona poem with an historical character as the narrator, the old rule that poets should never write anything they wouldn't say in conversation is worth keeping in mind.

Clichés

Clichés are often just dead metaphors—analogies that have lost their punch through decades or even centuries of repetition: *black as coal, white as snow, dark as night.*

Some metaphors are so obvious that it's hardly worth repeating them: the comparison of sexual passion to fire, for example, or the linking of someone's beauty to a flower. Here are some familiar locutions that have lost their zip and should be avoided:

- Stars like diamonds
- Drowning in sorrow
- Aflame with passion
- Her soul was laid bare

- His mind took flight
- My heart sings
- Love is blind
- Looking into my very soul
- As dense as fog
- Pierced my heart
- Reaching new heights, scaling new heights
- My weary soul (wandering soul or almost any kind of lonely soul)
- Broken heart, lonely heart, fickle heart, heavy heart, cold heart, or almost any kind of unhappy heart
- Silken hair, apple cheeks, ruby lips, emerald eyes
- Time heals all wounds
- Time goes by

Though the guidelines we've just discussed are important to our understanding of the role of word choice in the craft of poetry, there's no general rule that governs the selection of words for a poem. Some voices require "plain speech" while others need a broader or more formal lexicon. The only guideline that applies to all poems and all poets is that it's essential to bring a high level of attention and awareness to our relationship with language. If we want to make our poems as exciting, enjoyable, and meaningful as possible, we have to be willing to develop our skills by expanding our lexicon. Searching out interesting and useful words by reading widely and by listening to the "language of the street" is the first step toward developing such a broad and rich repertoire.

EXERCISES

Exercise 6/1: Working with Connotations

Provide three better words for each of the following. Make your choices concrete, precise, and original. If there's no appropriate synonym, use your imagination and reach for a metaphor.

- tree (evergreen, distorted by wind) apple tree, birch,
- mountain (barren, relatively small)
- old man
- manual worker
- soft rain
- hard rain
- infatuation

- confusion
- corrosion
- small talk
- relaxation
- disillusionment

Exercise 6/2: The Imaginary Dictionary

Imagine you've been given the task of arranging all the words in the English language into some order. What system of organization would you use?

You're already familiar with a couple of books that organize large numbers of English words: the dictionary and the thesaurus. Dictionaries arrange words alphabetically. That's a useful method if you want to find out how to spell a word or what its meanings might be. You can locate the desired word easily; all you need to know is the order of letters in the alphabet. In a thesaurus, words are clustered purely in terms of their meaning: various words with similar denotations or connotations are arranged in a brief list, and these clusters are grouped into a larger general category. These categories and subcategories are called "semantic fields." In Peter Mark Roget's original *Thesaurus of English Words and Phrases* of 1852, these "big" categories included "space," "matter," "intellect," "abstract relations," and "volition."

In a rhyming dictionary, words are arranged into clusters of rhymed words. One could imagine dictionaries of words that share a similar vowel sound or that have a natural anapaestic metre. All these methods of organization are (or might be) useful to poets.

Dictionaries sometimes provide information about the origin of a particular word. Does it come from the Latin, for example, or the Old English? It would presumably be possible to organize large numbers of modern English words in terms of derivation. All the Latinate words could go into one list, all the foreign loan words into another, and so on. It's also possible to imagine more fanciful categories: words organized according to the type of weather they describe or evoke, words that suit a particular mood, words that have organic or mechanical associations, words that occur in the speeches of Benjamin Disraeli or in the song lyrics of Taylor Swift, and so on.

Some poets design their own poetic forms by imposing "constraints" on the language they use. Poets have, for example, restricted themselves to using only those words that do not contain the letter "s."

Working alone or in groups of two or three, devise your own system for arranging and classifying English words. Use your imagination. Your new system may not be useful or even very sensible, but it should be imaginative and fun.

Exercise 6/3: Recognizing Slang and Jargon

Step 1: Slang Generations

Each of the following samples lists slang terms from one decade of the twentieth century—the 1920s, 1950s, 1960s, and 1980s. Working in groups or alone, try to identify the decade, and see how many of the slang terms you can understand and define. List or highlight any of these words that are still in use.

> Sample 1: Blast, cat, chariot, burn rubber, mint, cool, square, cube, duck-ass, flat-top, winkle-pickers, handle, horn, kookie, lid, nowhere, pad, pound, passion pit, ragtop, threads, strides, rumble.

> Sample 2: Bad, bomb, boss, bread, bummer, burned, chick, choice, head, crash, dork, dove, dropout, fab, gear, fink, freak, fox, funky, fuzz, gas, hang loose, hang-up, happening, hassle, heat, hip, laid back, far out, later, mod, off the wall, out of sight, righteous, rip off, uptight, vibes, threads.

> Sample 3: bee's knees, cat's pyjamas, cheater, gaspers, egg, yegg, jake, mazuma, know your onions, on a toot, spifflicated, tomato, zozzled, vamp, blind pig, Bronx cheer, jack, meat wagon, ace, deuce, fin, saw-buck, beat it, big cheese, bump off, busthead, bootleg, bushwa, gams, get-up, lollapalooza, sap, shiv, razz.

> Sample 4: totally, tubular, gnarly, grody, radical, bag your face, psyche, Betty, bitchin', bite me, boho, bounce, boy toy, chill, choice, couch potato, dank, deadly, dis, ditz, fave, fugly, gamer, get real, glam, Goth, hacker, hard core, harsh, headbanger, hella, homegirl, kickass, noob, ralph, wannabe, veg.

Step 2: Fields of Jargon

Each of the following lists includes jargon words from a particular profession, trade, or organization. Try to identify the source of all the words in each list. Which list is academic jargon, which is business jargon, which is education-related jargon, and which is military jargon?

> List 1: repurposing, transitioning, rebranding, paradigm shift, key metrics, impactful, deliverables, incentivise, core competencies, mission statement, leverage, reinvent the wheel, open the kimono, think outside the box, downsizing, blue-sky thinking, blamestorming.

List 2: metonymic, hermeneutics, commodified, contextualizing, perspectivizing, conceptualize, taxonomic, metacritical, polysemy, analepsis, metalepsis, indexical, reification, interstitial, valorize, diegetic, allegoresis, grammatology, oracy, aurality, centripetality.

List 3: heterogeneous groups, interpersonal intelligence, locus of control, methodology, motivational opening, musical-rhythmic intelligence, phonemic awareness, realia, remediation, rubric, summative evaluation, task orientation, stressor, prior knowledge, stimulus.

List 4: got your six, roger that, zero dark thirty, high and tight, hit the head, SOL, snafu, squared away, dog tags, hooch, back in the world, grunt, bandit, SOP, grease gun, honcho, deep six, ETA, gremlin, bug out, puddle jumper, sky pilot.

Exercise 6/4: Using Slang and Jargon in Poetry

Write a persona poem from the perspective of someone who would use one of the types of slang or jargon included in the lists in Exercise 6/3. Try to use as many of the slang or jargon words from the relevant list as you can, and add more to the list through your own research.

Exercise 6/5: Expanding Your Lexicon

Complete all three of the following lists, each containing at least five words.

- List 1 should consist of slang words used by your own generation.
- List 2 should be technical language from a branch of the sciences or technologies or from a craft.
- List 3 should be jargon from one particular profession, sport, or hobby.

When you've done this, share your list with the other members of your writers' group or workshop. Be prepared to discuss the origin and meaning of each word.

TAKEAWAY

- Words used in a poem should be a) precise, b) concrete and sensual, c) phonologically interesting, d) allusive, and e) original.
- Avoid abstract and general words such as "beautiful," "majestic," "breathtaking," or "courageous"—you're a poet, not a bureaucrat or a politician.
- Go as far down the abstraction ladder as possible. Get to the most specific, concrete word available. Never a "tree" when you know it's an "elm" or even a "red elm."
- Avoid clichés.
- Avoid pointlessly archaic or self-consciously "poetic" diction.
- Be aware of the lexical register that's appropriate to your poem.
- Consider dialect words, slang and jargon, loan words, even neologisms; poems often push the boundaries of standard usage, and poets are usually avid collectors of words.
- Look for interesting diction. Be prepared to do some research; researching the language connected to your central motif or governing metaphor is often a good place to start.

TERMS TO REMEMBER

- abstract nouns *cannot see/touch etc*
- abstraction ladder *hierarchy of nouns*
- clichés *dead/overused metaphors*
- concrete nouns *can use senses*
- connotation *feelings surrounding word*
- demotic *everyday speech*
- denotation *actual meaning*
- dialect *regional language/vocab*
- hieratic *literary*
- jargon *work words ex cash wrap*

- lexical register *how you talk*
- lexicon *vocab a person has*
- loan words *borrowed from other languages*
- neologisms *coined/made up words (brunch)*
- nominalization *verbs into nouns*
- noun-based poetry *using nouns*
- "nouns on wheels" *nouns into verbs*
- slang *generational vocab*
- verb-based poetry *using verbs*
- vernacular *colloquial speech*

CHAPTER SEVEN

Word Music

> *Poetry, like music, is to be heard. It deals in sound—long sounds and short sounds, heavy beats and light beats, the tone relations of vowels, the relations of consonants to one another . . . Reading in silence is the source of half the misconceptions that have caused the public to distrust poetry.*[1]
> —Basil Bunting

Poets build their poems around affinities between words. Two different words may sound alike or share the same final syllable. They may contain the same consonant or consonants that sound similar. They may reiterate a particular vowel or offer a selection of related but different vowel sounds.

Consider these two brief phrases. Which is more melodious?

> *green dream*
> *blue dream*

The first phrase, "green dream" consists of two words that *almost* rhyme. The "e" sounds echo each other, and the terminal consonants ("n" and "m") are similar in terms of their sound. Even the initial consonants ("g" and "d") are rhyming sounds. The second phrase lacks most of the musical effects we noticed in the first phrase. The "oo" vowel in "blue" doesn't chime well with the long "e" in "dream," and the first word ends in a fluting vowel sound while the second has that humming "m." The only striking similarity between the two words is that the initial consonants ("b" and "d") are both formed by pursing the lips and then letting the air escape in a small "explosion"—they're "bilabial plosives" in the jargon of linguistics. The word "blue" might chime more readily with a word such as "flute," which features a vowel sound similar to the "oo" in "blue."

> *green dream*
> *blue flute*

---

1 Quoted in *Basil Bunting: Complete Poems*, ed. Richard Caddel (Newcastle-upon-Tyne: Bloodaxe Books, 2000), 9.

The above example illustrates an important aspect of the craft of poetry: poets arrange vowel and consonant sounds to create a kind of music, and that music is a central feature of any successful poem. Let's look at another example and see if we can chart the "word music" running through the poem.

Little Boy Blue

> Little boy blue, come blow your horn.
> The sheep's in the meadow; the cow's in the corn.
> But where is the boy who looks after the sheep?
> He's under a haystack, fast asleep.
> Will you wake him? No, not I,
> For if I do, he's sure to cry.

You may be familiar with this simple nursery rhyme. If not, you've heard poems and lullabies that work in the same way as "Little Boy Blue." One thing that unites us as human beings is that we all love to hear songs and rhymes, and we use them to entertain, soothe, and educate our kids. Nursery rhymes and most folk songs and popular songs rely on the same limited but very effective set of techniques: rhyme, metre, alliteration, assonance, consonance, and repetition.

Let's start with the external "envelope" of this poem. There's a predictable rhyme scheme. The first line ends with "horn," which rhymes with the last word of line 2, "corn." The next two lines also rhyme, and so do the last two. We're looking at couplet rhyme, an *aabbcc* rhyme scheme, which is one of the most common patterns. If we say the poem aloud and listen for the stresses, we'll notice that each line has four fairly clear "beats." Laid out the way we see it above, the poem is in tetrameter. (You'll sometimes see the same little poem laid out differently, by the way, with twelve short dimeter lines instead of six long ones. The change in design doesn't have any important effect on the sound of the poem.)

Okay, that takes care of the poem's envelope: rhyme and metre. Now let's see what else is going on.

Line 1 contains alliteration: "Little *b*oy *b*lue, come *b*low your horn." The repeated "b" sounds give the line a percussive feel, as if we were hearing a drum or a tuba.

Line 1 also includes some interesting vowel sounds: *boy, come, blow, your,* and *horn* all feature variations on the same vowel sound—"o." Notice that the vowel sounds aren't identical, but they're similar enough to chime in our ears as we listen to the poem. Then there's the repeated "l" of *little, blue,* and *blow.*

Line 2 has more alliteration, this time on the hard "c" sounds of *cow* and *corn.* Those two words continue the "o"-sound motif we encountered in the first line. That phenomenon is called **assonance**; it simply means the repetition or patterning of similar or identical vowel sounds. There's another example of assonance in line 2: *sheep* and *meadow* contain similar vowel sounds, and the second syllable of *meadow* adds to the chorus of "o" sounds in the line. Notice, by the way, how those two words mimic the lowing of sheep.

Getting the idea? See if you can pick out the instances of alliteration, assonance, and consonance in lines 3 and 4.

Babies and toddlers aren't literary critics—nor, thankfully, are most people—but they enjoy the craft that went into the composition of nursery rhymes on an intuitive, sensual level. Rhymes and bouncy rhythms are fun, and so is the subtler music of vowels and consonants chiming together. Whoever composed the original versions of those rhymes (the authors' names are unknown) probably wasn't a literary critic either, and they probably weren't fretting about trochees and assonance while making up the poem. Probably the long-lost amateur poets behind nursery rhymes did what most poets and lyricists do—they used their *ears*.

Poets develop remarkably good ears for the sounds of language. They use the techniques of "word music" that we're discussing here to create a sonic tapestry that supports the theme of the poem and to excite their readers or auditors on a sensual level. The moral of this story is very simple: if you want to write poetry well, you have to *listen* well; you have to train your ear to pick up phonological nuances in much the same way that a musician must train his or her ear to grasp subtle differences in pitch and tone. As any musician will tell you, training your ear takes practice. It's also useful, when you're learning to navigate the sonic landscape of the human voice in general and the English language in particular, to be familiar with the basic concepts that govern the field of "word music" so that you can communicate effectively with editors and fellow poets.

If your interests lie exclusively in writing free verse, you may be asking yourself what all this jive about rhyme, metre, and "word music" has to do with you. Free verse doesn't make use of predictable end-rhyme and predictable metre to provide a symmetrical envelope for the poem. The lack of those elements doesn't mean that free-verse poems aren't structured; it simply means that free-verse poets have to rely more heavily on the remaining types of "word music"—assonance, consonance, alliteration, and repetition, for example. Writing free verse requires just as sharp an ear as writing traditional rhymed and metred verse. Learning about prosody and "word music" can be as useful to a free-verse poet as it can to a writer of rhymed, metric poems.

Let's consider the resources we can use to bring a sense of musicality to our poems. Our lungs, throats, and mouths function as built-in musical instruments. That's obvious if we think in terms of singing, but it may not occur to us that we're making music with our voices every time we speak, scream, hiss, or growl.

Writing represents speech, and when we read we subconsciously engage the physical mechanisms of speech. When we read a poem silently to ourselves, we can still "hear" the music of the language.

When you're drafting and revising a poem, look for opportunities to develop "word music." Do you notice any groups of similar vowel or consonant sounds that might be clarified and developed? Be suspicious if you're not finding any instances of "word music" at all or if the musical effects are confined to one part of a poem.

EXPLORING THE SONIC PALETTE

English makes use of fewer sounds than some other languages, but it does provide a wide range of sonic possibilities. Poets must be acutely aware of the full range of sounds, as we use them to create the music of our poems. English words consist of vowels and consonants. Vowels are formed with the vocal tract "open" while consonants require the constriction of the tract with the tongue, teeth, or lips. We can exploit those possibilities in a few different ways.

Here's a brief review of some important techniques:

In **alliteration**, a consonant is repeated (often on stressed syllables) to create a sense of structure and a musical motif. Anglo-Saxon poets, writing in "Old English," used alliteration as a structural tool, in the same way that later poets use rhyme, and quite a few modern free-verse poets still make creative use of that technique.

Most of us were taught that there are five (or maybe six) vowels in English; in fact, there are at least fourteen distinct vowel sounds. (Some linguists list twenty vowel sounds, but the number varies according to dialects and systems of analysis.) We use different combinations of letters to differentiate between the various sounds. For example, is the "a" in *car* the same as the "a" in *care*? In any case, there's a much wider range of options than the five letters we use to denote vowels would suggest, and that's really all we poets need to know—we'll do the rest by ear.

The following sentence contains 14 common English vowel sounds:

WHO WOULD KNOW AUGHT OF ART MUST
LEARN, ACT, AND THEN TAKE HIS EASE.

If we think of this range of vowels as being analogous to the stops or keys on a musical instrument, we can begin to see how poets use arrangements of similar or different vowel sounds in order to create a kind of music within the poem.

Poets, song writers, and even the composers of advertising jingles orchestrate similar vowel sounds within stanzas in a technique called assonance. The opening stanza of William Wordsworth's "I Wandered Lonely as a Cloud" is structured around a simple *abab* rhyme scheme, but its musicality derives as much from the repeated "o" sounds within the lines as from the end-rhyme.

> I wandered lonely as a cloud
> That floats on high o'er vales and hills,
> When all at once I saw a crowd,
> A host, of golden daffodils;
> Beside the lake, beneath the trees,
> Fluttering and dancing in the breeze.[2]

Think of **consonance** as a subtler form of alliteration, one that depends on the orchestration of similar rather than identical consonants.

Here's a brief list of common consonant sounds. (Note, by the way, that this list and the table that follows are greatly simplified adaptations of the categories used by students of linguistics. We're painting in broad strokes here in order to illustrate a poetic technique; anyone interested in studying linguistics will need to look elsewhere for a more comprehensive and detailed discussion of the subject.) Notice that the consonants are organized into pairs: each pair consists of a voiced consonant and an unvoiced consonant. Voiced consonants use "breath" (i.e., engage the larynx); unvoiced consonants don't. In other words, we hum a little when we utter some consonants but not others. (Put your fingers on your throat and say "bee" and then "pee" and you'll get the idea.) Poets use clusters of paired consonants ("t" and "d," for example, may be used together to produce an effect not far from alliteration). They also use clusters of voiced or unvoiced consonants—"f" and "s" might go together in one part of a poem, and "v" and "z" might be used together elsewhere in the poem.

Table 7.1: Voiced and Unvoiced Consonants

UNVOICED	P	T	K	F	S	
VOICED		B	D	G	V	Z

The following table organizes consonants somewhat differently than the previous one: here the consonants are arranged in linked pairs (voiced and unvoiced)

---

2 William Wordsworth, "I Wandered Lonely as a Cloud," in *The Broadview Anthology of British Literature: The Concise Edition, Volume B* (Peterborough, ON: Broadview P, 2006), 145.

or singly according to the action of the organs of speech. Some consonant sounds require that we put both lips together to make the right sound, so they're called "bilabial"—"bi" meaning two or both and "labia" meaning lips. Others are formed by touching the tongue to the roof of the mouth near the teeth, while still others (those classified as "velar") require us to touch our tongues to the back of the palette, the "velum." Try sounding out each consonant and noting how we move our lips and tongues to make each sound.

The columns of the table indicate the manner in which air is released from the organs of speech in order to make the consonant sounds. "Plosives" involve, as the name implies, making air "explode" from the pursed lips. "Fricatives" are formed by forcing air through a narrow opening, such as between the lip and teeth, thus creating friction—make the sound "f" and you'll see how that works. Nasals direct air through the nasal passage rather than the mouth. Try holding your nose and saying "n," and then do the same with another consonant such as "p" or "b"; you'll notice the difference.

Table 7.2: Consonant Formation

	PLOSIVE	FRICATIVE	NASAL
BILABIAL (both lips hold and release air)	P, B		M
LABIODENTAL (lower lip touches upper teeth)		F, V	
DENTAL, ALVEOLAR (tongue touches the roof of the mouth near the teeth)	T, D	S, Z	N
VELAR (tongue touches the soft palate, known as the "velum"—that's the back of the roof of your mouth.)	K, G	X	

Sibilance is a special form of consonance in which "s" sounds are repeated, as in this line from Edgar Allan Poe: "And the silken, sad, uncertain rustling of each purple curtain."[3] Notice how the "s" and soft "c" sounds create a fluid, almost hissing music in the line.

The following four lines from John Keats's "The Eve of St. Agnes" create a flowing, sensuous music by ladling on the sibilance with "s" and soft "c" sounds: "lucent," "syrops," "cinnamon," "argosy," "transferred," "spiced," "silken," "Samarkand," "cedar'd." The other prominent sound is the repeated "f" ("transferred," "From," "Fez," "From"); as we can see from Table 7.2, the "f" sound is a fricative much like "s" sounds.

> And lucent syrops, tinct with cinnamon;
> Manna and dates, in argosy transferr'd
> From Fez; and spiced dainties, every one
> From silken Samarkand to cedar'd Lebanon.[4]

Alliteration, assonance, and consonance repeat a sound or highlight the similarities between sounds. **Dissonance** occurs when we emphasize the *differences* between words by juxtaposing sounds that clash. It's a useful technique for reinforcing violent or disturbing imagery or for creating moments of tension in a poem.

The quatrain below, from the *Pied Piper of Hamelin* by Robert Browning, contrasts sharply with the lines from Keats. While Keats selected soft-sounding sibilance and similar sounds, Browning goes for a rougher, more aggressive feel by leaning toward "d," "b," "g," and "k" sounds that rely on explosions of breath. (There's some variety in the lines, of course—note the sibilance in line 3). Put the harsh consonants together with the *ka-thump ka-thump* rhythm, and you've got a poem that practically bounces off the page, a very different effect from the smooth, seductive music of the Keats passage.

> Rats!
> They fought the dogs and killed the cats,
> And bit the babies in the cradles,
> And ate the cheeses out of the vats,
> And licked the soup from the cooks' own ladles,

---

3 Edgar Allan Poe, *The Raven*, in *Edgar Allan Poe: Selected Poetry and Tales* (Peterborough, ON: Broadview P, 2012), 61.

4 John Keats, "The Eve of St. Agnes," in *The Broadview Anthology of British Literature Volume 4: The Age of Romanticism*, 2nd edition, 818–24 (Peterborough, ON: Broadview P, 2010), 822.

> Split open the kegs of salted sprats,
> Made nests inside men's Sunday hats . . .[5]

Try reading those two passages aloud and consider how they differ in terms of their use of assonance and consonance.

Onomatopoeic words mimic the sound they represent. Words such as "smash," "bang," "ring," "buzz," "hum," "rattle," "crash," "clank," and "chirp" are familiar examples. Some words aren't as obviously onomatopoeic as those, but they still convey something of their meaning in their little cluster of sounds—"flutter," "shatter," "ratchet," "dribble," "sludge," "chop," "crush." These words suggest one of the ways that language came into being, through the simple imitation of sounds in our environment, and they can add a visceral punch to a poem. Onomatopoeic words don't have to be isolated moments in a poem; we can create a more complex "word music" by using them as touchstones and building larger structures (phrases, lines, and stanzas) that echo and elaborate their sounds. These lines from Lord Tennyson's *The Princess* illustrate the use of onomatopoeic effects in poetry.

> The moan of doves in immemorial elms,
> And the murmuring of innumerable bees.[6]

There are only a couple of obviously onomatopoeic words, "moan" and "murmuring," but the other words in each line complement those two key words. The "o" of "doves" chimes with the "o" sound of "moan," and then the "m" sound of "immemorial" and "elms" picks up the "m" in "moan." Similarly, it's easy to hear the connections between "murmuring" and "innumerable"—the first two syllables of "murmuring" almost rhyme with the middle syllables of "innumerable." When we put these effects together, we get a powerful and coherent sonic tapestry: everything moans in the first line, and everything murmurs in the second. We don't just "see" an image of doves and bees as we read the poem; we hear them as well.

---

5 Robert Browning, *The Pied Piper of Hamelin*, illustrated by Arthur Rackham (Philadelphia: J.B. Lippincott & Co., 1934), 10.
6 Alfred, Lord Tennyson, *The Princess*, in *The Broadview Anthology of British Literature: The Concise Edition, Volume B*, 656–57 (Peterborough, ON: Broadview P, 2006), 657.

"WORD MUSIC" AND THE CONVERSATIONAL VOICE

In some poems, "word music" is the main attraction; in others, it's one aspect of a broader technical palette and shouldn't announce itself or overwhelm the conversational quality of the voice. Getting that balance right is important. In a poem such as "On the Steps of the Met" (following), the voice is conversational and the diction generally understated. The use of assonance, consonance, and sibilance doesn't hit us in the face, but those techniques are important structural tools that help to build the musical dimension of the poem. Note, for example, the alliteration of "f" and "p" sounds in the opening line, the sibilant "skin"/"silvered"/"Pepsi" sequence later in that stanza, and the "a" sounds of "Manhattan," "cab," and "way" in stanza 3. There's also some tasty juxtaposing of unusual sound clusters: "greasy knish," for example. Stephanie Bolster's subtle use of "word music" techniques is typical of much modern free-verse poetry.

> *On the Steps of the Met*
> by Stephanie Bolster
>
> When the first wasp would not stop flying near me I sat still
> and let it stay. All thin legs and yellow, it did not find my skin
> but the silvered mouth of the Pepsi can. It crawled inside
>
> and then another joined it there. I let those two
> fill themselves while I finished my greasy knish and thought
> how I would soon not be here and how painful
>
> not wanting anyone. One wasp staggered out
> and flew, and then the other, and in Manhattan
> they were two cabs on their way in one direction. Inside,
>
> what I had loved most: the folds of the woman's scarf
> in Vermeer's portrait, their depth of shadow,
> how the fabric came so close to itself without touching.

EXERCISES

Exercise 7/1: Parsing the Nursery

Here's another familiar nursery rhyme that uses some of the techniques we encountered in "Little Boy Blue" and adds a couple of new ideas.

Humpty Dumpty

Humpty Dumpty sat on a wall,
Humpty Dumpty had a great fall.
All the king's horses and all the king's men
Couldn't put Humpty together again.

The little rhyme above tells the sad tale of Humpty Dumpty, who is often depicted as an egg with a face, limbs, and even a hat and shoes. Humpty falls off a stone wall and, being an egg, comes to grief when he lands on the ground below. The rhyme was first published, in a slightly different version, in 1797, and it was already popular throughout the nineteenth century.

Like "Little Boy Blue," "Humpty Dumpty" seems a simple little rhyme, but in fact it's quite technically complex. Read the poem aloud and then list at least five examples of rhyme, repetition, assonance, consonance, or alliteration.

Exercise 7/2: The Onomatopoeia Factory

Think of some of the sounds you've heard that haven't been tagged with a single word, and invent your own onomatopoeic words to denote those sounds. What single word could you imagine that would embody the sound of steamed milk being added to a latte? How about the sound of a car refusing to start or a ping-pong ball landing in a glass of beer? Make a list of five new coinages, and then congratulate yourself on having added some new words to the English language. If you're part of a group or workshop, share your sound words with your colleagues.

Exercise 7/3: Onomatopoem

Write a brief (one or two stanzas) poem using the onomatopoeic words you invented in Exercise 7/2. Add some slang words or jargon from the lists in Exercise 6/3 if you wish, or simply invent a few more words. Try to make your poem scan (have a regular metre) and rhyme. Consider whether your stanzas could be developed into a poem for children.

Exercise 7/4: Univocalism

A "univocalism" is a document that excludes all vowels except one. It's a species of "constrained" form, and we'll be discussing that sort of formalism in a later chapter. For now, all we need to know is that we'll be collecting some "univocal" words and building a poem around them.

Make a list of at least fifteen words that contain the same vowel (and no other vowels). Your list could, for example, consist of words that contain "a" and that do not contain "e," "i," "o," or "u."

When you've compiled your list, try to use those words in a short verse or prose poem. (The words on your list will probably suggest a topic or theme.) You may find it useful to expand your repertoire of sounds a little by finding words that contain other vowel sounds that chime well with your "governing" vowel—in other words, move from a univocal (single-vowel) technique to a broader sense of assonance. Then think about options for using other "word music" techniques such as alliteration and consonance.

Exercise 7/5: Nonsense Verse

Lewis Carroll's "Jabberwocky" is a classic example of **nonsense verse**.

Jabberwocky
by Lewis Carroll

'Twas brillig, and the slithy toves
Did gyre and gimble in the wabe:
All mimsy were the borogoves,
And the mome raths outgrabe.

"Beware the Jabberwock, my son!
The jaws that bite, the claws that catch!
Beware the Jubjub bird, and shun
The frumious Bandersnatch!"

He took his vorpal sword in hand:
Long time the manxome foe he sought —
So rested he by the Tumtum tree,
And stood a while in thought.

And, as in uffish thought he stood,
The Jabberwock, with eyes of flame,

Came whiffling through the tulgey wood,
And burbled as it came!

One two! One two! And through and through
The vorpal blade went snicker-snack!
He left it dead, and with its head
He went galumphing back.

"And hast thou slain the Jabberwock?
Come to my arms, my beamish boy!
Oh frabjous day! Callooh! Callay!"
He chortled in his joy.

'Twas brillig, and the slithy toves
Did gyre and gimble in the wabe:
All mimsy were the borogoves,
And the mome raths outgrabe.

Notice that Carroll's poem is gibberish in semantic terms but familiar sounding in terms of its syntax. It's as if he's taken a perfectly sensible narrative poem and substituted nonsense words for most of the nouns, verbs, and modifiers, leaving the structure words—prepositions, conjunctions, and articles.

In Chapter 6, Exercise 6/5, you were asked to compile three lists of interesting words. Take some or all of the words from your lists and arrange them into at least four lines of a draft poem. Use the words in any order you wish, and add a few more words if you want to, but try to group words into interesting sonic clusters. When you've finished this exercise, you should have an extremely strange little poem full of interesting diction. Don't worry if it doesn't make sense! Concentrate on employing the techniques of "word music" that we've been discussing in this chapter.

If you're working with other poets in a discussion group or workshop, you might find it interesting to do this exercise in small groups of two or three writers. You can then add to your "word hoard" by trading words or borrowing some from your fellow group members' lists. When your group has finished its poem, appoint a scribe, whose job it will be to write the poem on a blackboard or white board, post it online, distribute it through an email list, or display it with a data projector. In addition to the scribe, you'll need an orator who can read the poem aloud to the workshop as a whole or perform it on a video. After each poem is read (and you've all stopped laughing), try to point out examples of "word music" in each group's poem.

TAKEAWAY

- A poem is a musical composition as well as a narrative, argument, or description.
- The English language offers a wide range of vowel and consonant sounds from which we can create "word music."
- Poets use phonological techniques such as alliteration, assonance, consonance, and dissonance to structure the music of their poems.

TERMS TO REMEMBER

- alliteration
- assonance
- consonance
- dissonance
- nonsense verse
- onomatopoeia / onomatopoeic
- sibilance

CHAPTER EIGHT

Traditional Prosody

acceptable

Most **canonical** poetry of the twentieth century is written in free verse, and there's a certain snobbery among free-verse poets, some of whom believe that rhymed verse is either antiquated or lowbrow. Rhymed formalist poetry has made a surprising and overdue comeback in recent years, however, and some literary magazines have become battlegrounds for the debate between the modernist and formalist camps. Just as the Pounds and Williamses of a century ago delighted in rejecting the conventions of traditional prosody, contemporary formalists seem to take considerable pleasure in their status as rebels against the hegemony of *vers libre*. Those poets would agree with Valéry that "not the least of the pleasures of rhyme is the rage it inspires in those poor people who think they know something more important than a *convention*."[1]

Poetry is an ancient art; its roots are in the beginnings of human language. Writing is a relatively modern innovation. Scientists have postulated that human language began well over 40,000 years ago, while the first writing system (Sumerian cuneiform) dates from about 7,000 years ago. More important, most languages were purely oral until recently—within the last millennium—and the majority of the world's languages still do not have a system of writing. Living in an oral culture poses a challenge that print cultures have to some degree overcome: how do you preserve information from one generation to the next or transmit it from one location to another? One answer to that question is the use of mnemonic devices to make spoken language more memorable. Mnemosyne was the goddess of memory in ancient Greece, and a **mnemonic device** is any strategy that aids memory. Two of the most common mnemonic devices are rhyme and regular rhythm. Rhymed verse with a predictable metre tends to stick in the mind remarkably well. Verses we heard as children are sometimes still with us in old age. Song writers depend heavily on these devices to make their songs memorable: most popular songs are tightly rhymed, and most offer a memorable chorus that "hooks" into our minds and won't let go. Writers of advertising slogans and jingles use the same techniques.

Our ancestors noticed that the sounds of language could be analyzed and arranged in patterns. We could, for example, count syllables and arrange them

---

1 Paul Valéry, *The Art of Poetry*, trans. Denise Folliot (New York: Random House/ Vintage, 1961), 179.

into lines, each line containing a certain number of syllables. As some syllables (in English and some other languages, at least) tended to be stressed more than others when we spoke, we could also count the number of stresses and let that number determine the length of a line. We could build patterns based on the similarity of sounds. Putting words with similar or identical terminal syllables—rhyming words—together provided another obvious pattern. Words that contained similar or complementary consonants or vowels or that almost (but not quite) rhymed produced still more patterns.

The study of intonation, stress, and rhythm is called **prosody.** Every practising poet (and any enthusiastic reader of poetry) should be familiar with the basics of prosody. More important, every poet should be attuned to the sound of words, phrases, and lines. Improving our sense of sound requires practice: writing verse often, editing carefully, and speaking poems aloud are probably the best ways of honing our listening skills.

Learning the intricacies of prosody can be interesting, but it's not always directly relevant to the needs of poets. Our interest is in technique, not in taxonomy. For most practising poets, it's sufficient to understand the basic concepts and to be familiar with the terms for those ideas. Ultimately, we need to train our ears to recognize phonological patterns in much the same way that musicians train themselves to be sensitive to rhythm and pitch. If prosody intrigues you and you'd like to learn more about it, print and online guides to literary terms are widely available.

RHYME

We're all familiar with the idea of rhyme. Some words sound like other words, or at least the terminal syllables of some words sound like the endings of other words. That phenomenon is called perfect rhyme and is also known as full rhyme or true rhyme.

Rhyme can serve a number of purposes in a poem.

- Enhance the music of the poem by emphasizing the metric units
- Emphasize certain ideas as rhyming words.
- Link related ideas by rhyming them
- Link disjunctive ideas or words for ironic or comic effect
- Provide a structure for the poem by establishing a pattern of rhyme words
- Link the poem to a particular tradition by echoing familiar formal strategies
- Create the impression of an orderly mind and an orderly world (Just as rhyme is cognate with music, it is also cognate with logic.)

Rhymes can be as simple as the clichéd "moon-June" pairings of Tin Pan Alley pop songs, but they can also be complex and entertaining in themselves. Note the witty polysyllabic rhymes in this eighteen-century poem.

A Receipt to Cure the Vapours
by Lady Mary Wortley Montagu (1689–1762)

I

Why will Delia thus retire,
    And idly languish life away?
While the sighing crowd admire,
    'Tis too soon for hartshorn tea.

II

All those dismal looks and fretting
    Cannot Damon's life restore;
Long ago the worms have ate him,
    You can never see him more.

III

Once again consult your toilette,
    In the glass your face review:
So much weeping soon will spoil it,
    And no spring your charms renew.

IV

I, like you, was born a woman,
    Well I know what vapours mean:
The disease, alas! is common;
    Single, we have all the spleen.

V

All the morals that they tell us,
    Never cured the sorrow yet:
Choose, among the pretty fellows,
    One of honour, youth, and wit.

VI

> Prithee hear him every morning
>   At least an hour or two;
> Once again at night returning—
>   I believe the dose will do.

Songwriters can be as inventive as most poets, but it's hard to deny that many of them rely on clichéd rhymes of the "our love" and "stars above" variety. Poets take the opposite approach, reaching for rhymes that startle us into a heightened awareness of the language rather than lulling us to sleep with shopworn connections that lost their sparkle generations ago. Contemporary poet Ken Babstock connects a wildly unlikely gathering of words into a dance that's as energetic as, well, a tarantella.

Tarantella
by Ken Babstock

Having just watched my dogs suffer their bordatella
winding, having just flashed back to my own spiking, as a girl,
                against rubella,

I was serving him Nutella
on dinky bread, this guy, whose ex once serenaded—and
                beautifully, apparently—a harbour seal with Ella

Fitzgerald songs from a kayak, proffering up strips of fat-striped
                mortadella
and pitted cherries. And from within the darkened crescent my
                patio umbrella

made, I wondered who and why this fella
might up and tell a

girl, a girl already suffering from, like, *l'angoscia del hora della
posta* due to debt racked up with Visa, the library, and a man who
                resembles Danny Aiello,

a thing so intimate as to make her Cosa Bella
itch. And *so soon!* So soon after the portobello

mushrooms had come off the grill a
little darker, crispier than is my usual, ah,

preference. I bought some minutes by casting down my gaze
      intoning *la illaha illa Allah,*
till he noted no burka, and pressed on, pushing his Costello

frames up with a forefinger, *a barrel, a*
steamer trunk, a shipping container couldn't hold what I have to tell you . . .

More sure of his own worth was this dude than even Cela,
he could, I decided, fork it in alone, hold forth alone, sit alone at
      his own Valhalla

and spare me the blah and the blah,
so I gathered the dogs and waltzed off to work on my libretto. Tra-la.

Mapping a Rhyme Scheme

In poetry or song, it's common for rhyme words to be arranged into patterns: for example, the last word of line 1 rhymes with the last word of line 3, and perhaps the last words of lines 2 and 4 also rhyme with each other. That pattern is called a rhyme scheme, and we can quantify it by assigning letters to each rhyme: in the pattern I've just described, lines 1 and 3 are "*a*" rhymes while lines 2 and 4 are the "*b*" rhymes; thus the rhyme scheme is *abab*. A typical pop song or advertising jingle may not need to go beyond that simple pattern, but in verse poetry things can get a lot more complicated.

    The letters after the lines of the following poem map the pattern of end-rhymes:

Snowbirds
by Archibald Lampman (1861–99)

Along the narrow sandy height (a)
    I watch them swiftly come and go, (b)
      Or round the leafless wood, (c)
    Like flurries of wind-driven snow, (b)
Revolving in perpetual flight, (a)
    A changing multitude. (c)

Nearer and nearer still they sway, (d)
And, scattering in a circled sweep, (e)
Rush down without a sound; (f)
And now I see them peer and peep, (e)
Across yon level bleak and gray, (d)
Searching the frozen ground,— (f)

Until a little wind upheaves,
And makes a sudden rustling there,
And then they drop their play,
Flash up into the sunless air,
And like a flight of silver leaves
Swirl round and sweep away.

Each stanza in Lampman's poem repeats the same rhyme scheme. Line 1 rhymes with line 5; line 2 rhymes with line 4; and line 3 rhymes with line 6. Well, okay, in the first stanza there's a half-rhyme between "wood" in line 3 and "multitude" in line 6, but apparently Lampman felt he was close enough on the rhyme to maintain the pattern. Map the rhyme scheme of the final stanza and compare it to the rest of the poem.

Slant Rhyme

As we noted in relation to Lampman's poem, some words contain similar sounds but don't quite rhyme. Although they don't qualify as rhyme words, they can still be used to connect different parts of a poem or to create patterns in a poem. For example, "sun" and "moon" have vaguely similar vowel sounds and the same terminal consonant. Connecting these "sort-of-rhyming" words is called **slant rhyme**, but it's also known as **half-rhyme** or **imperfect rhyme** or **oblique rhyme** or **off-rhyme** Some literary scholars define this technique more narrowly than we have here: for them, slant rhyme refers to linking words that have only the final consonant sound in common. For practising poets, the exact definition of the term isn't important: what concerns us is the application of the technique in our poems. So why and when would we use slant rhyme instead of full rhyme or no rhyme at all?

Slant rhyme can be more suitable to some poems than full rhyme might be. If, for example, we want to vary the rhythm in a poem, then full rhyme and a set rhyme scheme might not be appropriate, as the full rhymes might clash with the less-predictable rhythm. Any poem that communicates a sense of the poet's struggle to articulate a dark or troubling theme might also benefit from the use of slant rhyme rather than full rhyme. Some early modernists wrote poems that are *almost* as orderly as the rhymed verse of their formalist contemporaries, but those poems seemed poised on the brink of chaos, the slant rhymes barely cohering into a rhyme scheme.

Srikanth Reddy's "First Circle" uses both full rhyme and slant rhyme: "crows" in line 2 rhymes with "grows" in line 4, but the other lines of the first two stanzas are linked with a half-rhyme ("man" and "again") or alliteration ("grows" and "gray"). As you read the poem, try to map the subtle use of phonological effects such as slant rhyme, consonance, and alliteration.

First Circle
by Srikanth Reddy

It's dark in here, the dark inside of a man
in the dark. It's not night. One hears crows
overhead, dawn fowl caws, the shod soles again

treading their sunlit plots above. One grows
dotish-fond of such things. Long live the things,
their ways, their roots pushed goatish & gray

through the skull, in this earth that gaily spins
though one has crossed its smutted green threshold
to reign in a crate. We have done no wrong,

my friends, & yet we find ourselves soiled,
sold, carbonized teeth in a moss-riven jaw.
Once I sat on a stool as my grandmother told

me of heaven. She cleaned fish for our living. I saw
how her rusty black knife unseamed the sunset
in each belly—coral, ochre, carmine, raw,

lice-infested sunsets in a pail. So many nights.
Night in the kitchen shack, night at the crumbling edge
of our milk-pond province, a blade, lone cricket

raving in the lawn.

Internal Rhyme

Rhyming words aren't invariably placed at the ends of lines. Rhyming the final word of a line with a word in the middle of the same line complicates and reinforces the musical and mnemonic effects of rhyming. The first two stanzas of Edgar Allan Poe's famous Gothic poem *The Raven* make constructive use of internal rhyme to create an obsessive, hypnotic atmosphere. Note that Poe doesn't just rhyme a midline word with the final word of the same line; on occasion, he'll add a third rhyming word in the middle of the next line. No wonder this poem has stuck in readers' minds for generations!

> Once upon a midnight dreary, while I pondered, weak and weary,
> Over many a quaint and curious volume of forgotten lore—
> While I nodded, nearly napping, suddenly there came a tapping,
> As of someone gently rapping, rapping at my chamber door.
> "'Tis some visitor," I muttered, "tapping at my chamber door—
>   Only this, and nothing more."
> Ah, distinctly I remember it was in the bleak December,
> And each separate dying ember wrought its ghost upon the floor.
> Eagerly I wished the morrow;—vainly I had sought to borrow
> From my books surcease of sorrow—sorrow for the lost Lenore,
> For the rare and radiant maiden whom the angels name Lenore,
>   Nameless *here* for evermore.

Chain Rhyme

Chain rhyme links stanzas by rhyming a word in one stanza with a word in the next stanza. Verse forms such as *terza rima* and the villanelle are built using a chain rhyme. Here's the first canto of Percy Bysshe Shelley's "Ode to the West Wind," which is written in *terza rima*. Notice how the word that ends line 2 of the first stanza sets the rhyme for lines 1 and 3 of the next stanza and how that pattern continues throughout the poem. It's interesting to compare Shelly's *terza rima* to the related but more varied approach of "First Circle" (presented previously).

> O, wild West Wind, thou breath of Autumn's being,
> Thou, from whose unseen presence the leaves dead
> Are driven, like ghosts from an enchanter fleeing,

Yellow, and black, and pale, and hectic red,
Pestilence-stricken multitudes: O, thou,
Who chariotest to their dark wintry bed

The winged seeds, where they lie cold and low,
Each like a corpse within its grave, until
Thine azure sister of the spring shall blow

Her clarion o'er the dreaming earth, and fill
(Driving sweet buds like flocks to feed in air)
With living hues and odours plain and hill:

Wild Spirit, which art moving every where;
Destroyer and preserver; hear, O, hear!

The term **chain rhyme** is also used to refer to a different technique: rhyming a word at the end of one line to the word that starts the next line. The chain metaphor is appropriate in either instance.

Cascading Rhyme, Eye Rhyme, and Rime Riche

Anyone who listens to rap will recognize the rapid-fire rhyming over multiple lines (*aaa*, *bbbb*, etc.) that often characterizes that popular genre. A **cascading rhyme** flows from one line to the next and can be sustained for as long as the poet (singer, rapper) wishes to play out the string. The use of cascading rhyme in poetry and song is far from new: Robert Southey's "The Cataract of Lodore," quoted in Chapter 6, is a classic example of (far too much!) cascading rhyme—it's a technique that should be used judiciously.

An **eye rhyme** connects two words that *look* as if they should sound the same but don't: come and home, slaughter and laughter, or temperate and date, for example. *Rime riche* (or *rhyme riche*) is a French term that describes rhymes between words that sound exactly alike such as *write* and *right*, *phase* and *faze*, *aloud* and *allowed*, and so on. The term can also refer to pairs of words that share a final syllable, as in *command* and *demand* or *complement* and *implement*.

Rhyme without Reason: A Classic Mistake

Beginning poets sometimes make the mistake of assuming that anything that contains enough rhymes must be a worthwhile poem. They push that erroneous assumption to the point of absurdity, producing poems that rhyme obsessively but that don't make sense or that don't have anything interesting to say. Song-writers, rappers, and "spoken word" performers are frequently prey to the same affliction, and regrettably their audiences are often too uncritical to care.

Rhyme should feel natural; it should never intrude into our reading of the poem. More important, we should avoid letting the rhyme scheme dictate our choice of words. Never use a word simply because you need a rhyme. That sort of "reaching for a rhyme" can reduce your poem to gibberish.

There's a temptation to achieve a rhyme by reversing or otherwise compli-cating the syntax of a line. The most common trick is to use the emphatic form of a verb rather than the simple form: "I did go" instead of "I went." That's a gesture we all recognize from folk songs, and within the context of that genre it usually sounds okay. In a poem that doesn't obviously reference folk music, it seems awkward. Keep the syntax appropriate to the voice of the poem.

If you start a poem with a fixed rhyme scheme, you have to be cautious about deviating from the pattern. Rhyme schemes get into our heads and stick there. Once the reader gets on that horse and starts galloping, it's going to be a shock if he or she is thrown off. If you start a poem with a rhymed quatrain or two and then wander into free verse, your readers may be justified in assuming that you've lost the plot and forgotten what you set out to accomplish. The human mind loves a pattern, and if you give us a pattern and then junk it, we're likely to suspect incompetence rather than intention. You have to ease us out of the pattern gradually or provide some clue to the transition—a visual break such as a division between cantos or a system of indentations might work.

STRESS AND SCANSION

Why do poets put so much emphasis on rhythm? The short answer is that people have always been captivated by patterned sound. As Arthur Koestler puts it, "rhythmic periodicity is a fundamental characteristic of life. All auto-matic functions of the body are patterned by rhythmic pulsations: heart-beat, respiration, peristalsis, brain-waves are merely the most obvious ones."[2] We recognize the rhythms we encounter in nature: the lapping or crashing of waves on a shoreline, the patter of raindrops, the trembling of leaves in a mild wind, or the shaking and screeching of boughs in a gale.

Rhythm, then, is a fundamental characteristic of poetry. Learning to hear the stresses in a line of verse is as important to a poet as learning to hear rhythm is to a musician. It's surprising, however, how difficult it is for many people to find the stresses in a line of verse. It's particularly strange that the rhythms of verse are so difficult for people to grasp when the majority of them

2 Arthur Koestler, *The Act of Creation* (London: Pan/Picador, 1970), 311.

enjoy listening to music that's characterized by simple four-four rhythms, often emphasized by heavy bass lines and pounding drums. How can they listen to a million repetitions of the standard ballad-stanza form in pop songs and not be able to recognize it when they're reading a poem? The answer is that there's a difference between enjoying rhythms passively and thinking about them analytically. As readers, we can probably be content with the former approach, but as poets we need to ramp up our level of awareness so that we can develop and refine the music of our poems. We should be able to map the pattern of stresses in our lines and to recognize when those patterns should be made more consistent or more varied and subtle. Finding a "base rhythm" in a draft can help us to build the poem.

Mapping the pattern of stresses in a poem is called **scansion**. If we're writing a poem in metric verse or blank verse, we have to make the lines **scan**. That is, we have to ensure that the metre is sustained. If we set out to write a poem with a regular metre, we have to make absolutely sure that there are no unintentional lapses in that metre. There are few things more disconcerting than trying to read a poem that doesn't scan—it's like listening to an incompetent musician or watching a clumsy dancer who keeps stumbling and losing the beat. Similarly, we should apply the same principle of continuity to metre as we did to rhyme. If we write a stanza or two with a regular metre, the pattern of stresses—the "beat"—will get into our readers' heads, and they'll expect it to continue or to change in a meaningful and musically attractive fashion.

Metrical Feet

English is a "**stress**" language: we tend to emphasize one syllable in a **disyllabic** (two-syllable) word more than the other, and in a **polysyllabic** (many-syllable) word we may emphasize one or more syllables. Consequently, English prose is inherently rhythmic. This rhythm is generated naturally by the interplay of stressed and unstressed syllables in successive words in a phrase or sentence.

The way we emphasize one syllable or another in a word can affect auditors' understanding of the word, and it can also tell auditors where we come from or where we learned the language. In some instances, stress differentiates between a noun and a verb. For example, a "*pro*ject" is a noun, but to "pro*ject*" is a verb. Similarly, to "re*cord*" is a verb, but the result of that action is a noun, a "*re*cord." As well, the various dialects of English have their own rules for assigning stress. In the UK, the car is parked in the "ga*rage*" for the "week*end*," while in the US and Canada, it would be in the "*ga*rage" for the "*week*end."

Poetic metre takes the natural rhythm of speech and organizes it into a system. In metric composition, the rhythms of everyday speech are analyzed in terms of metrical units made up of stressed and unstressed syllables called "feet." Each foot includes at least one syllable, and most include at least one stress. These feet are themselves the product of a process of abstraction: in a foot, the various levels of stress that linguists have discerned in speech are reduced to a binary opposition of stress or no stress.

The most common metrical feet are the iamb, the trochee, the anapaest, the dactyl, the amphibrach, and the spondee. There are others, but Thomas Campion was probably on target when he noted, in his *Observations in the Art of English Poesie* of 1602, that "Diuers other feete I know are by the Grammarians cited, but to little purpose."[3]

The **iamb** is a two-syllable foot in which the second syllable takes the stress—"in*vent*," "en*gage*," "de*pict*," "in*spire*." Elizabethan poets and dramatists were, as everyone knows, inordinately fond of iambic pentameter—that's five iambs in a line. English leans toward stressing the second syllable in a word, so it's not surprising that quite a few English poems are predominantly iambic. The opening lines of Christopher Marlowe's "The Passionate Shepherd to His Love" provide a good example of that tendency, though the poem is in tetrameter, not pentameter:

> Come *live* with *me* and *be* my *love*
> And *we* will *all* the *plea*sures *prove*

The **trochee** is the opposite of the iamb: a trochee begins with a stressed syllable, which is followed by an unstressed syllable—"*plain*tiff," "*al*ways," "*din*ner," and "*in*jure."

W.H. Auden chose a sombre trochaic drumbeat for this passage from his elegy to another famous poet, W.B. Yeats:

> Earth, receive an honoured guest:
> *Will*iam *Yeats* is *laid* to *rest*:
> *Let* this *Irish* *ves*sel *lie*
> *Empt*ied of *its* po*et*ry.

The **anapaest** is an elongated iamb: two unstressed syllables followed by a single stress—"over*come*," "under*stand*," "contra*dict*," and "ana*paest*." We use a lot of prepositional phrases in English, and quite a few of them scan as anapaestic feet: "through the *field* to the *house* of the *cat*."

---

3 Thomas Campion, *Observations in the Art of English Poesie*, in *The Prelude to Poetry: The English Poets in Defence and Praise of Their Own Art*, ed. Ernest Rhys, 61–85 (London: J.M. Dent & Sons: 1927), 66.

The *dactyl* is the opposite of the anapaest: stressed / unstressed / unstressed—"*man*nequin," "*scor*pion," "*hor*rible," and "*sud*denly." Classical epics such as *The Iliad* and *The Odyssey* were written in dactylic hexameter, but of course they weren't written in English. Writing a poem that relies heavily on dactyls in modern English is a bit of a headache. Lord Tennyson's rousing "The Charge of the Light Brigade" includes several dactylic lines such as this famous and highly quotable passage:

> *Theirs* not to *make* reply,
> *Theirs* not to *rea*son why,
> *Theirs* but to *do* and die:

A line made up of either or both of the two common feet that end with a stress—the iamb and the anapaest—is said to be in **rising rhythm,** as the foot "rises" towards the final stress. Lines based on the trochee and the dactyl, conversely, are in **falling rhythm**—the feet seem to "fall away" from the initial stress. Rising rhythms are more common in English verse than falling rhythms, simply because most English dialects tend to lean more heavily on the end of a word than the beginning.

Other feet are less common but still worth knowing about:

The **spondee** is two stresses—"football," "childhood," "aircraft," and "heartbreak." The spondee is often used for emphasis—it's like underlining a point in a speech by whacking your hand on the podium. Some poems end (or end a stanza) with a spondee to nail down the resolution.

The **amphibrach** is three syllables with the stress on the middle syllable: unstressed / stressed / unstressed—"ac*cept*ed," "re*gard*less," "stac*ca*to," and "pu*tres*cent." The amphibrach should sound familiar, as it's the foundation of the limerick, the durable and amusingly disreputable verse form that decorates washroom walls all over the English-speaking world.

> There *was* a | *young* fool | from *Chic*ago
> Who *thought* he | was *Doc*tor | Zhi*va*go.

The amphibrach also features prominently in the comic verses of Edward Lear and Doctor Seuss. There must be something inherently funny about that da-*dum*-da rhythm.

You can analyze any English phrase in terms of its constituent metric feet. Even proper names embody a sequence of stressed and unstressed syllables. *El*vis *Ar*on *Pres*ley had an unusual name in metric terms: three trochees. (The King isn't dead; he's just trochaic.) *Mud*dy *Wa*ters had a trochaic stage name, but his real name, McKinley Morganfield, was an amphibrach followed by a dactyl. Imagine a pop-music supergroup called the Amphibrach Sisters: Rhianna, Madonna, Beyoncé.

Counting the Feet: Stress and Metre

Metre is an abstraction and an exaggeration of speech rhythms. Yes, we stress some syllables more emphatically than others when we speak; no, we don't arrange those stresses into a predictable pattern. Metre makes music of the raw material of speech, but it can also distort the reality of our speaking voices. That contradiction presents poets with a challenge: how can we make our lines of verse both musical and *real*? Most modern poets—and in fact most poets of previous eras—don't adhere too closely to a prescriptive pattern of metre and rhyme: they play with the pattern, establishing a counterpoint between strict metre and patterned rhyme, on the one hand, and a more conversational, subtle, and personal voice, on the other. Formalists aren't, whatever the name implies, limited by a strict formula; they use the formula as a musical centre or "home base" and dance around it.

Metre is measured in feet—the number of feet in a line determines the metre.

Table 8.1: Common Metres

monometer = one foot	pentameter = five feet
dimeter = two feet	hexameter = six feet
trimeter = three feet	heptameter = seven feet
tetrameter = four feet	octameter = eight feet

Anything longer than pentameter (five feet) is relatively rare in modern English poetry. Dimeter and monometer are more likely to be used in comic verse than in poems addressing more serious subjects, but those rhythms do have their uses. If you're a hip-hop aficionado, you'll be familiar with the dimeter rhythm of quite a few raps.

Amanda Jernigan's "Encounter" uses occasional rhyme, linking lines 2 and 4, for example, and lines 8 and 12 with end-rhyme while using slant rhyme and consonance to marry other lines. The full rhyme between "thin" and "in" at the end of the poem underlines the resolution. Notice how the iambic pentameter rhythm surfaces in the last half of the poem. Read the poem (preferably out loud) and see if you can map the stresses and the moments in which the poet has chosen to vary the pattern. "Leonov," incidentally, refers to Alexey Leonov, a Russian cosmonaut of the 1960s.

Encounter
by Amanda Jernigan

A friend, seeing his babe in ultrasound,
imagined it an astronaut, "behind
glass dome reflections, lost in space . . .,"
and so I had that image close to mind
when the technician finally tipped her screen
to me, revealing—not an astronaut, but Earth,
so "small, light blue, so touchingly alone."
Thus Leonov. It was a commonplace,
back then, that once we had the earth in sight,
the isolation of the planet "known,"
we would clean up our act, would mend our ways—
a kind of cosmic recognition scene.
So much for that, the skeptic in me says.
And yet as I beheld you floating there
I felt myself grow small, the air grow thin,
as if I were the one adrift in space,
and you the one who might yet pull me in.

EXERCISES

Exercise 8/1: Chant Poem

The chant may be the most ancient and universal poetic form. Many cultures (perhaps most cultures) worldwide perform chants as part of their sacred or artistic traditions. The structure of a chant is very simple: one line of a free-verse couplet is repeated over and over. This "chant line" may be varied to some degree, but its rhythm and memorable phrasing are generally constant.

Write a chant poem consisting of at least six couplets with the chant line repeated in each couplet. Vary the pattern if you feel that the poem will benefit from being a little less symmetrical, but stick reasonably closely to the original template. *Make your chant rhythmic.* You should be able to pound out a steady rhythm on a tabletop while you read the poem aloud.

Exercise 8/2: Getting Stressed about Your Name

Where do you want people to place the emphasis when they use your name? Our names can be divided into syllables (or single-syllable words) and analyzed in terms of whether the syllables are stressed or unstressed. So where do the stresses fall?

In the name "Susan," the stress falls at the beginning of the word, which sounds like its diminutive form, "Sue." In the similar name "Suzanne," the stress is usually placed on the second—"anne"—syllable.

Some popular names have only one syllable. If your name is "Grace Wong" or "Joe Craig," both words of the name should be stressed. Your full name then, is a spondee. (The rapper LL Cool J may have the ideal stage name—in terms of metre, at least—for someone in his line of work. Spondees show up in a lot of raps, and his name is two spondees.) Polysyllabic names may correspond to other metric feet: if your name is "Dominque Elliott," your metric pattern is a pair of dactyls—not to be confused with a pterodactyl.

Write your full name (first name, any middle names, last name or names), and then sound the whole name out and decide where the stresses fall. Does your name correspond to any of the common metric feet or any sequence of various feet?

When you've done that, try to write a few lines that echo the stress pattern of your name.

Exercise 8/3: Rhyming Gibberish

Using a rhyming dictionary (available online), pick three or four interesting words and then list as many rhyme words for each as you can. Then arrange your list into a brief rhyming poem. Fill in your lines with as few non-rhyming words as possible. Make your poem scan. Don't worry if it doesn't make sense.

Exercise 8/4: Rhyme Schemes and Chain Rhyme

Invent a system of rhyme for a hypothetical lyric poem. Your scheme should repeat a pattern over at least three stanzas, and it should include a rhyme that links each stanza to another stanza. Throw in some internal rhyme if you wish.

Exercise 8/5: Writing in Metre

Step 1: Write about 25 words about the weather and/or your plans for the day. The number of sentences doesn't matter, but the style should be conversational and the language unremarkable. Then arrange the passage you've written into at least two lines of *iambic tetrameter*. You can rearrange the words, add words, or delete words as required by the rhythm. Try, however, to keep the feel of natural, conversational language.

Step 2: When you've done that, form into groups of two or three (if you're in a writers' group or workshop) and edit each other's lines, or just get a friend and fellow poet to trade drafts with you. Try to make sure that the lines scan and that they sound regular and rhythmic. You can throw in the occasional anapaest if you wish to, but try to avoid inversion and to stick to a rising rhythm.

Step 3: Next, working with your editorial group, arrange the same passage into at least two lines of *iambic trimeter*.

Step 4: Feeling brave? If you've finished parts 1 and 2, try to arrange the passage into one or two lines with a falling rhythm (trochaic or dactylic feet). You could shoot for *trochaic trimeter*, for example.

TAKEAWAY

- The study of intonation, stress, and rhythm is called *prosody*.
- *Rhyme* is used as a structural tool and a means of signifying in traditional verse and (less often and less obviously) in free verse.
- Rhymes can be organized into a pattern called a *rhyme scheme*.
- Words that almost (but not quite) rhyme form a *slant rhyme*, also known as half-rhyme, imperfect rhyme, off-rhyme, or oblique rhyme.
- A rhyme between words within the same line is called *internal rhyme*.
- English is a stress language: we emphasize some syllables more than others.
- A *foot* is a group of consecutive stressed and unstressed syllables. Common feet include the iamb, the trochee, the anapaest, the dactyl, the amphibrach, and the spondee.
- *Metre* is an abstraction of the natural rhythms of speech.

TERMS TO REMEMBER

- amphibrach *³ stress on middle & unstressed & stressed*
- anapaest/anapaestic
- canonical
- cascading rhyme *(appealing?)*
- chain rhyme *last word in line rhymes w/ 2ⁿᵈ coming*
- *1 stress & unstressed* dactyl/dactylic
- dimeter *2 feet*
- disyllabic *2 syllables, stressing 1*
- *look like they should* eye rhyme
- falling rhythm *feet fall away from stress*
- feet/foot *words??*
- full rhyme (<u>perfect</u> rhyme, true rhyme)
- iamb/iambic *2ⁿᵈ syllable stressed*
- internal rhyme *middle/end in line*
- metre
- mnemonic device

- occasional rhyme
- pentameter
- polysyllabic
- prosody
- *rime riche / rhyme riche*
- rhyme scheme
- rising rhythm
- scan, scansion
- slant rhyme (half-rhyme, off-rhyme, imperfect rhyme, oblique rhyme)
- spondee/spondaic
- stress
- tetrameter
- trimeter
- trochee/trochaic

CHAPTER NINE

Line, Stanza, Canto

Although poems can be written in prose paragraphs, most English-language poetry is written in verse, that is, in language that has been organized into lines and (possibly) stanzas. Verse lines provide opportunities for highlighting the inherent rhythms of English, for emphasizing rhyme words, for communicating a sense of the narrator's speech patterns or thought processes, and for playing cat-and-mouse games with the reader's expectations. Where and when (and most importantly *why*) to break lines is one of the most basic questions in poetic technique.

Beginning poets often instinctively adopt one of two strategies for breaking lines of verse: they either write everything in simple metres with end-rhyme (rhyming couplets, typically, or *abcb* quatrains), or they chop their prose sentences into phrase-generated units of free verse. Sometimes they combine these two approaches with predictably unhappy results. Learning more sophisticated and subtle techniques for lineation is an important step toward becoming a better poet.

LINE AND GRAMMATICAL STRUCTURE

A line of a poem can be a complete sentence; it can also be a smaller unit such as a phrase or clause or even a single word. Beyond that simple formula, a line can be a fragment of a phrase or clause, an incomplete idea that cries out for resolution.

If you're writing poetry, it's useful to be clear about the difference between phrases, clauses, and sentences:

- a *sentence* is constructed around a subject and verb and expresses a complete proposition or question;
- a *clause* also has a subject and verb, but it's used as part of a larger sentence;
- a *phrase* is any group of words that doesn't have a subject and verb.

A line, then, can consist of a word, a phrase, a clause, or a sentence. (Obviously, a line can combine two or more of those possibilities, but it's best to start by thinking of your lines in relation to the four basic grammatical units.)

Writing lines of verse that are also complete sentences—**sentence-generated lines**—can lend a booming, oratorical quality to a poem; it's a technique that chimes well with the public voice of a politician or a prophet.

Clause-generated lines consist of one complete clause per line. The clauses may be dependent or independent in relation to the larger sentences of which they form a part. Clause-generated lines offer something of the solidity and strength of sentences, but they also allow poets to break long sentences into their constituent clauses and thus to make the lines more flexible than sentence-generated lines might be. Blank-verse stanzas might naturally fall into clause-generated lines with a pentameter rhythm, taking advantage of the natural iambic and anapaestic feel of English clauses.

One of the most common mistakes that writers of free-verse poetry make is relying too heavily on **phrase-generated lines**. Too many phrase-generated lines make a poem seem plodding and predicable; the routine progression of phrase after phrase takes the energy out of the language.

Word-generated lines consist of a single word per line. The effect is a little like drops of water dripping from a tap, and it's a technique that's as likely to be annoying as intriguing. Single-word lines are best used selectively, as points of emphasis.

Let's take a random sentence and see how it looks and sounds as a line of verse.

Sentence-generated
All night the dogs barked, and the wind ruffled the feathers of
the elms.

The above sentence consists of two parallel clauses joined by a conjunction ("and"). Each clause contains an active verb ("barked" and "ruffled") that directly follows the subject, so there's an opportunity to highlight that parallel structure by breaking the sentence in half and making each clause a separate line.

Clause-generated
All night the dogs barked,
And the wind ruffled the feathers of the elms.

The voice is now more controlled and contemplative than the "prophetic" voice of the sentence-generated line. We can dice things up even more finely by isolating the phrases within the two parallel clauses. The sentence begins with an adverbial phrase that tells us when the events occurred ("All night") and it ends with another phrase ("the feathers of the elms") that tells what was getting ruffled. We can further divide that longish phrase into two units: the object of the second clause ("the feathers") and an adjectival phrase that tells us something about those feathers (i.e., that they belong to the elms). Now we have five shorter lines instead of one long line or two medium-length lines. The voice has become intimate, echoing the sound of someone speaking quietly or even whispering. By breaking the lines, we've changed the voice from public oratory to private conversation, and we've also made the rhythm more sparse and tentative.

> *Phrase-generated*
> All night
> The dogs barked,
> And the wind ruffled
> The feathers
> Of the elms.

It's possible, though probably not advisable, to break the sentence up even more finely: we could make each word a separate line. The effect here is whimsical, even comic, and we're risking trying our readers' patience as they try to piece together the proposition expressed by the sentence as a whole.

> *Word-generated*
> All
> Night
> The
> Dogs
> Barked,
> And
> The
> Wind
> Ruffled
> The
> Feathers
> Of
> The
> Elms.

Though quite a few poems lean heavily on one type of line generation, it's also possible to orchestrate a poem more subtly by mixing the styles, provided that there's a method to our madness in the sense that the shifts in texture mirror movements in the subject, theme, and voice.

Short lines tend to imply emphasis, while long lines de-emphasize the words and phrases within them. Imagine that you're a garden designer, and you're laying out a cobblestone pathway through a rose garden. There are some spots in the garden you'd like to highlight—a particularly beautiful rose bush, for example. Other stretches of the pathway pass through relatively uninteresting parts of the garden. You have to decide where to place stepping stones in order to make a pathway through the garden. If you want your visitors to pass through a stretch of the garden quickly, you might place the stones relatively far apart, so people will have to stretch their legs to stay on the stones. Conversely, if you want visitors to slow down and admire a particularly interesting flower bed, you might place the stones closer together in that area.

There's a downside to using short lines, however. As a general rule, *every line in a poem should offer something interesting to the reader*: there shouldn't be any "slack" lines. Very short lines imply emphasis, so it's important to make sure that the language of those short lines is worth emphasizing. Beginning poets sometimes forget that criterion and isolate uninteresting or transitional words or phrases in short lines.

Enjambed Lines and End-Stopped Lines

You'll have noticed that the examples above divide the original sentence into its natural grammatical units. None of the options we've explored cut into those units. Only the sentence-generated lines are genuinely "end-stopped" in the sense that the end of a line is also the end of a sentence, but none of the lines conflict with the grammatical structure.

In a passage of prose, there's really only one organizing system: phrases and clauses are combined into sentences, and the sentences are arranged into paragraphs. In a verse poem, there are two distinct organizing principles: 1) sentences and paragraphs and 2) lines and stanzas. Think of these systems as independent "grids."

In some poems, every line is a sentence or a complete clause or phrase. In those poems, the "sentence grid" and the "line grid" are identical. There's no conflict between the two grids. That lack of conflict communicates a sense of harmony and balance. That's okay, as long as it's what you want your poem to communicate. As Marcel Proust said, "The superimposition of two systems, thought and metre, is a primary element of ordered complexity, that is to say, of beauty."[1] If you're writing a poem about an unhappy love affair or the horrors of war, implying a state of harmony may not be the best strategy. You may want to introduce a note of tension and conflict by breaking some lines *against* the

---

1 Quoted in Arthur Koestler, *The Act of Creation* (London: Pan/Picador, 1978), 312.

grammatical "grid." You can do that by starting a sentence, clause, or phrase on one line and ending it on the next line—a technique called enjambment. An enjambed line cannot communicate an idea by itself; in order to get the full meaning, we have to read the following line or lines.

Enjambment often has implications for the rhythm or metre of the lines. If we enjamb a sentence onto the next line, we might then end that sentence in the middle of the second line, creating a caesura. That pause further complicates the rhythm of the poem and offers the opportunity to develop a more complex, jazzy rhythm than is possible in sentence-, clause-, or phrase-generated lines. Every poet should be skilled at introducing enjambment and caesura into poems when they're appropriate to the theme.

Janet McNally's "The Wicked One Goes to the Makeup Counter" is composed of sentences and sentence fragments arranged in tercets with reasonably regular line lengths. The sentence grid and the line grid are at odds throughout the poem, and the enjambed lines and strong caesuras are as important to the reader's experience of the poem as the rich diction and the engaging voice.

The Wicked One Goes to the Makeup Counter
by Janet McNally

You can't argue beauty's not an accident, the particular heft and angle
of a chromosome's spin. A tarted spangle, bright lanyard twist, the slip
of cells weighting this boat uneven from stern to prow. We're all

skittery as marbles on a marble floor. Beauty stays, then goes;
it *fades*, we say, something about years and sun, the nights we slept
in makeup and left mascara like ashes on the pillowcase. We burned

through every one of our dreams. I wasn't always a stepmother, you know.
There were whole years when I was a girl. But now, these ladies
sell me moisturizer, stand close in their lab coats, pretending at science

in a fog of perfume. They wield a contour brush and my cheekbone pops.
The magic settles uneasy; it turns out fairy dust was always
fake. And the lipstick's made from beetles, shells crushed vermillion.

My color is Fleshpot, they say, it's Folie or Fixation. It's Wilderness;
it's Artificial Earth. They can't quite make themselves care.
We'll waste it, they know, whatever we've been given.

Enjambment can be used to produce a kind of "double exposure" in the reader's mind. The reader understands, or thinks he or she understands, the meaning of a line, but when the sentence is completed in the next line, the meaning is changed or contradicted. This rationale for breaking lines is grounded in the perception that readers process language in phrases, clauses, and sentences rather than in individual words. When we read the beginning of a sentence (or a shorter unit such as a phrase or clause), our minds leap ahead, forming assumptions about the rest of the sentence. This process is like the "autocomplete" feature in most word-processing programs and Internet search engines. Poets can engage readers in a game of "cat and mouse" by setting up an "autocomplete" and then enjambing the line and completing the syntactic unit in an unexpected way. The enjambments have to be constructed so that they complement the music of the lines and the voice of the narrator, of course. When employed creatively, enjambments can add witty moments to your poems or facilitate shifts from the tragic to the comic or from the literal to the figurative or ironic.

Playing around with the possibilities of harmony and conflict offered by the juxtaposition of the two grids—syntax and lineation—is an important part of the craft of writing poetry. The range of possibilities afforded poets by the existence of these two distinct grids is surprisingly wide.

There are two ways of enjambing lines. We can break the "big" grammatical units, such as sentences and clauses, at the end of lines while keeping the "small" units—phrases—intact. That sort of enjambment opens up possibilities for rhythmic variety and tension, but it doesn't make the music of the poem seem jagged and dissonant.

> We move with the music
> of the spheres, dancing carefully
> with a quiet abandon, watching
> our step from star to star.

Conversely, we can break lines in the middle of phrases or after the initial conjunction, article, or preposition. That sort of "radical enjambment" produces a dissonant, jagged tone. It can also give the reader a sense of the writer's mind groping for the next thought and forming ideas actively, right on the page. We can even use "word splitting" to make the enjambment more radical still.

We move with the
music of the
spheres, dancing care-
fully, with a
quiet abandon, watch-
ing our
step from
star to
star.

Compare the lineation of Janet McNally's poem (above) with that of Jennifer Chang's "Pastoral" (Chapter 1), in which single words dangle at the ends of lines and some words are split over two lines by radical enjambment.

COMMON LINE FORMS

It's useful to consider the ways that poets have configured verse lines at various moments in the history of English poetry. Modern poets still use techniques from the earliest English (Anglo-Saxon or "Old English") poetry of the Dark Ages and from all the periods between then and now. In the arts, new ideas come along from time to time, but they don't necessarily eclipse the old ideas or render them obsolete. Sometimes, "innovation" is really a matter of resurrecting ancient techniques.

Accentual Verse

Anglo-Saxon (Old English) poems were usually structured around alliteration rather than rhyme. In addition to alliteration, Anglo-Saxon poets often used a predictable number of stressed syllables in each line. The standard Old English line had four stresses, with a pause (caesura) between the first two stresses and the last two. Anglo-Saxon poets counted only the stressed syllables when patterning their poems; they didn't factor in the unstressed syllables. This strategy is called accentual verse. They also made extensive use of alliteration, repeating a consonant within a line to emphasize the stresses and to create a musical motif. In Old English poems, alliteration serves as a structural tool in the same way that rhyme does in (later) traditional verse. Consequently, Anglo-Saxon poetry is also known as alliterative verse, as is the technique of counting stresses to shape a line.

Cassidy McFadzean channels the form of Anglo-Saxon riddle poems in her "The Magician Wove." Her poem gives us a sense of the four-stress line and strong caesura that was typical of Anglo-Saxon accentual verse.

The Magician Wove
by Cassidy McFadzean

I found a wise   and weird creature
   seated in a tall,   secluded tower,
a spire overlooking   vast seas and fields,
  working in silence   her solitary task.
She toiled through   threadbare nights,
  her finger's tired   twill weaving
  droplets of red   dye into filament,
her blood into fibre,   body into thread.
This magician wove   the warp and weft,
  transformed ply into   pictures divine,
  her tapestry spoke   unspeakable words,
  spun into cotton   like clouds onto sky.
Who is this servant,   ever spinning twine
stringing sentences,   speech into time?

answer: poet

Modern writers sometimes make use of accentual verse and alliterative techniques. Consider the use of alliteration in Gerard Manley Hopkins's "Pied Beauty," and try to count the stresses as you read.

Pied Beauty
by Gerard Manley Hopkins (1844–89)

Glóry be to God for dappled things—
   For skies of couple-colour as a brinded cow;
      For rose-moles all in stipple upon trout that swim;
Fresh-fīrecoal chestnut-fálls; fínches' wings;
   Lándscape plotted and piecèd—fold, fallow, and plough;
      And áll trádes, their gear & tackle & trim.

Áll things counter, original, spáre, stránge;
   Whatever is fickle, frecklèd, (who knows how?)
      With swíft, slów; sweet, soūr; adázzle, dím;
He fathers-forth whose beauty is pást chánge:
                    Práise hím.

Syllabic Verse

While the Anglo-Saxon poets counted only stressed syllables, some modern poems are constructed around the idea of counting the syllables in a line without regard for the stresses. In syllabic verse, each line of a stanza is allotted a specific number of syllables—the first line might, for example, have ten syllables, the second line eight, the third line five, and the fourth line seven. This pattern forms a kind of grid (line 1 = 10 syllables; line 2 = 8; line 3 = 5; line 4 = 7) that's repeated in each stanza of the poem. This technique will seem familiar to anyone who has written a haiku. That popular Japanese verse form consists of a syllabic grid of 5-7-5 syllables distributed over three lines. Some modern poets have made use of syllabic grids in their poetry: the American modernist Marianne Moore was particularly noted for her syllabic-verse poetry, and one well-known example of a syllabic-verse poem is Dylan Thomas's "Fern Hill."

Syllabic verse is in some sense the opposite of accentual verse: instead of putting the emphasis solely on the number and position of stresses, syllabic verse ignores the issue of stress and instead organizes the line in terms of a fixed number of syllables. The effect of syllabic verse is usually to deaden the rhythm and make the lines sound flat and prosaic, although Thomas's syllabic lines miraculously seem highly rhythmic, especially if Thomas himself recites them.

It's debatable, of course, whether it's possible to "kill the rhythm" in an English-language poem, syllabic or otherwise. The poet and translator Burton Raffel didn't think so. In his *How to Read a Poem*, he stated rather vehemently that "it is impossible for any utterance in English *not* to be governed by the rise and fall of stressed and unstressed syllables. Let me repeat: this is not a matter that can be debated, nor is it a matter of syllabics being merely difficult. Syllabics are literally impossible in English, poetry being no more exempt from basic linguistic rules than is any other artifact of language."[2]

Raffel's point notwithstanding, syllabic forms have been popular among English-language poets for some time. William Blake occasionally wrote in fourteen-syllable lines (called "fourteeners"), and Algernon Charles Swinburne managed a poem in eleven-syllable lines. His "Hendecasyllabics" (1866) applies the form to a stichic (single stanza) poem that employs the imagery of autumn.

---

2 Burton Raffel, *How to Read a Poem* (New York: Meridian, 1984), 243.

Hendecasyllabics
by Algernon Charles Swinburne (1837–1909)   11 syll.

In the month of the long decline of roses
I, beholding the summer dead before me,
Set my face to the sea and journeyed silent,
Gazing eagerly where above the sea-mark
Flame as fierce as the fervid eyes of lions
Half divided the eyelids of the sunset;
Till I heard as it were a noise of waters
Moving tremulous under feet of angels
Multitudinous, out of all the heavens;
Knew the fluttering wind, the fluttered foliage,
Shaken fitfully, full of sound and shadow;
And saw, trodden upon by noiseless angels,
Long mysterious reaches fed with moonlight,
Sweet sad straits in a soft subsiding channel,
Blown about by the lips of winds I knew not,
Winds not born in the north nor any quarter,
Winds not warm with the south nor any sunshine;
Heard between them a voice of exultation,
"Lo, the summer is dead, the sun is faded,
Even like as a leaf the year is withered,
All the fruits of the day from all her branches
Gathered, neither is any left to gather.
All the flowers are dead, the tender blossoms,
All are taken away; the season wasted,
Like an ember among the fallen ashes.
Now with light of the winter days, with moonlight,
Light of snow, and the bitter light of hoarfrost,
We bring flowers that fade not after autumn,
Pale white chaplets and crowns of latter seasons,
Fair false leaves (but the summer leaves were falser),
Woven under the eyes of stars and planets
When low light was upon the windy reaches
Where the flower of foam was blown, a lily
Dropt among the sonorous fruitless furrows
And green fields of the sea that make no pasture:
Since the winter begins, the weeping winter,
All whose flowers are tears, and round his temples
Iron blossom of frost is bound for ever."

Accentual-Syllabic Verse

Accentual-syllabic verse is a combination of the two previously mentioned techniques. (Actually, the historical background is more complicated than that, but for our purposes it's enough to think of accentual-syllabic or "metric" verse as poetry in which the line length is determined by the number and type of feet.) To write accentual-syllabic verse, we count both stressed and unstressed syllables. We do this by grouping the syllables into units of two or three stressed or unstressed syllables called "feet," just as we discussed in the previous chapter. Accentual-syllable verse dominated English-language poetry from the time of Chaucer (fourteenth century) to the late-Victorian period (nineteenth century).

Long, End-Stopped Lines ("Stave Prose" or "Rhetorical Rhythm")

The ubiquity of metric verse before the twentieth century wasn't quite absolute. A small number of poets explored other possibilities for shaping a line. American poet Walt Whitman wrote in long, flowing, rhythmic lines that echoed the rhythmic prose of the King James Bible. This technique has been termed stave prose or rhetorical rhythm. Whitman was the quintessential American voice in poetry, and his influence on American poets from Carl Sandburg and Vachel Lindsay to "Beat poets" such as Allen Ginsberg was enormous.

Facing West, from California's Shores
by Walt Whitman (1819–92)

Facing west, from California's shores,
Inquiring, tireless, seeking what is yet unfound,
I, a child, very old, over waves, towards the house of maternity,
    the land of migrations, look afar,
Look off the shores of my Western sea—the circle almost circled;
For, starting westward from Hindustan, from the vales of Kashmere,
From Asia, from the north, from the God, the sage, and the hero,
From the south, from the flowery peninsulas and the spice islands,
Long having wander'd since, round the earth having wander'd,
Now I face home again, very pleas'd and joyous;
(But where is what I started for so long ago?
And why is it yet unfound?)

So we now have four distinct ways of thinking about line:

- the accentual (just count stresses);
- the syllabic (forget the stresses and count every syllable);
- the accentual-syllabic (count metric feet, with each foot consisting of two or three stressed or unstressed syllables);
- long end-stopped lines that produce a flowing if unpredictable rhythm.

We can add a few modern alternatives to that list: note that each of these modernist techniques makes creative use of the white space of the page as poets began to explore the possibilities offered by a new technology—the age of the typewriter replacing the era of the pen.

Triadic Lines (aka "Stepped Lines" or "Visual Rhythm")

Visual rhythm makes use of the white space of the page, indenting lines varying distances from the margin. This technique is associated with American modernist William Carlos Williams, some of whose best-known poems are written in three-line stanzas with the second line indented from the left margin and the third line indented still farther, so the stanza resembles a staircase with three steps. Williams called his three-line visual rhythm stanzas triadic-line poetry, though the term stepped lines is more descriptive. Williams's theory was that each stepped line could be heard as a foot, essentially substituting a musical phrase for the traditional foot determined by counting stressed and unstressed syllables. The term "visual rhythm" can also be used to refer to other arrangements of indented lines, such as tercets in which the middle line of each stanza is indented while the first and third lines are flush left. Matthew Rader uses both conventional stepped lines and the reverse strategy, indenting successive lines away from the left margin and then moving back toward it.

> Fastest Man on the Planet
> by Matthew Rader
>
> *Citius, altius, fortius*
>
> Over before you know it. A curve
>   in the space-time continuum and so
>   quick he's looking himself in the back
>   of the head just as the race is about to
>   begin. He's already won, or will win,

> once the race is run, but from the couch
> at home, where we've just recently tuned in,
> the announcer is cautioning us not to rush
> to judgment on this one. Anything can
> happen between now and then, he says,
> which is where our runner is at this very
> instant, vanished from our TV set, like
> so much of our lives given over to watching
> this dreck. Hard to believe we'd take
> the bet given the odds things would turn out
> different from the way they will or did, but
> who's kidding who, we've covered the spread
> and are ready to kick back and crack a beer,
>
> the fastest man on the planet was just here.

Split Lines

The technique of adding space between words or phrases to indicate a pause or breath—a strong caesura—within a line is a fairly common one in modern poetry. It's a device (known as a split line) that's associated with American poet James Dickey, though in fact it recalls Anglo-Saxon poetry. (See, for example, Cassidy McFadzean's riddle poem.) The space within the line can take the place of a comma, a semicolon, a dash, or even a period or colon and is termed a **visual caesura**.

"Open Field" Composition

Open field composition or projective verse was popularized in the 1950s by poets associated with Black Mountain College in the eastern United States—Charles Olson, Denise Levertov, Gary Snyder, Robert Creeley, and others. Put (very) simply, open field composition extends the modernist concern for writing in the "musical phrase" rather than in metric units by using the white space of the page as a field on which phrases, sentences, and single words can be arranged visually without reference to margins. Think of the words of the poem as notes in a musical composition and the white space of the page as silence.

Ocean Vuong's "Aubade with Burning City" uses varied indentations, italicized passages, and fragments set off with ellipses or dashes to create a poem that locates itself in visual space—the "open field" of composition.

Aubade with Burning City
by Ocean Vuong

South Vietnam, April 29, 1975: Armed Forces Radio played Irving Berlin's "White Christmas" as a code to begin Operation Frequent Wind, the ultimate evacuation of American civilians and Vietnamese refugees by helicopter during the fall of Saigon.

Milkflower petals on the street
                        like pieces of a girl's dress.

May your days be merry and bright . . .

He fills a teacup with champagne, brings it to her lips.
        Open, he says.
                    She opens.
                                Outside, a soldier spits out
            his cigarette as footsteps
                    fill the square like stones fallen from the sky. *May all
                        your Christmases be white* as the traffic guard
            unstraps his holster.

                        His hand running the hem
    of her white dress.
                    His black eyes.
            Her black hair.
                    A single candle.
                        Their shadows: two wicks.

A military truck speeds through the intersection, the sound of children
                    shrieking inside. A bicycle hurled
        through a store window. When the dust rises, a black dog
                lies in the road, panting. Its hind legs
                                crushed into the shine
                of a white Christmas.

On the nightstand, a sprig of magnolia expands like a secret heard
                            for the first time.

The treetops glisten and children listen, the chief of police
              facedown in a pool of Coca-Cola.
                         A palm-sized photo of his father soaking
      beside his left ear.

The song moving through the city like a widow.
           A white . . . A white . . . I'm dreaming of a curtain of snow

                      falling from her shoulders.

Snow crackling against the window. Snow shredded

               with gunfire. Red sky.
           Snow on the tanks rolling over the city walls.
A helicopter lifting the living just out of reach.

        The city so white it is ready for ink.

                      The radio saying run run run.
Milkflower petals on a black dog
        like pieces of a girl's dress.

May your days be merry and bright. She is saying
      something neither of them can hear. The hotel rocks
        beneath them. The bed a field of ice
                     cracking.

Don't worry, he says, as the first bomb brightens
          their faces, *my brothers have won the war*
                and tomorrow . . .
        The lights go out.

I'm dreaming. I'm dreaming . . .
               to hear sleigh bells in the snow . . .

In the square below: a nun, on fire,
        runs silently toward her god—

      Open, he says.
          She opens.

The visual arrangement of words we encounter in Olson and other twentieth-century poets, such as e e cummings, depends to a significant degree on the advent of the typewriter. As Olson himself put it, "It is the advantage of the typewriter that, due to its rigidity and its space precisions, it can, for a poet, indicate exactly the breath, the pause, the suspensions even of syllables, the juxtapositions even of parts of phrases, that he intends."[3]

Some poets link the "open field" technique to the concept of proprioception. That's a term from kinesiology, and it originally referred to the feedback between perception and physical movement that allows us to be aware of the position of our extremities and the motions required to perform tasks. Olson refers to proprioception as "the data of depth sensibility."[4] In the context of poetics, proprioception places emphasis on the process of composition and the open-ended interaction between the consciousness of the poet and the language of the emerging poem. Thus the poem exists not only as an art object but as a record of the creative process from which it emerged. The reader receives the poem by following the poet through that process and living it with him or her.

STANZAS AND CANTOS

Line breaks are one way of using visual space to organize a verse poem; *stanza breaks* are another. Some poems consist of one long passage of verse; the term for these poems is **stichic** (pronounced *stick-ik*). Most verse lyrics, however, are organized into groups of lines called **stanzas**. A stanza is a line or group of lines that's visually separated from the other stanzas. The term "stanza" comes from the Italian "*stanza*," meaning a room. A **stanza break** is a visual space between adjacent stanzas. The convention is to leave a blank line between stanzas; more than one line suggests a very long pause or even a shift in topic or technique.

Stanzas and the stanza breaks between them are important tools for building and developing your poems. Stanzas can make your poem more accessible than it might be in stichic form by allowing your readers to process the information one "roomful" at a time. A stanza functions on both auditory and visual levels: stanza breaks help to orchestrate our reading of a poem as they indicate a longer pause than the pause at the end of a line. They also provide a visual clue to the poem's theme: repetition of the same stanza form communicates a sense of symmetry and balance, while irregular stanza forms suggest an informal and discursive tone.

---

3 "Biography: Charles Olson, 1910–1970," *Poetry Foundation*,
http://www.poetryfoundation.org/poems-and-poets/poets/detail/charles-olson.
4 Charles Olson, *Proprioception* (San Francisco: Four Seasons Foundation, 1965), 17.

A stanza in a verse poem isn't the same thing as a paragraph in a prose document. A paragraph is a unit of punctuation; a break between paragraphs signals a shift from one subtopic to another and thus works as a way of organizing subject matter. A stanza, on the other hand, divides a poem into units of sound: stanza breaks are more a matter of music than of meaning. Stanza breaks will sometimes fall in the middle of a passage of narrative or in a subsection of an argument or even in the middle of a sentence, making the function of a stanza strikingly different from that of a paragraph. Paradoxically, some poems are written not in stanzas but in "verse paragraphs." Like a paragraph of prose, a verse paragraph defines a unit of meaning and is only incidentally related to the orchestration of sound. Verse paragraphs, as opposed to stanzas, usually show up in lengthy narrative or dramatic poems, where they perform the same function as paragraphs in prose fiction. Verse paragraphs begin with an indented line; stanzas usually do not.

It's often worth revising your poem into regular stanzas of different lengths: try it in couplets, then tercets, and so forth. Sometimes a draft of the poem will offer a clue to the best arrangement of stanzas: a particularly strong passage may fall naturally into a tercet or quatrain form, and shaping the other passages into the same form may involve pruning off unnecessary verbiage and thus making the poem not only more symmetrical but also more efficient. We'll look at some common stanza forms in another chapter.

A canto is a section of a poem. Cantos consist of one or more stanzas. If a stanza is vaguely analogous to a paragraph in a prose work, then a canto is like a chapter. Dividing a poem into cantos may seem to be appropriate only for long poems, but even short lyrics can sometimes benefit from being organized into separate sections. Recognizing the need to divide your poem into cantos is a useful skill.

Cantos are usually separated by Roman or Arabic numerals or dingbats (printed characters other than letters or numerals), though sometimes poets use headings or subtitles. Numerals imply sequence, which in turn implies narrative or logical progression. If you don't want to imply that your cantos are part of a sequence, then dingbats are probably the best option. A dingbat can be anything from a simple asterisk to a more ornate glyph. Most word-processing programs include a "Dingbats" or "Wingdings" font that will supply you with a range of interesting characters.

When should you consider dividing your poem into cantos? If you want to approach a theme in a few different ways, then sectioning the poem into cantos would give you that latitude. You could tell a story in one canto, use a listing technique in another, and so on. If your draft includes more than one field of imagery, it's likely to seem muddled and incoherent, but you might be able to get around that problem by dividing the draft poem into cantos.

EXERCISES

Exercise 9/1: Reverse Engineering

Select two or more poems from this book and analyze each in terms of the poet's use of lines. Are lines phrase, clause, or sentence generated? As an experiment, try to rewrite at least one of these poems using a different strategy than that employed by the poet. Refer to the examples of phrase-, clause-, and sentence-generated lines given in this chapter. When you've done this, consider the relative effectiveness of your strategy and that used in the original poem. If you're working with a workshop or writers' group, try having everyone analyze the same poems and then compare strategies.

Exercise 9/2: The "Topography Test"

Topographers map the relative height of landforms in a region. If you turn a poem on its side, you'll see a "mountain range" (or maybe just a plateau), as lines of different lengths will resemble the peaks and valleys of a landscape.

If you're writing a traditional verse poem, the topography test may not tell you much. Your lines are likely to be fairly regular in length, or the length will vary according to the constraints of a fixed form. Stanza lengths are probably also going to conform to the demands of the form. Obviously, a notable irregularity in line lengths is probably an indication that something is amiss or at least unusual: time to check your scansion or to listen carefully to the rhythm of the lines.

Checking the relative line and stanza lengths of free-verse poems can often be quite instructive. If your lines are getting progressively longer or shorter, perhaps you're losing control of the music of the poem. It's not uncommon to run across poems that seem to wander off and devolve into prose; the poet has lost his or her sense of a base rhythm or is becoming more interested in the narrative dimension of the poem than in its music.

Select two of your own draft poems and apply the topography test. What did you learn?

Exercise 9/3: Revising Lineation

Write a paragraph of about fifty to seventy-five words, and then revise it into a brief free-verse poem by breaking the lines wherever you feel they should be broken. Your poem can be any number of lines, and the lines can be of any length. Don't add or delete words; just arrange the words into lines.

If you're in a workshop or writers' group, exchange sheets with another poet or workshop member and try to revise each other's lineation by making changes to the line breaks. Consider, as well, whether deleting or adding a word here and there would improve the poem. After you've shared your draft with the group, try a few different versions of the poem, modelling each version on one of the strategies for lineation that we've just discussed—start with long, end-stopped lines, and then try clause-generated lines or a mixture of clauses and phrases; then try enjambing. Look for a strategy that seems to work well in at least one part of the poem, and try applying it throughout the poem.

Exercise 9/4: Syllabics

Create a syllabic grid and use it as a template for writing a short lyric poem. Your template might require, for example, that the first line of each stanza be six syllables long while the second line is ten syllables, line 3 is nine syllables, line 4 also nine syllables, and lines 5 and 6 seven syllables. Thus the syllabic grid for each six-line stanza would be 6, 10, 9, 9, 7, 7. Hint: Start by writing a few lines and counting the syllables; then consider how you could develop a grid that would include those lines. You might find that you have to modify the lines (and thus the template) as you draft successive stanzas, but at least you'll have something to work from.

Exercise 9/5: Sound and Visual Design— Exploring the Open Field

Print a copy of one of your lyric poems or of a paragraph of your prose. Then record yourself reading the poem or prose passage. Next, cut the printed text up into individual words or short phrases. Play the recording of your reading, and try to place the words on a fresh sheet of paper (use a big sheet if you need to) in a design that mirrors the way you recited the text. Use white space to indicate pauses of various durations, and arrange phrases into positions that visually represent their relationship to each other and to the poem as a whole. When you've done all that, paste the words to the sheet, or (better yet) type up a new draft that incorporates the visual arrangement you've just created.

If you want to push this exercise one step further, try doing it in reverse: place the words on the page in an interesting visual design, and then read the results aloud, paying careful attention to the pauses you've indicated with white space.

TAKEAWAY

- The three most common traditional line forms are the accentual, syllabic, and accentual-syllabic. *Accentual verse* counts stresses; *syllabic verse* counts syllables; *accentual-syllabic verse* combines the first two approaches.
- Lines can be phrases, clauses, sentences, or, less commonly, a word.
- Lines that consist of a complete grammatical unit such as a clause or sentence are called *end-stopped lines.* Some poets use long, flowing, rhythmic, and usually end-stopped lines to create a sense of public oratory.
- *Enjambment* is the technique of breaking lines *within* grammatical units.
- Enjambing lines creates pauses within lines. A pause within a line is called a *caesura.* A caesura can be signalled with a period, a comma, or a split line (visual caesura).
- Modern poets have experimented with alternate strategies for organizing lines such as visual rhythm (triadic or "stepped" lines), split lines, and open field composition.
- Poems that consist of one continuous sequence of lines are termed *stichic.* Many poems, however, are divided into groups of lines called *stanzas.*
- Poems—particularly longer poems—may be further divided into groups of stanzas called *cantos.*

TERMS TO REMEMBER

- accentual verse
- accentual-syllabic verse
- alliterative verse
- caesura
- canto
- clause-generated lines
- dingbats
- end-stopped
- enjambment
- open field composition
- phrase-generated lines
- projective verse
- proprioception
- rhetorical rhythm
- sentence-generated lines
- split line
- stanza break
- stanzas
- stave prose
- stepped lines
- stichic
- syllabic verse
- triadic-line poetry (triads)
- verse paragraph
- visual caesura
- visual rhythm
- word-generated lines

CHAPTER TEN

Working with Fixed Forms

A "fixed form" or "form poem" conforms to a set of requirements regarding, typically, its metre or lineation or stanza forms or rhyme scheme or some combination of those and other elements. Writing a form poem is a little like doing a crossword puzzle: you're given some blanks to fill, and you have to fit your language to the number and arrangement of spaces. Form poems fall into four general categories: traditional European forms, forms from non-European literatures, newly minted "nonce forms," and experimental constrained forms. European forms tend to be in metric verse and usually (but not always) include a rhyme scheme. Asian forms tend to be syllabic. Forms involving repetition of a word or phrase come from many different languages and cultures.

Why would we want to adhere to a fixed pattern rather than letting each poem determine its own form? Some poets find working in a fixed form constricting and limiting, but others find that the form provides a stimulus to creativity. Fitting voice, language, and form together works as a kind of "forced inspiration" exercise; we stretch our imagination and linguistic abilities in order to meet the demands of the formula. Trying out a new fixed form can give us a fresh take on poetic technique; the unfamiliar pattern forces us to rethink our style and to take some risks in order to meet new challenges. Working in fixed forms is also a great way to develop our writing skill and our knowledge of the craft. As well, there's an enjoyable sense of being part of a tradition: when we write a sonnet, we're walking in the footsteps of Thomas Wyatt and Mary Wroth and John Donne and Elizabeth Barrett Browning, and we're fitting our intellectual and perceptual processes into the same mould that they used to forge their justly famous poems—that's kind of a cool idea.

Some fixed forms bring with them a certain mode of thought. The Italian sonnet is constructed around an argument: the octave puts forward a theory or problem, and the sestet provides the resolution. The English version of that form encapsulates the resolution in a witty final couplet. The villanelle's cycling repetitions give that form an incantatory quality that suits it to a prayer or confession. English-language adaptations of the Malaysian pantoum often marry that form's interlocking stanzas to surreal imagery. A haiku can take us from sense perception to insight in three brief lines.

COMMON STANZA FORMS

Couplet: a two-line stanza. Normally, the term "couplet" refers to two lines that are "coupled" by end-rhyme. The term can also be used to refer to any two-line stanza. Couplets that express a complete thought and end with a period are called "closed couplets." Couplets in pentameter are called "heroic couplets" because of their association with heroic themes in poetry. This epistolary poem by early American poet Anne Bradstreet is written in rhyming couplets:

> *A Letter to Her Husband, Absent Upon Publick Employment*
> by Anne Bradstreet (1612–72)
>
> My head, my heart, mine eyes, my life, nay more,
> My joy, my magazine of earthly store,
> If two be one, as surely thou and I,
> How stayest thou there, whilst I at Ipswich lie?
> So many steps, head from the heart to sever,
> If but a neck, soon should we be together.
> I like the Earth this season, mourn in black,
> My Sun is gone so far in's zodiac,
> Whom whilst I 'joyed, nor storms, nor frosts I felt,
> His warmth such frigid colds did cause to melt.
> My chilled limbs now numbed lie forlorn;
> Return, return, sweet Sol, from Capricorn;
> In this dead time, alas, what can I more
> Than view those fruits which through thy heat I bore?
> Which sweet contentment yield me for a space,
> True living pictures of their fathers face.
> O strange effect! now thou art southward gone,
> I weary grow, the tedious day so long;
> But when thou northward to me shalt return,
> I wish my Sun may never set, but burn
> Within the Cancer of my glowing breast,
> The welcome house of him my dearest guest.
> Where ever, ever stay, and go not thence,
> Till natures sad decree shall call thee hence;
> Flesh of thy flesh, bone of thy bone,
> I here, thou there, yet both but one.

Tercet (or triplet): a three-line stanza. The term "triplet" is used interchangeably with the more common term "tercet," though some poets restrict the meaning of "triplet" to a three-line stanza in which all three lines rhyme. Tercet stanzas are also popular among free-verse poets, as they apply a useful sense of balance and organization to poems that might seem too dense or too discursive in stichic form. *Terza rima* is an Italian form in which the first and third lines of each stanza rhyme with each other and the second line of the first stanza rhymes with the first and third lines of the next stanza. This interlocking pattern (*aba, bcb, cdc, ded,* and so on) or "chain rhyme" was used in Dante Alighieri's epic *The Divine Comedy* (*Divina commedia,* 1308–20) and in P.B. Shelley's "Ode to the West Wind" (1820). The **blues stanza** is a tercet rhymed *aaa* with the first line repeated (often with some changes) as the second line.

Quatrain: Perhaps the most popular stanza form in English verse is the four-line stanza. The four lines can be interwoven in a variety of ways. Rhymed quatrains are common throughout the history of English verse, and the quatrain lends itself to a few simple patterns of end-rhyme. The **ballad stanza** consists of alternating tetrameter and trimeter lines rhymed *abcb*. A quatrain rhymed *aabb* is called a **couplet quatrain,** as it seems to consist of two couplets. Quatrains can also be rhymed *abba*; this arrangement is called an **envelope stanza** as the rhymed first and last lines seem to "envelop" the middle two lines. It's a good idea to be familiar with the various permutations of the quatrain, as quatrains are easy to balance rhythmically and are often employed in light-verse poems and even in free verse. Quatrains also resemble the verses of a song and provide a link to traditional and popular song structures. A **free-verse quatrain** is simply an unrhymed four-line stanza.

Here's a poem by Wilfred Owen that's structured around envelope quatrains.

Shadwell Stair
by Wilfred Owen (1893–1918)

I am the ghost of Shadwell Stair.
    Along the wharves by the water-house,
    And through the cavernous slaughter-house,
I am the shadow that walks there.

Yet I have flesh both firm and cool,
    And eyes tumultuous as the gems
    Of moons and lamps in the full Thames
When dusk sails wavering down the pool.

Shuddering the purple street-arc burns
    Where I watch always; from the banks
    Dolorously the shipping clanks
And after me a strange tide turns.

I walk till the stars of London wane
    And dawn creeps up the Shadwell Stair.
    But when the crowing syrens blare
I with another ghost am lain.

The **Sapphic stanza** (or simply "Sapphic") is named for the ancient-Greek poet Sappho, although it was employed by other poets of her time such as Alcaeus of Mytilene. Thomas Campion (1567–1620) mentions **Sapphics** in his *Observations in the Art of English Poesie,* so the form was of interest to English poets of Shakespeare's time. Victorian poet A.C. Swinburne wrote a number of Sapphics, and despite its complexities, the form remains popular. The template for the modern English-language adaptation of the Sapphic stanza calls for three **hendecasyllabic** (eleven-syllable) lines followed by a five-syllable line called the "Adonic." In case that's not challenging enough, there's also a metric pattern: each of the long lines should consist of two trochees, a dactyl, and then two more trochees. The Adonic (final line) should be a dactyl followed by a trochee.

Unlikely as it may seem, quite a few good poems have been crafted in Sapphic stanzas, though some, such as Cowper's "Lines Written During a Period of Insanity," take a few liberties with the prescribed pattern.

Lines Written During a Period of Insanity
by William Cowper (1731–1800)

Hatred and vengeance, my eternal portion,
Scarce can endure delay of execution,
Wait, with impatient readiness, to seize my
        Soul in a moment.

Damned below Judas: more abhorred than he was,
Who for a few pence sold his holy master.
Twice betrayed, Jesus me, the last delinquent,
        Deems the profanest.

Man disavows, and Deity disowns me:
Hell might afford my miseries a shelter;
Therefore hell keeps her ever-hungry mouths all
    Bolted against me.

Hard lot! encompassed with a thousand dangers;
Weary, faint, trembling with a thousand terrors,
I'm called, if vanquished, to receive a sentence
    Worse than Abiram's.

Him the vindictive rod of angry justice
Sent quick and howling to the centre headlong;
I, fed with judgment, in a fleshly tomb, am
    Buried above ground.

A five-line stanza is called a **cinquain** or **quintet** and is less common in English verse than the couplet, tercet, or quatrain. Five-line stanzas do show up in some free-verse examples and have specific applications in fixed forms. The **limerick** consists of one five-line stanza rhymed *aabba*, and the **mad song** uses an *abccb* rhyme scheme that isolates a floating opening line, thus contributing to the wandering, slightly incoherent quality that gives the form its name. This stanza is from the anonymous sixteenth-century "Tom O'Bedlam's Song":

I know more than Apollo,
For, oft when he lies sleeping,
    I behold the stars
    At bloody wars,
And the wounded welkin weeping.

Six-line stanzas or **sestets** can usually be broken down into three rhymed couplets or a rhymed quatrain and a couplet, and of course in free verse they are simply any grouping of six lines. There are, as well, some relatively complex six-line stanza forms: the following poem by Aphra Behn makes use of the Portuguese-Spanish **sextilla** form—a six-line stanza rhymed *ababcc*.

The Libertine
By Aphra Behn (1640–89)

A thousand martyrs I have made,
    All sacrificed to my desire,
A thousand beauties have betray'd

That languish in resistless fire:
The untamed heart to hand I brought,
And fix'd the wild and wand'ring thought.

I never vow'd nor sigh'd in vain,
    But both, tho' false, were well received;
The fair are pleased to give us pain,
    And what they wish is soon believed:
And tho' I talk'd of wounds and smart,
Love's pleasures only touch'd my heart.

Alone the glory and the spoil
    I always laughing bore away;
The triumphs without pain or toil,
    Without the hell the heaven of joy;
And while I thus at random rove
Despise the fools that whine for love.

Seven-line stanzas—septets—occur in free verse but rarely as a regular stanza form; usually, one or more stanzas of the free-verse poem may be seven lines long, but other stanzas may be any other length. Rime royal is a seven-line iambic pentameter stanza rhyming *ababbcc*.

An **octave** is an eight-line stanza; the Petrarchan or Italian sonnet begins with an eight-line exposition (usually rhyming *abbaabba*) and ends with a sestet. *Ottava rima* is an eight-line iambic pentameter stanza rhymed *abababcc*. W.B. Yeats chose that complex form for his classic poem "Sailing to Byzantium."

The **Spenserian stanza** consists of nine lines: eight iambic pentameter lines rhymed *ababbcbc* and one final hexameter line, also rhymed. The form is named for sixteen-century poet Edmund Spenser (1522–99), who used it in his epic *The Faerie Queene* of 1590–96.

In free-verse poems, it's not uncommon to see a single-line stanza. This technique is often used to emphasize or isolate a particular moment in the poem. Quite a few free-verse lyrics end with a single-line stanza as the isolated line highlights the resolution—a technique that recalls the final couplet of a Shakespearean sonnet.

POPULAR EUROPEAN FORMS

Ballad

The **ballad** is an ancient, and very simple, verse form. The ballad form is the foundation of folk song and—more recently—pop songs. Anyone who wants to be a song writer would do well to study the history and structure of the traditional ballad.

The form of the ballad is straightforward, though some interesting variants have been developed over the years. The basic pattern goes like this: a ballad has a variable number of quatrains with a rising rhythm (iambic or sometimes anapaestic) organized in alternating lines of tetrameter and trimeter. The rhyme is usually *abcb* or *abab* or (less commonly) *aabb*. One typical variation is to add a fifth line that simply repeats the fourth line in order to create a "chant" or refrain effect. The metre of a folk song may not adhere strictly to the tetrameter-trimeter pattern.

Many well-known ballads have been around for hundreds of years. They've been preserved by folklorists and given new life by singers who are drawn to their simplicity and drama. (One of the most famous collections of ballads is Thomas Percy's *Reliques of Ancient English Poetry*, published in 1765; another is *The English and Scottish Popular Ballads*, collected by Francis James Child and first published in 1860.) The Welsh poet David Jones said that the popular ballad "Barbara Allen" was the unofficial national anthem of Great Britain: folk songs like this one, passed along through the generations, bind a community or a culture together, along with the legends and history they embody and preserve. (Note that, over the years, many different versions of folk songs develop; the US Library of Congress collected recordings of 30 American versions of "Barbara Allen" between 1933 and 1954.) The tetrameter-trimeter rhythm and *abcb* (occasionally *abab*) rhyme scheme is typical of the ballad.

> *Barbara Allen*
> as performed by Joan Baez
>
> 'Twas in the merry month of May
> When green buds all were swelling,
> Sweet William on his death bed lay
> For love of Barbara Allen.
>
> He sent his servant to the town
> To the place where she was dwelling,
> Saying you must come, to my master dear
> If your name be Barbara Allen.

So slowly, slowly she got up
And slowly she drew nigh him,
And the only words to him did say
Young man I think you're dying.

He turned his face unto the wall
And death was in him welling,
Good-bye, good-bye, to my friends all
Be good to Barbara Allen.

When he was dead and laid in grave
She heard the death bells knelling
And every stroke to her did say
Hard-hearted Barbara Allen.

Ballads are narrative poems—poems that tell a story—and the story they tell is often a dramatic tale of betrayal, revenge, lost love, death, and even murder. The traditional folk ballad "Silver Dagger," which exits in many versions under various titles, has a typically dramatic theme:

Silver Dagger
as performed by Joan Baez

Don't sing love songs, you'll wake my mother
She's sleeping here right by my side
And in her right hand a silver dagger,
She says that I can't be your bride.

All men are false, says my mother,
They'll tell you wicked, loving lies.
The very next evening, they'll court another,
Leave you alone to pine and sigh.

My daddy is a handsome devil
He's got a chain five miles long,
And on every link a heart does dangle
Of another maid he's loved and wronged.

Go court another tender maiden
And hope that she will be your wife
For I've been warned, and I've decided
To sleep alone all of my life.

Ballads in English may have originated in medieval England, Ireland, or Scotland, but they've travelled well. Most folk songs and a great many pop songs are constructed around the *abcb* rhyme scheme and the tetrameter or tetrameter-trimeter rhythm of the traditional ballad. Pop songs (and many folk songs) typically repeat one verse as a **chorus**, and some repeat the last line of each stanza as a refrain. As well, pop-song writers often add an additional verse that varies the rhythm and rhyme; that's called a **bridge**. Quite a few very good poets double as song writers (Leonard Cohen is the obvious example), and some poets start out by writing song lyrics and then find that they want to concentrate on language rather than doubling as musicians.

Try printing the lyrics to a couple of your favourite songs (ignore the printed lyrics sheets you'll find in some CDs and vinyl albums; the designers often get the line breaks wrong). Can you see the resemblance to the traditional ballad form?

Sonnet

The **sonnet** originates in Italy and is associated with Petrarch (Francesco Petrarca, 1304–74), though it may have been invented by an earlier Italian poet, Giacomo Da Lentini. The form drifted north and west into France and then England, where it was adapted for English verse by Sir Thomas Wyatt; Henry Howard, Earl of Surrey; and other poets of Henrican times. Sonnets and sonnet sequences of various lengths were popular in the late sixteenth and early seventeenth centuries. The most famous sonnet sequences from that time are by William Shakespeare, Mary Wroth, John Donne, and Sir Philip Sydney, but there were a great many others that were published or circulated in manuscript. Since then, sonnets have come (with some exceptions) in two flavours: Italian ("Petrarchan") and English (sometimes called "Shakespearean"). In either case, the name refers to the formal envelope of the poem. An Italian sonnet is divided into two parts: the octave and the sestet, with a change of tone or subject called a "turn" (*volta*) between the two parts of the poem. An English sonnet is organized something like a song, with three quatrains and a final couplet. The rhyme scheme is *abab, cdcd, efef, gg*.

Christina Rossetti's sonnet, which follows, conforms to the pattern of the Italian sonnet, with the octave consisting of two *abba* quatrains and the sestet rhymed *cdecde*. Notice the striking change of mood and imagery between the octave and sestet as Rossetti moves from the exposition to the resolution.

A Dream (Sonnet)
by Christina Rossetti (1830–94)

Once in a dream (for once I dreamed of you)
  We stood together in an open field;
  Above our heads two swift-winged pigeons wheeled,
Sporting at ease and courting full in view.
When loftier still a broadening darkness flew,
  Down-swooping, and a ravenous hawk revealed;
  Too weak to fight, too fond to fly, they yield;
So farewell life and love and pleasures new.
Then as their plumes fell fluttering to the ground,
  Their snow-white plumage flecked with crimson drops,
    I wept, and thought I turned towards you to weep:
  But you were gone; while rustling hedgerow tops
Bent in a wind which bore to me a sound
    Of far-off piteous bleat of lambs and sheep.

The English (aka Shakespearean) sonnet offers different strengths than its Italian counterpart. There may be less sense of a structured argument moving from exposition to resolution, but that final couplet provides a strong, often epigrammatic, kicker. Christina Rossetti's brother, the poet and painter Dante Gabriel Rossetti, used a variation (note the envelope rhyme in the first two quatrains) of the English sonnet form in this example from his sonnet sequence, *The House of Life.*

The Sonnet
by Dante Gabriel Rossetti (1828–82)

A Sonnet is a moment's monument—
  Memorial from the Soul's eternity
  To one dead deathless hour. Look that it be,
Whether for lustral rite or dire portent,
Of its own arduous fulness reverent:
  Carve it in ivory or in ebony,
  As Day or Night may rule; and let Time see
Its flowering crest impearl'd and orient.

A Sonnet is a coin: its face reveals
  The soul—its converse, to what Power 'tis due—
Whether for tribute to the august appeals

> Of Life, or dower in Love's high retinue,
> It serve; or, 'mid the dark wharf's cavernous breath,
> In Charon's palm it pay the toll to Death.

The sonnet's popularity among poets has never waned. Contemporary poet Karen Volkman uses slant rhymes and creative lexical choices to put a new spin on the time-honoured pattern.

Sonnet [Laughing below, the unimagined room]
by Karen Volkman

> Laughing below, the unimagined room
> in unimagined mouths, a turning mood
> speaking itself the way a fulling should
> overspilling into something's dome,
>
> some moment's edging over into bloom.
> What is a happening but conscious cloud
> seeking its edge in a wound or word
> pellucidity describing term
>
> as boundary, body, violated bourne
> no sounding center, circumscription turn.
> Mother of mirrors, angel of the acts,
>
> do all the sighing breathing clicking wilds
> summon the same blue breadth the sense subtracts,
> the star suborning in its ruptured fields.

A **sonnet crown** is a suite of anywhere from three to fourteen sonnets (seven is common) in which the last line of each stanza becomes the first line of the next stanza and the last line of the seventh stanza becomes the first line of the first stanza, making a the poem as a whole a complete circle or "crown." Famous examples include Mary Wroth's "A Crown of Sonnets Dedicated to Love" and John Donne's "La Corona."

The most recent evolution of the sonnet form is the **free-verse sonnet,** which is loosely defined as any fourteen-line lyric poem. Although that criterion may seem too vague to qualify a free-verse poem as a sonnet, modern poets often capture something of the tone of the traditional sonnet in their free-verse adaptations. They also make effective use of "word music" techniques in order to make their poems as sonically complex as their intricately rhymed cousins. The following poem, by a contemporary American poet, hovers close to pentameter blank verse—a distant echo of Elizabethan sonnets—and includes enjambed lines, repeated phrases (such as "so many . . . so many" and "summers . . . summers"), occasional rhyme ("you" with "into"), consonance ("more" and "Tabernacle"), and alliteration to create a densely woven, highly musical composition.

Ark
by Camille T. Dungy

I will enter you as hope enters me,
through blinding liquid, light of rain, and I
will stay inside until you send me out;
I will stay inside until you ground me.
We cannot outrun the rain. So many
summers I have tried. So many summers.
But when the rumble calls after the spark
there can be no escape. No outstripping
the drench soak, the wet sheath, the water caul.
This is more than you want to hear. Much more
than I want to tell you. Tabernacle
transporting my life from the desert, you,
the faith I am born and reborn into,
you, rescuer, deliverer of rain.

Villanelle

Like the sonnet and several other popular verse forms, the villanelle originated in the Mediterranean countries and found its way north to England. In English usage, at least, the villanelle is a fixed form consisting of five three-line stanzas followed by a quatrain and having only two rhymes. In the stanzas following the first, the first and third lines of the first stanza are repeated alternately as refrains; they then become the final two lines of the concluding quatrain.

For the Punk Rock Boys
by Elizabeth Bachinsky

The stars engraved your names indelibly
as ink under my skin, you valley boys:
Sean and Shaun and Michael, Paul and Steve.

How often fifty fingers tried to free
my half-formed breasts on nights you boys,
like stars, engraved your names indelibly

with knives into the bark of a pine tree
or a park bench. The parks filled with your noise.
Sean and Shaun and Michael, Paul and Steve.

how strange you were, above me—strange like thieves
one frightens in a heist. You were just boys
with stars engraved, like names, indelibly

along your boyish veins. You stood out green
under your flesh. You tasted like a choice.
Sean and Shaun and Michael, Paul and Steve.

you wore your anger as you wore your need,
as politic or fashion, such little joy—
and yet, the stars inscribed your names. Indelibly,
Sean and Shaun and Michael, Paul and Steve.

Some poets prefer a looser version of the villanelle form, one that drops the requirement for rhyme and relies solely on the pattern of stanza forms and repeated lines for its formal symmetry.

Rondeau

The **rondeau** adds an interesting twist to the usual patterns of fixed-form poems: its three stanzas are all of different lengths. The poem begins with a quintet, which is followed by a quatrain, which is in turn followed by a sestet. In addition to this formal requirement, the rondeau uses only two rhymes to create a complex rhyme scheme, and the initial line repeats in truncated form in the second and third stanzas. The poem below, written by a physician during World War I, is probably the most famous of Canadian poems. Note that most lines are in iambic tetrameter, while the final line of each of the last two stanzas is dimeter. Modern rondeaux can also be written in syllabic verse.

In Flanders Fields
by Dr. John McCrae (1872–1918)

In Flanders fields the poppies blow
Between the crosses, row on row,
    That mark our place; and in the sky
    The larks, still bravely singing, fly
Scarce heard amid the guns below.

We are the Dead. Short days ago
We lived, felt dawn, saw sunset glow,
    Loved and were loved, and now we lie,
    In Flanders fields.

Take up our quarrel with the foe:
To you from failing hands we throw
    The torch; be yours to hold it high.
    If ye break faith with us who die
We shall not sleep, though poppies grow
    In Flanders fields.

Sestina

A **sestina** uses six six-line stanzas before its final tercet. The final words of the lines repeat a sequence of six words in a different order in each sestet; this eccentric pattern of organization has been associated with numerology, though it may spring from some poet's interest in dreaming up challenging puzzles. Given the difficulty of the form, it's surprising how many sestinas have been (and are still being) written.

Rudyard Kipling used the sestina form for his dialect poem narrated by an English gentleman of the road. There's a certain disconnect between the sophisticated form and the rough-hewn narrator, but the poem remains enjoyable nonetheless. The order of key words in this poem will give you an idea of the standard pattern of the form.

Sestina of the Tramp-Royal
by Rudyard Kipling (1865–1936)

Speakin' in general, I 'ave tried 'em all—
The 'appy roads that take you o'er the world.
Speakin' in general, I 'ave found them good
For such as cannot use one bed too long,

But must get 'ence, the same as I 'ave done,
An' go observin' matters till they die.

What do it matter where or 'ow we die,
So long as we've our 'ealth to watch it all—
The different ways that different things are done,
An' men an' women lovin' in this world;
Takin' our chances as they come along,
An' when they ain't, pretendin' they are good?

In cash or credit—no, it aren't no good;
You 'ave to 'ave the 'abit or you'd die,
Unless you lived your life but one day long,
Nor didn't prophesy nor fret at all,
But drew your tucker some'ow from the world,
An' never bothered what you might ha' done.

But, Gawd, what things are they I 'aven't done?
I've turned my 'and to most, an' turned it good,
In various situations round the world—
For 'im that doth not work must surely die;
But that's no reason man should labour all
'Is life on one same shift; life's none so long.

Therefore, from job to job I've moved along.
Pay couldn't 'old me when my time was done,
For something in my 'ead upset me all,
Till I 'ad dropped whatever 'twas for good,
An', out at sea, be'eld the dock-lights die,
An' met my mate—the wind that tramps the world!

It's like a book, I think, this bloomin' world,
Which you can read and care for just so long,
But presently you feel that you will die
Unless you get the page you're readin' done,
An' turn another—likely not so good;
But what you're after is to turn 'em all.

Gawd bless this world! Whatever she 'ath done—
Excep' when awful long—I've found it good.
So write, before I die, "'E liked it all!"

Triolet

The triolet, like the villanelle, combines a rhyme scheme with a pattern of repetition. The poem consists of eight lines rhymed *abaaabab,* with the first line repeating as the fourth and seventh lines and the second line repeating as the last line. Thomas Hardy made effective use of the form in his "How Great My Grief." Australian poet "Banjo" Paterson, however, took a dim view of the triolet.

> How Great My Grief
> by Thomas Hardy (1840–1928)
>
> How great my grief, my joys how few,
>   Since first it was my fate to know thee!
> —Have the slow years not brought to view
> How great my grief, my joys how few,
> Nor memory shaped old times anew,
>   Nor loving-kindness helped to show thee
> How great my grief, my joys how few,
>   Since first it was my fate to know thee?

> A Triolet
> by Andrew Barton "Banjo" Paterson (1864–1941)
>
> Of all the sickly forms of verse,
>   Commend me to the triolet.
> It makes bad writers somewhat worse:
> Of all the sickly forms of verse
> That fall beneath a reader's curse,
>   It is the feeblest jingle yet.
> Of all the sickly forms of verse,
>   Commend me to the triolet.

Kyrielle

Kyrie eleison (roughly, "Lord, have mercy") is a prayer in Christian liturgy, and, as the name implies, the kyrielle was originally associated with hymns or prayers. The form consists of three or more end-rhymed quatrains, the last line of which repeats as a refrain. Line length can be construed as either eight syllables or iambic tetrameter, take your pick. Thomas Campion and other Elizabethan poets wrote kyrielles, and Queen Elizabeth herself employed a variation of the form in her "When I was Fair and Young." This poem substitutes hexameters for the standard tetrameter, eight-syllable line length. If you happen to be a divine-right monarch, you can do the same.

> *When I Was Fair and Young*
> by Elizabeth I, Queen of England (1533–1603)
>
> When I was fair and young, and favour graced me,
> Of many was I sought their mistress for to be,
> But I did scorn them all and answered them therefore,
> "Go, go, go, seek some other where. Importune me no more."
>
> How many weeping eyes I made to pine in woe,
> How many sighing hearts I have not skill to show,
> But I the prouder grew and still this spake therefore,
> "Go, go, go, seek some other where. Importune me no more."
>
> Then spake fair Venus' son, that proud victorious boy,
> Saying, "You dainty dame, for that you be so coy,
> I will so pluck your plumes as you shall say no more,
> 'Go, go, go, seek some other where. Importune me no more.'"
>
> When he had spoke these words, such change grew in my breast
> That neither night nor day since that I could take any rest.
> Wherefore I did repent that I had said before,
> "Go, go, go, seek some other where. Importune me no more."

Epigram

An **epigram** is a brief—often no more than a line or two—verse poem or prose passage that encapsulates a witty or intellectually stimulating idea. Quite a few poets have written memorable epigrams, and most poets are connoisseurs of the epigrammatic turn of phrase. Samuel Taylor Coleridge summed up the genre neatly in—what else?—an epigram.

> *What is an Epigram?*
> by Samuel Taylor Coleridge (1772–1834)
>
> What is an Epigram? a dwarfish whole,
> Its body brevity, and wit its soul.

Acrostic

An acrostic is a species of "puzzle poem" in which the initial letters of each line spell out a word or phrase when read vertically from top to bottom. In Lewis Carroll's "A Boat Beneath a Sunny Sky," the letters of the lines combine to spell the name of the subject of the poem, Alice Pleasance Liddell, thought to be the model for the heroine of *Alice in Wonderland*.

> *A Boat Beneath a Sunny Sky*
> by Lewis Carroll (1832–98)
>
> A boat beneath a sunny sky,
> Lingering onward dreamily
> In an evening of July —
>
> Children three that nestle near,
> Eager eye and willing ear,
> Pleased a simple tale to hear —
>
> Long has paled that sunny sky:
> Echoes fade and memories die:
> Autumn frosts have slain July.
>
> Still she haunts me, phantomwise,
> Alice moving under skies
> Never seen by waking eyes.
>
> Children yet, the tale to hear,
> Eager eye and willing ear,
> Lovingly shall nestle near.
>
> In a Wonderland they lie,
> Dreaming as the days go by,
> Dreaming as the summers die:
>
> Ever drifting down the stream —
> Lingering in the golden gleam —
> Life, what is it but a dream?

Glosa and Cento

A glosa begins with a sort of homage. The opening quatrain is quoted from an existing poem by another poet; the rest of the poem expands on the theme of that first stanza or reacts to it. Originally, the form, which dates from the late medieval period, required a set stanza form and rhyme, but there are many variations. Kim Addonizio's "The First Line is the Deepest" (Chapter 5) begins with a parody of a line from Robert Frost, and could thus be described as a comic take on the glosa.

The **cento** is a collage of quoted sources—the term comes from the Greek word for a patchwork garment. Lines from several poems are combined to make a new poem.

SOME INTERESTING FORMS FROM OUTSIDE THE EUROPEAN TRADITION

The **haiku** is easily the most popular foreign form among English-language poets. A Japanese form, the haiku was originally intended to reflect on some aspect of nature, but modern poets apply the form to almost any subject. English-language haiku usually consist of three unrhymed lines of five, seven, and five syllables, though there are numerous variants, notably the five-six-four pattern favoured by some modernists such as Ezra Pound and Amy Lowell. Some poets cast their haiku as single-line poems in imitation of the original Japanese form. Other poets write verse poems that ignore the standard syllable count while trying to embody the spirit of the haiku in four or five short lines. Despite the form's brevity, some haiku are divided into two sections with a "turn" from one subject or perspective between the sections—some poems, for example, move from impressionistic description to rhetoric between the first two lines and the last line; others vary that pattern. The imagery of the traditional haiku was related to nature; however, poems following a related form, called **senryu**, were cast in the same syllabic pattern but tended to dwell on personal and social concerns, often with a comic twist.

"October Aspens" employs the 5-7-5 grid while marrying autumnal imagery to a carpe diem motif.

from *October Aspens*
by Richard Arnold

Earth's tugging us down
let's lie here, buy each other:
green's not for saving.

The **tanka** is a Japanese syllabic form that dates from the seventh century, making it one of the oldest poetic forms still in common use. The form usually consists of five lines with a syllabic grid of 5-7-5-7-7, although the tanka can also be arranged in different ways, including as one long line. Like the sonnet, the tanka has a two-part structure—essentially a haiku followed by a two-line coda—and this arrangement provides an opportunity to shift from exposition to resolution or to take a paratactic "leap" between subjects.

The **haibun**, a Japanese form that dates back to the seventeenth-century poet Matsuo Bashō, combines prose and verse poetry. The prose is sometimes narrative but often imagistic and even surreal. The verse section consists of a haiku or some related syllabic form and acts as a coda to the prose. The haibun lends itself well to a "journaling" approach. Keeping a travel journal, commonplace book, or diary in the form of a series of haibun is a good way to develop a long poem or simply to practise your craft.

The **renga** traditionally began with a *hokku* (haiku) of 5-7-5 syllables followed by a two-line stanza with seven syllables in each line. The third stanza returned to the haiku form, while the fourth mirrored stanza 2 with two seven-syllable lines. In English-language practice, the stanza forms are usually retained but the lines aren't always syllabic: some poets write free-verse versions of the renga. A **chain renga** is a collaborative poem in the renga form written by two or more poets who take turns composing stanzas. Each stanza embodies one poet's take on the previous stanza, which was written by one of his or her collaborators.

The **ghazal** is an Arabic and Persian form that has enjoyed a vogue among modern poets, a notable example being John Thompson's book-length collection *Stilt Jack*, a few cantos of which are quoted in our chapter on the long poem. A ghazal is composed of five or more couplets. In the original Arabic and Persian usage, the ghazal has a repeated word or phrase (the *radif*) at the end of the second line of each couplet and rhymes *aa ba ca da*, etc. In English versions of the form, both repetition and rhyme scheme may be omitted.

Red Ghazal
by Aimee Nezhukumatathil

I've noticed after a few sips of tea, the tip of her tongue, thin and red
with heat, quickens when she describes her cuts and bruises—deep violets and red.

The little girl I baby-sit, hair orange and wild, sits splayed and upside down
on a couch, insists her giant book of dinosaurs is the only one she'll ever read.

The night before I left him, I could not sleep, my eyes fixed on the freckles
of his shoulder, the glow of the clock, my chest heavy with dread.

Scientists say they'll force a rabbit to a bird, a jellyfish with a snake, even
though the pairs clearly do not mix. Some things are not meant to be bred.

I almost forgot the weight of a man sitting beside me in bed sheets crumpled
around our waists, both of us with magazines, laughing at the thing he just read.

He was so charming—pointed out planets, ghost galaxies, an ellipsis
of ants on the wall. And when he kissed me goodnight, my neck reddened.

I'm terrible at cards. Friends huddle in for Euchre, Hearts—beg me to play
with them. When it's obvious I can clearly win with a black card, I select a red.

I throw away my half-finished letters to him in my tiny pink wastebasket, but
my aim is no good. The floor is scattered with fire hazards, declarations unread.

The **pantoum** is a traditional Malaysian verse form that has been adapted to
English-language poetry. Like the villanelle, the pantoum requires the repetition of complete lines. In the pantoum, the second and fourth line of the
first quatrain repeat as the first and third lines of the second quatrain. Then
lines two and four of stanza two become lines one and three of the following
stanza, and so on. Ideally, the pantoum resolves by inverting the only lines
that haven't been repeated (lines 1 and 3 of stanza 1) as lines 2 and 4 of the
final stanza. A pantoum can be of any length. The cycling repetitions of the
pantoum make the form a good choice for surreal imagery, as the cycles tend
to break up narrative through lines or coherent arguments. They also lend an
incantatory, obsessive feel to the poem.
    As the following poem illustrates, it's common for poets to vary the word-
ing of the repeated lines slightly.

pantoum: landing, 1976
by Evie Shockley

dreaming the lives of the ancestors,
you awake, justly terrified of this world:
you could dance underwater and not get wet,
you hear, but the pressure is drowning you:

you're awake, but just terrified of this world,
where all solids are ice: *underwater boogie,*
you hear, but the press sure is drowning you:
the igbo were walking, not dancing:

where all solids are ice, *underwater boogie*
is good advice, because they're quick to melt:
the igbo were straight up walking, not dancing:
and you've still got to get through this life:

take my advice, quickly: they're melting:
you could dance underwater and not get wet:
and you've got to, to get through this life still
dreaming the lives of the ancestors

The *rubáiyát* **quatrain** is an adaptation of a Persian form and requires an indeterminate number of quatrains rhymed *aaba*. Edward FitzGerald's *The Rubáiyát of Omar Khayyám* (1859, revised 1868–89), a free translation from the medieval Persian poem, is one of the most famous poems of the nineteenth century. Fitzgerald's translation encompasses one hundred and one quatrains, each numbered as a separate canto.

The Korean *sijo* is a syllabic form consisting of three lines, with each line anywhere from fourteen to sixteen syllables long, though longer versions are also popular. In the standard three-line format, each line has a specific purpose: introduction, development, resolution. The original Korean form required that the lines consist of groups of syllables, each with a specific purpose. English-language adaptations are sometimes printed in a six-line format to reflect those internal divisions. The *sijo* was originally intended to be sung to musical accompaniment, giving it something in common with the Greek lyric of Sappho's time.

NONCE FORMS

Anyone can invent a new verse form by combining some or all of the technical aspects of verse poetry: line length, number of lines, rhyme scheme, number and type of stanza, syllable count, word count, and so on. Recently minted verse forms are called "**nonce forms**," as in the archaic expression "for the nonce," meaning "for the moment." Some nonce forms reconfigure the same basic elements as traditional fixed forms; others impose arbitrary constraints on the language that can be deployed in the poem.

The American **cinquain** was invented by New York poet Adelaide Crapsey (1878–1914). The form is syllabic and consists of five lines (one cinquain) with 2 syllables in the first line, 4 in the second, 6 in the third, 8 in the fourth, and 2 in the fifth. Cinquains lend themselves to an imagistic approach and the delineation of one moment of perception, much like the Japanese haiku.

Although the cinquain is a simple form, there are some more complex variations. The "reverse cinquain" reverses the syllabic grid of the standard form: 2, 8, 6, 4, 2. The "butterfly cinquain" melds two cinquains into a nine-line form with the fifth line (2 syllables) shared by both cinquains. The syllabic grid works like this: 2, 4, 6, 8, 2, 8, 6, 4, 2. The "mirror cinquain" combines a standard cinquain with a reverse cinquain, producing a visually symmetrical two-stanza poem.

2, 4, 6, 8, 2
by Shaleeta Harper

Green Nose
of strawberries
poking from brown grass, like
groundhogs snatching at your feet: beg
you, stay.

The **fib** is a modern poetic form that has become popular on Internet poetry forums. Fibs are similar to haiku in that both forms are short and syllabic. The syllable count for the fib is based on the Fibonacci sequence, a mathematical formula that governs the geometry of a wide variety of natural phenomena such as the spiral of a snail's shell and the shape of a spiral galaxy. In a Fibonacci sequence, each number is the sum of the previous two. The name derives from the thirteenth-century Italian mathematician Leonardo of Pisa, who was also known as "Fibonacci." The typical fib is a six-line, twenty-syllable poem with a syllable count of 1, 1, 2, 3, 5, 8.

Constrained Forms—Oulipo

A group of (mainly French) poets and mathematicians who called themselves "Oulipo" devised several systems for generating form poems. (The group's name derives from *Ouvroir de littérature potentielle* or "Workshop of potential literature.") These formulas include "constraints" such as the one that produces the **snowball poem**, in which each line is only one word long but each successive word is one letter longer than the last; the **lipogram**, in which one or more letters of the alphabet are excluded; and the **univocalism**, in which only one vowel can be used throughout the poem.

EXERCISES

Exercise 10/1: Villanelle

Writing a villanelle is a good way to develop your skill as a poet, and many excellent poets (Sylvia Plath comes to mind) have honed their craft by exploring that challenging form.

Getting the first stanza right is crucial to crafting a good villanelle. The first and third lines of that stanza will cycle throughout the poem, so they should be memorable and rhythmic. Imagine those lines as a kind of chant. Choose a reasonably common rhyme for the end of those lines, by the way: you'll be using it throughout the poem. Check your rhyming words in an online rhyming dictionary and make sure that you have some good options.

If you're having trouble with the intricate rhyme scheme, you can simplify the pattern by ignoring the "*b*" rhyme—that's the last word of the second line of each stanza; your poem won't quite conform to the villanelle template, but if you maintain a strong rhythm, it could still be a good poem.

Exercise 10/2: Pantoum

Write a pantoum of no fewer than ten stanzas. Choose a subject that you consider appropriate to the form—think, for example, about cycles and spirals. Remember to invert lines 1 and 3 as lines 2 and 4 of your final stanza. Try to make the poem rhythmic as well as imagistic: given the pattern of repetition, establishing a fluid rhythm can be challenging.

Exercise 10/3: Butterfly Fib

A butterfly fib puts two fibs together to create the shape of a butterfly. The first fib is "upside down" with the long line at the beginning rather than the end. Then write a "normal" fib, starting with one syllable and working up to the final thirteen-syllable line. When you put the first poem above the second, you'll see the butterfly.

Exercise 10/4: Inventing Your Own Form

Write a lyric poem in an original fixed form. Your form could require a set number of lines, a syllabic grid, and a particular metre, rhyme scheme, pattern of repetition, or two or more of those options.

Alternate Possibility: The Form Exchange

When you've created your own nonce form, exchange it for that of a fellow poet or another member of your workshop or writers' group. Then write a poem in his or her form while he or she tackles your form. If you really want to drive yourselves crazy, set a time limit for composing a draft of the poem. When you're both finished your drafts, check each other's poem to make sure that it conforms to the requirements of your form. Oh, and don't forget to give your form a name—hey, it might become popular!

Exercise 10/5: Ballad or Song

Following the template for the ballad form, write a ballad of not less than six quatrains. Your ballad should rhyme, scan, and tell a story. The story can be topical (based on current-day events) or historical, or it can be based on a legend or myth. Give your ballad a memorable title (many ballads are entitled "The Ballad of . . ."). Include a refrain if you wish. If you'd like to write a song (i.e., with a verse-chorus-bridge structure) instead of a "print" ballad, go ahead. If you're in a workshop group, perform your new song for your colleagues.

TAKEAWAY

- Techniques such as repetition, rhyme, metre, or syllable count can be combined into a pattern for a poetic form.
- English-language writers often work in traditional European forms, but they also enjoy adapting forms from other literary traditions: Asian and Middle-Eastern forms are particularly popular.
- Any poet can invent a fixed form or modify existing forms.
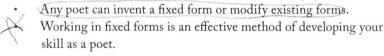 Working in fixed forms is an effective method of developing your skill as a poet.

TERMS TO REMEMBER

- acrostic
- ballad / ballad stanza
- blues stanza
- bridge
- cento
- chain renga
- chorus
- cinquain
- couplet / couplet quatrain
- envelope stanza
- epigram
- fib
- free-verse quatrain
- free-verse sonnet
- ghazal
- glosa
- haibun
- haiku
- hendecasyllabic
- kyrielle
- limerick
- lipogram
- mad song
- nonce forms
- octave
- *ottava rima*

- Oulipo
- pantoum
- quatrain
- quintet
- *radif*
- renga
- rime royal / rhyme royal
- rondeau
- *rubáiyát* quatrain
- Sapphic stanza / Sapphics
- senryu
- septets
- sestets
- sestina
- sextilla
- *sijo*
- snowball poem
- sonnet, sonnet crown
- Spenserian stanza
- tanka
- tercet
- *terza rima*
- triolet
- univocalism
- villanelle

CHAPTER ELEVEN

Writing Free Verse

Free verse—from the French *vers libre*—became the dominant genre of English poetry between the wars and has continued to be the default setting for most aspiring and professional poets. The term "free verse" implies a complete lack of structure, but in fact the adjective "free" simply refers to the fact that free verse doesn't rely on fixed forms, a set metre, or a rhyme scheme. "Free" does not mean chaotic, sloppy, arbitrary, or lacking in craft; it simply refers to the fact that many modern poets use the technical repertoire of poetry in more subtle ways than some traditional-verse poets do.

Here's Ezra Pound's definition of the difference between traditional verse and free verse: "As regarding rhythm: to compose in the sequence of the musical phrase, not in sequence of a metronome."[1] That's a fairly succinct statement of the aims of free-verse poets, specifically from the perspective of Pound's era (roughly the beginning of World War I to the late 1920s) when poets were beginning to feel the limitations of metric verse and to wish to expand their technical vocabulary. Pound's contemporary and friend T.S. Eliot wrote: "[N]o verse is free for the man who wants to do a good job."[2] (Had he been writing today, he'd no doubt have said "man or woman," and one suspects that poets of both genders would agree with him.)

Before we get into the technical nuts and bolts of free-verse composition, it's worth digressing for a moment to consider the origins of free verse. Modern English free verse stems from three quite distinct antecedents. The first was the influence of continental (mainly French) experiments in *vers libre* associated with late nineteenth-century poets such as Stéphane Mallarmé. Mallarmé brought the impressionism of Monet and Renoir in painting and Debussy and Ravel in music into the realm of the written word. His free-verse lines are musical phrases of varying durations rather than parades of predictable beats. The second important influence was the verse of Civil War–era American poet Walt Whitman (1819–92). Whitman's poems are structured around long, rhythmic end-stopped lines that create a sense of oratory and even prophecy. The third influence on the evolution of free verse was the interest of early

---

1 Ezra Pound, "A Retrospect," in *The Literary Essays of Ezra Pound*, ed. T.S. Eliot, 3–14 (New York: New Directions, 1918), 3.
2 T.S. Eliot, *On Poetry and Poets* (New York: Octagon Books, 1975), 31.

twentieth-century English-language poets in the poetic traditions of Asia, Africa, and the Middle East. That interest in itself was nothing new: Edward FitzGerald's *The Rubáiyát of Omar Khayyám*, a free translation of a Persian classic, was popular in the mid-to-late nineteenth century, and English-language poets have drawn inspiration from the poets of other languages and nationalities for a very long time. Modern free-verse poets were more interested in the formal aspects of foreign-language poetries than in their exotic subject matter. The syllabic lines of the Japanese haiku, renga, and other traditional forms provided an alternative to the European emphasis on stress and rhythm: syllabic verse tends to "flatten" the rhythm of the line and thus to encourage a more subtle music than does metric verse. The modernists shifted the focus of poetry from the ear to the eye, freeing it from the roots of English verse in song and story, and in Japanese poetry they found an aesthetic that privileged description over narrative.

TECHNIQUES FOR STRUCTURING FREE VERSE

Free verse can be as patterned as any fixed form, but the patterns are generally less obvious. We have to train our eye and ear to notice them. Free-verse poets develop a repertoire of techniques for patterning their poems and making them symmetrical. Here are some of the more common structural tools for writing free verse.

- repetition (chant lines, refrains, anaphora)
- parallelism and chiasmus
- lists and litanies
- half-rhyme and occasional rhyme
- enjambment and caesura
- inversion
- circularity
- parataxis

All or most of these techniques are also used in traditional metric verse; trad verse differs from *vers libre* in that it adds metre and predictable rhyme to the mix. Techniques for creating "word music"—assonance, consonance, dissonance, alliteration—are also used extensively in both genres. Let's consider each of these strategies in relation to free verse.

Repetition

The chant is perhaps the most ancient and common poetic form. Many cultures worldwide perform chants as a part of their sacred or artistic traditions. If you've ever been to a championship game or a political rally, you're already familiar with the attraction of the chant form and its connection to strong feelings and communal identity.

The basic structure of a chant is very simple: one line of a couplet is repeated over and over. This "chant line" may be varied to some degree, but its rhythm and phrasing are generally constant. These stanzas will give you a sense of the structure of a typical chant.

> The stain of rust where the leaves have fallen
> Rain washes away
>
> The hour of light before night encroaches
> Rain washes away
>
> The weight of our past and the shadows behind us
> Rain washes away

Some free-verse poems are variations and elaborations of the chant form; others just use the idea of a repeated line to bring a sense of symmetry to the poem and to emphasize an important idea or motif. The following poem uses the fugue-like repetition of phrases as a structural tool.

> *In a Beautiful Country*
> by Kevin Prufer
>
> A good way to fall in love
> is to turn off the headlights
> and drive very fast down dark roads.
>
> Another way to fall in love
> is to say they are only mints
> and swallow them with a strong drink.
>
> Then it is autumn in the body.
> Your hands are cold.
> Then it is winter and we are still at war.

The gold-haired girl is singing into your ear
about how we live in a beautiful country.
Snow sifts from the clouds

into your drink. It doesn't matter about the war.
A good way to fall in love
is to close up the garage and turn the engine on,

then down you'll fall through lovely mists
as a body might fall early one morning
from a high window into love. Love,

the broken glass. Love, the scissors
and the water basin. A good way to fall
is with a rope to catch you.

A good way is with something to drink
to help you march forward.
The gold-haired girl says, *Don't worry*

about the armies, says, We live in a time
full of love. You're thinking about this too much.
Slow down. Nothing bad will happen.

Some poets structure the lines of their poems around anaphora, the use of a
repeated initial word or phrase. The following passage from a poem by Walt
Whitman is a good example of how effective this technique can be:

Out of the cradle endlessly rocking
Out of the mockingbird's throat, the musical shuttle,
Out of the Ninth-month midnight,
Over the sterile sands and the fields beyond, where the child
    leaving his bed wander'd alone, bareheaded, barefoot,
Down from the shower'd halo,
Up from the mystic play of shadows twining and twisting
    as if they were alive,
Out from the patches of briars and blackberries,
From the memories of the bird that chanted to me,
From your memories sad brother, from the fitful risings
    and fallings I heard,

From under that yellow half-moon late-risen and
    swollen as if with tears,
From those beginning notes of yearning and love there in the mist,
From the thousand responses of love there in the mist,
From the thousand responses of my heart never to cease,
From the myriad thence-aroused words,
From the word stronger and more delicious than any,
From such as now they start the scene revisiting,
As a flock, twittering, rising, or overhead passing,
Borne hither, ere all eludes me, hurriedly,
A man, yet by these tears a little boy again,
Throwing myself on the sand, confronting the waves,
I, chanter of pains and joys, uniter of here and thereafter,
Taking all hints to use them, but swiftly leaping upon them,
A reminiscence sing.[3]

Parallelism and Chiasmus

Poets use parallel sentence structures to lend a sense of order to their work and
to make their words and ideas memorable. A form of parallelism can be seen
in this couplet from W.B. Yeats's "Sailing to Byzantium," in which the list of
three words in the beginning of the first line of the couplet is echoed by the
three-word list at the end of the last line:

    Fish, flesh, or fowl commend all summer long
    Whatever is begotten, born, and dies.[4]

The echoing of syntax is called **chiasmus** (*kay-ahs-muss*). That term is sometimes
used to refer to a similar technique called **antimetabole** (*anti-meh-tab-eh-lee*),
in which the words are repeated as well as the sentence structure. Chiasmus
is a good general term for any syntactic reversal: the word derives from the
Greek letter *chi*, which is the equivalent of "X." and it's that crossing of one
clause into another that characterizes the rhetorical strategy. Orators often

---

3 Walt Whitman, "Out of the Cradle Endlessly Rocking," in *The Oxford Book of American Poetry*, ed. David Lehamn and John Brehm (Oxford, UK: Oxford UP, 2006), 136.
4 William Butler Yeats, "Sailing to Byzantium," in *The Broadview Anthology of British Literature, The Concise Edition: Volume B* (Peterborough, ON: Broadview P, 2006), 1156.

employ chiasmus and related figures. President John F. Kennedy used a parallel structure in his famous line, "And so, my fellow Americans: ask not what your country can do for you—ask what you can do for your country." Another president, Richard M. Nixon, liked to quote the catchphrase "When the going gets tough, the tough get going." The two men may have been at opposite ends of the political spectrum, but they were both aware of the power of parallel structures.

When you're drafting a poem, look for opportunities to develop **parallelism** and to highlight parallel grammatical structures by making them visually as well as grammatically parallel. If you've written sentences with similar structures, consider enhancing the parallelism by placing the repeated elements in parallel locations—at the beginning or end of consecutive lines or indented to the same tab stop.

Lists and Litanies

A list poem is simply that: a list of related things or ideas. We all make lists from time to time, and we probably don't think of a list as a rhetorical form. We may make a list as an aid to memory (to remind us what groceries we need to pick up at the supermarket, for example) or as an exercise in ranking (our fifty favourite blues songs, perhaps, or the five best burger joints in our home town). But we may not have considered the list as a structure for poetry.

Rebecca Lindenberg's "Catalogue of Ephemera" makes effective use of a listing technique, and it also employs anaphora and parallelism:

Catalogue of Ephemera
by Rebecca Lindenberg

You give me flowers resembling Chinese lanterns.

You give me *hale*, for yellow. You give me *vex*.

You give me lemons softened in brine and you give me cuttlefish ink.
You give me all 463 stairs of Brunelleschi's dome.

You give me seduction and you let me give it back to you.
You give me *you*.

You give me an apartment full of morning smells—toasted bagel and black coffee and the freckled lilies in the vase on the windowsill.
You give me 24-across.

You give me flowers resembling moths' wings.

You give me the first bird of morning alighting on a wire.
You give me the sidewalk café with plastic furniture and the boys
with their feet on the chairs.
You give me the swoop of homemade kites in the park on Sunday.
You give me afternoon-colored beer with lemons in it.

You give me D.H. Lawrence,
and he gives me pomegranates and sorb-apples.

You give me the loose tooth of California, the broken jaw of New York City.
You give me the blue sky of Wyoming, and the blue wind through it.

You give me an ancient city where the language is a secret
everyone is keeping.

You give me a t-shirt that says all you gave me was this t-shirt.
You give me pictures with yourself cut out.

You give me lime blossoms, but not for what they symbolize.

You give me *yes.* You give me *no.*

You give me midnight apples in a car with the windows down.
You give me the flashbulbs of an electrical storm.
You give me thunder and the suddenly green underbellies of clouds.

You give me the careening of trains.
You give me the scent of bruised mint.

You give me the smell of black hair, of blond hair.

You give me Apollo and Daphne, Pan and Syrinx.
You give me Echo.

You give me hyacinths and narcissus. You give me foxgloves
and soft fists of peony.

You give me the filthy carpet of an East Village apartment.
You give me seeming not to notice.

You give me an unfinished argument, begun on the Manhattan-bound F train.

You give me paintings of women with their eyes closed.
You give me grief, and how to grieve.

Internal Rhyme, Half-Rhyme, and Occasional Rhyme

The essential quality of "free verse" is the lack of a set rhyme scheme. That doesn't mean that free-verse poems never include rhyme. Free-verse poems employ rhyme selectively, usually in the form of occasional rhyme, internal rhyme, or slant rhyme. These selective uses of rhyme provide a counterpoint to the overall "freedom" of the poem's structure.

Rhyme joins ideas together by linking words that echo the same sound or sounds, and that potential for linking one part of a poem to another through rhyme can be used effectively even in free verse. Rather than using end-rhyme, free-verse poems may link a word at the end of one line with a rhyme word in the middle of a subsequent line or link two words in the same line; that sort of internal rhyme is common in traditional rhymed verse as well as in free verse.

Words that don't quite rhyme also suggest a linkage and add to the music of the poem. Half-rhyme (also called slant rhyme or off-rhyme) can be effective in free-verse poetry as it fits in well with the doctrine of the "musical phrase" that early modernists considered a desirable alternative to metric verse. Slant rhymes create a subtle, jazzy music in a poem. Consider the following example, by the English modernist Mina Loy:

> *Moreover, the Moon — — —*
> by Mina Loy (1882–1966)
>
> Face of the skies
> Preside
> over our wonder.
>
> Fluorescent
> truant of heaven
> draw us under.
>
> Silver, circular corpse
> your decease
> infects us with unendurable ease,

touching nerve-terminals
to thermal icicles

Coercive as coma, frail as bloom
innuendoes of your inverse dawn
suffuse the self;
our every corpuscle become an elf.

At first glance, Loy's poem seems loosely structured. Line lengths vary considerably, and there's no set stanza form—the tercets eventually give way to a couplet and a quatrain. Notice, however, the sneaky "almost-rhymes" that hold the poem together: skies/preside, decease/ease, terminals/icicles. These slant rhymes serve much the same purpose as end-rhyme in a more traditional poem, but they're less obtrusive, and much better suited to the surreal imagery and informal tone of the poem.

The slant rhyming isn't the only tricky use of sound-alike words in Loy's poem. There's an "occasional" rhyme between "wonder" in line 3 and "under" in line 6. That rhyme suggests a pattern, but no set rhyme scheme emerges. On an even more subtle level, "Moreover, the Moon" employs the "word music" of assonance and consonance within the lines and between one line and another: "infects" in line 9 is echoed by "innuendoes" and "inverse" in line 13. Then there's the alliterated hard "c" sounds of "circular corpse" and "coercive coma." Our loosely woven free verse poem is in fact a carefully crafted musical composition. It's more like jazz than chamber music, but it's wonderfully musical all the same.

Notice, by the way, that Loy only goes for a full rhyme when she wants to emphasize the resolution. That's the old trick of ending a lyric poem with a rhyming couplet, a reliable move that refers back to the English sonnet of Elizabethan times and that a surprising number of modern free-verse poets still find useful.

Free Verse and Lineation

Controlling line is the crucial skill in writing free verse. We've already discussed the varieties of line forms in an earlier chapter. In relation to free verse, we can benefit from considering line breaks as a mechanism for generating either harmony or conflict and tension in a poem. In *The Origins of Free Verse*, Henry Tompkins Kirby-Smith divides free verse into five types: phrase-reinforcing, phrase-breaking, word-breaking, word-jamming, and the prose poem. Phrase-reinforcing free verse consists of "lines parallel to natural phrasal units" while phrase-breaking free verse breaks lines within phrases or clauses.[5] Kirby-Smith is referring to the familiar opposition between phrase-generated, clause-generated, or end-stopped lines on the one hand and enjambed lines on the other. The first category reinforces the natural grammatical units that make up sentences, while the second type—"phrase-breaking"—creates suspense and tension by enjambing and thus splitting up those units.

"Word-Jamming" and "Word-Breaking"

Kirby-Smith's taxonomy of free-verse embraces some radical methods of creating musical effects. The word-breaking method involves splitting a single word with a hyphen so that the word begins on one line and ends on the next. The word-jamming method, conversely, combines two or more words into single compound words. Gerard Manley Hopkins deploys both techniques in "The Windhover."

The Windhover:
to Christ our Lord
by Gerard Manley Hopkins (1844–89)

I caught this morning morning's minion, king-
    dom of daylight's dauphin, dapple-dáwn-drawn Falcon, in his riding
    Of the rólling level úndernéath him steady air, and striding
High there, how he rung upon the rein of a wimpling wing
In his ecstasy! then off, off forth on swing,
    As a skate's heel sweeps smooth on a bow-bend: the hurl and gliding
    Rebuffed the bíg wind. My heart in hiding
Stírred for a bird, —the achieve of, the mástery of the thing!

Brute beauty and valour and act, oh, air, pride, plüme, here
    Buckle! AND the fire that breaks from thee then, a billion
Tímes told lovelier, more dangerous, O my chevalier!

    No wönder of it: shéer plód makes plóugh down síllion
Shine, and blue-bleak embers, ah my dear,
    Fall, gáll themsélves, and gásh göld-vermílion.

---

5 Henry Tompkins Kirby-Smith, *The Origins of Free Verse* (Ann Arbor: U of Michigan P, 1996), 46.

Parataxis

Poets are risk takers. They broach original ideas, and sometimes they even evoke original *ways of thinking*. Though we're generally taught to focus on the logical and linear modes of thought, poets are just as likely to explore the analogical and intuitive. A poet's mind can jump *sideways* as well as moving straight ahead. In order to read poetry, we have to be willing to follow those exhilarating lateral leaps, and if poets want to develop their abilities as fully as possible, they have to consider how they can move from perception to perception or insight to insight without any "connective tissue" in between.

The technique of jumping laterally from one idea to another in a poem is called **parataxis**. Its opposite is **hypotaxis**—progressing logically, in linear fashion. These terms come from the Greek words *hupotassein* and *paratassein*, meaning to arrange (*tassein*) under (*hupo*) and beside (*para*).

The following poem initially offers a narrative about the poet-narrator's visit to a hairdresser. The voice shifts suddenly between straightforward narrative and perceptions about the general topic of appearance and beauty; some observations seem to have drifted in from other times and other episodes in the narrator's life, and some are dreamlike rather than realistic.

Xtraordinaire (722 Queen Street West) 1994–96
by Lynn Crosbie

I have never had a hairdresser before but things come to this.
Hand-carved crosses, piercing, face-slaps, lipliner.
He fits my hair with extensions, someone else's hair,

twice now, I wear this stranger's remains. My head scraped raw
with sutures, I sleep on my face, some fall out I am falling apart.

You look like a mermaid, Sook-Yin says when she sings to me.

He tells me about an associate, Ray, who almost died from fluorocarbons,
his aurora of hairspray, and leaves me under the dryer
while I think about glamour.

How angry I have been, lethal shoes talons corsets, you got to move on,
if you want to see glory, train train.

That glamour may be something else, walking slowly and painfully,
so there are no mistakes. The discomfort, the drag.
Of effacing yourself; the sublimation. Of recovering the grotesque.

I wonder at the hair of the skeleton, in museum glass, pulling a comb
through my own tangled *memento mori*.

I fought with my hairdresser once, viciously. Pretend I'm dead, I told him,
and slammed down the phone. Before we made up and since, I think
this is the most glamorous thing I have ever done:
his clips clattering to the floor—the nerve of that woman—my hair
alight, as I turn in an outrage, switching beauty's tail, to get moving.

It's worth remembering that there's a limit to how freely we can employ parataxis: at some point, shifts in focus may render a poem incomprehensible. One
should also consider the fact that any technique should be used for a good
reason, one that supports the theme of the poem. W.H. Auden warned Frank
O'Hara and John Ashbery (modern American poets who are both known for
their extensive use of parataxis) about "confusing authentic non-logical relations which arouse wonder with accidental ones which arouse mere surprise
and in the end fatigue."[6]

FREE VERSE AND ACCENTUAL VERSE

Quite a few "free-verse" poems are actually written in a loose form of accentual
verse. The poet isn't concerned about composing in a regular metre consisting
of both stressed and unstressed syllables; he or she is simply hearing the strong
beats in each line. It's useful, in fact, to ask yourself whether your "free-verse"
poem is close to being accentual verse. Try to sound out the stresses in your
poem. If the poem tends toward accentual verse of a particular metre, then
you might find it useful to make the form more regular. Conversely, you may
wish to vary or obscure that regular drumbeat if you feel it's not appropriate
to the poem. If your poem is accentual verse in some stanzas and free verse
in others, you should ask yourself what that variation is intended to signify;
if the formal variation doesn't improve the poem, then try making the form
more consistent.

---

6 Quoted in David LeHardy Sweet, "Parodic Nostalgia for Aesthetic Machismo: Frank
O'Hara and Jackson Pollock," *Journal of Modern Literature* 23, no. 3/4 (Summer 2000):
375–91, http://muse.jhu.edu/article/16588.

FINDING A RESOLUTION

Some fixed forms provide the technical resources, if not the intellectual ones, to bring about a satisfying resolution. The English sonnet ends with a rhyming couplet that generally offers a witty and memorable resolution to the argument that runs through the preceding quatrains. In a free-verse poem, finding a technique to bring the poem to a resolution may be more challenging.

Quite a few free-verse poems are resolved by a shift between modes: a poem that presents an argument can achieve a resolution by shifting from rhetoric to image at or near the end; the same can be true for a narrative poem. A poem that's primarily descriptive may be best resolved by a shift from image to rhetoric.

Some free-verse poems are circular. They end where they began. You can often find a good resolution for your poem by looking carefully at the way the poem begins.

PITFALLS AND PROBLEMS

We've been talking about the methods poets use to write free verse well; it's also worth reflecting on how some poets write free verse very, very badly. Just as there are a great many bad abstract paintings in the world, there are also an enormous number of bad free-verse poems. (The same, alas, is true of rhymed metrical poems and figurative paintings, and for similar reasons.) Too many poets approach free verse with a vague and inadequate sense of how the form works. They see poems that don't rhyme and don't have a predictable metre, and they assume that all you have to do to make a free-verse poem is to write some prose and chop it up into lines. If you wish to appear sophisticated, indent some lines or centre the whole the production. Bonus points are awarded for ornamental fonts and pretentious titles.

Perhaps the most common failing of aspiring free-verse poets is the tendency to divide poems into predictable phrase-generated lines. The result is a poem that sounds flat and lacking in rhythm and music or a poem that creates a singsong rhythm reminiscent of rhymed doggerel. Less common is the poem that consists largely of sentence-generated, end-stopped lines that lack the driving rhythm of a Whitman poem or the jazzy cadences of the Beat poets. Then there's the "close your eyes and hack it into lines" poem, in which lengthy complete sentences alternate with single words and everything in between without respect for either logic or musicality. Finally, there's the poem in which words are strewn around the page in a vague approximation of "open field" composition without any sensitivity to the relationship between visual arrangement, sense, and sound.

Ultimately, the key to writing free-verse poetry well is *awareness*: becoming aware of the various techniques available to free-verse poets and recognizing the potential of your draft for further development are essentials.

EXERCISES

Exercise 11/1: Poem Using Anaphora

Begin with a phrase, one that might be as simple as "The rain was falling . . ." or "After I spoke with you . . ." or "Nothing is as perfect as . . .," and try to write a number of possible sentences or lines beginning with that phrase. Use the lines you generate in this manner to construct a poem that, like some of Walt Whitman's poems, is structured around lines with a repeated initial word or phrase.

Exercise 11/2: Stone Poem

Write eight to ten lines (phrases, clauses, or sentences—any group of words can be a line), each containing the word "stone." If you're in a workshop or writers' group, trade at least two and no more than four lines with each member of your group. Using anaphora or other forms of repetition, shape your lines into a poem. If you wish to, write your "stone" poem as a ritual poem, using a command having something to do with stone. You could, for example, begin your poem with a command such as, "Take a stone and break it . . ." or "Throw a stone into water. . . ."

Exercise 11/3: List Poem

Write a free-verse poem that's based on a list of related things or ideas. Listing the contents of your pockets or of a drawer in an old dresser might produce interesting material for a poem. Consider all the things (or attitudes or people) you'd like to throw out of your life. Consider all the interesting things you could collect on a walk through the woods or along a beach.

Use anaphora or other forms of repetition. Remember that your list must be interesting to others and that it should engage the imagination.

Exercise 11/4: Collage Poem

Find an interesting book that *isn't* a book of poetry. Manuals, guidebooks, self-help books, and school textbooks (especially really old ones) work best. Now copy at least ten and no more than twenty lines from the book you've chosen, picking any line that seems intriguingly worded or that expresses an interesting or quirky idea. Next, assemble the lines into a poem. It probably won't make any sense, but don't let that bother you. When you've got your collage poem typed up, try to rearrange the lines into something that's intriguing and—so far as possible—meaningful. Delete lines and invent lines as you wish, but try to keep the highly paratactic quality of your first draft. Then, finally, change some of the diction—no more than twenty words in the entire poem. Give your poem or collage a title, and it's done!

Exercise 11/5: Free-Verse Renga

Write a free-verse renga of no fewer than six stanzas. (A free-verse renga retains the alternating two- and three-line stanzas of the traditional renga form but doesn't necessarily conform to the syllabic requirements.) Begin your renga with a description of some detail from the landscape, one that reflects the season. Try to take advantage of the opportunities for parataxis that are inherent in the renga form. Look for tangential ways of linking stanzas—you might, for example, find that a word or image in stanza 1 suggests an idea that you can use in stanza 2. Don't the afraid to "leap sideways" rather than connecting ideas into a linear narrative or argument.

TAKEAWAY

- Free-verse lyrics are the most popular form of modern poetry.
- The music of free verse is often more subtle and varied than that of traditional rhymed metric verse. Free-verse poets seek to "compose in the sequence of the musical phrase, not in sequence of a metronome."
- Free-verse poets employ a repertoire of techniques to structure their poems.
- When you write a free-verse poem, it's essential to make creative and constructive use of line breaks.
- Free-verse poems are often paratactic.

TERMS TO REMEMBER

- anaphora
- antimetabole
- chiasmus
- hypotaxis
- parallelism
- parataxis

- phrase-breaking
- free verse
- phrase-reinforcing free verse
- repetition
- word-breaking method
- word-jamming method

CHAPTER TWELVE

The Long Poem

Some poets are most comfortable working in the lyric form, just as some fiction writers prefer writing short stories to writing novels. Most poets, however, find the lyric form too limiting for some themes and subjects; they sometimes need to stretch their legs a little and work in a more expansive form. It's hard to think of a major poet who hasn't written a long poem at one time or another, and we can all learn something about the craft—and about ourselves as poets—by exploring longer forms.

WHAT IS A "LONG POEM"?

A long poem is more substantial (yes, *longer*) than a lyric; that's obvious. So how long is "long"? To some degree, the length of a long poem is determined by typical publication formats: if we think in terms of the usual page count of a chapbook—12 to 24 pages, say—or a single volume of poetry—typically 60 to 120 pages—we'll be reasonably close to describing most long poems. You'll have noticed that there's a considerable difference between 12 pages and 120. The book-length poem is a more ambitious project than the chapbook, at least in terms of sheer volume. Book-length "long poems" usually centre more on narrative than chapbooks, though their greater length may simply be symptomatic of a more general subject and theme. Journal poems, for example, can explore various aspects of a time or a persona, and their length is determined by a time frame rather than a theme. Robert Lowell's *Notebook* (1967–70) consists of a couple of hundred free-verse sonnets arranged into a suite—it's literally a notebook or journal. A chapbook-length "long poem," conversely, may simply expand on the concerns of a typical lyric, using the division of the poem into cantos as an organizational principle and an aid to reading.

The role of the epic poem has largely been taken over in the last century or so by the novel. Although there are some important modern epics by poets such as W.C. Williams, H. D. (Hilda Doolittle), and David Jones, the epic form is more commonly associated with poets of the ancient world, or with medieval and Renaissance writers such as Chaucer and Dante. Most modern long poems aren't epics: they're **lyric suites** or collages of various forms. A modern "long poem" resembles a nineteenth-century ode or a sonnet sequence more than it resembles an epic. Modern writers of long poems also borrow formal strategies from non-European traditions: the Japanese renga and haibun and the Persian or Arabic ghazal are popular choices.

The nineteenth century saw a vogue for **verse novels** such as Elizabeth Barrett Browning's *Aurora Leigh* (1856); Lord Byron's *Don Juan* (1818–24), sometimes called a "mock epic" as it parodies the conventions of the traditional epic; and Robert Browning's *The Ring and the Book* (1864–68). Verse novels are still with us: Les Murray's *Fredy Neptune: A Novel in Verse* (1998), Craig Raine's *History: The Home Movie* (1994), and Derek Walcott's *Omeros* (1990) are reasonably recent examples. There has also been some contemporary interest in verse novels for young adults, but these days the genre occupies a minor niche in the spectrum of modern literature.

In the **verse autobiography**, the poet recounts his or her life story in the form of a lengthy narrative poem: examples include William Wordsworth's *The Prelude* (1850) and James Merrill's *The Changing Light at Sandover* (1976–82). As Merrill's book and those of other modern poets such as Sir John Betjeman (*Summoned by Bells*, 1960) demonstrate, the verse autobiography is still a viable form, though it's often a summation of the poet's life and achievements.

As we've seen before, it's the diversity of poetic forms and strategies that strikes us, not the uniformity. The epic had a predictable structure and form, but modern long poems tend to be highly variable in terms of length and structure. Many are sequences of lyrics constructed around a theme or pattern. Some are narratives. Some are collages. The only useful definition of a modern long poem is that it's longer than a lyric and broader than a lyric in terms of its scope and theme.

TYPES OF LONG POEM

There are fundamentally two types of long poem: the spatial and the temporal or linear. Linear structures include narrative and argument, though the former is much more common in modern times than the latter—today, the poem as essay would likely seem a throwback to the eighteen century. Spatial forms are pictorial or architectural and rely on juxtaposition and counterpoint rather than on narrative continuity or logical shape.

Finding the balance between overarching linear structures such as narrative and the fugal interweaving of images and motifs is crucial to writing a long poem. Inevitably, the poem needs some forward motion to carry the reader along. Few readers will feel particularly comfortable with the idea of reading in a non-linear, non-sequential manner; books invite us to start at the beginning. Paradoxically, there's no real reason that a long poem shouldn't allow alternate methods of reading. A successful long poem should embed secondary patterns of signification within the overall structure: we should, in other words, be able to enjoy not only the forward motion of the poem but also the back-eddies, echoes, and reverberations created by recurring or contrasting images and motifs.

Many of the most famous long poems in English are linear narratives in verse. The alpha point of the Western canon has always been *The Iliad* (circa eighth century BCE), a narrative about the Trojan War, and many English-speaking poets have attempted to create their own epics based roughly on that model. Though the epic is the "high style" version of a verse narrative, there is an equally vibrant "folk poetry" tradition—the ballad. Tennyson's "Maud" (1855) is a good example of a self-consciously literary version of that most durable of narrative verse forms. Henry Wadsworth Longfellow, Rudyard Kipling, Robert Service, Australian Banjo Paterson and a host of other popular poets of the nineteenth and early twentieth centuries also employed variations on the ballad form for their narrative poems. Such lengthy verse narratives have been out of fashion for at least a century, replaced by the novella and novel.

The first few stanzas of Lord Tennyson's "Guinevere," from *Idylls of the King* (1859–85), will give you a sense of how a traditional narrative works. Take away the lineation and ignore the musicality of the language, and these opening stanzas could be the beginning of a prose romance or fantasy story. (If you've been drawn into this tale—and it's a great one—you should be able to find the rest of this poem, which is now in the public domain, on the Internet.)

from *Guinevere*
by Alfred, Lord Tennyson (1809–92)

Queen Guinevere had fled the court, and sat
There in the holy house at Almesbury
Weeping, none with her save a little maid,
A novice: one low light betwixt them burned
Blurred by the creeping mist, for all abroad,
Beneath a moon unseen albeit at full,
The white mist, like a face-cloth to the face,
Clung to the dead earth, and the land was still.

For hither had she fled, her cause of flight
Sir Modred; he that like a subtle beast
Lay couchant with his eyes upon the throne,
Ready to spring, waiting a chance: for this
He chilled the popular praises of the King
With silent smiles of slow disparagement;

And tampered with the Lords of the White Horse,
Heathen, the brood by Hengist left; and sought
To make disruption in the Table Round
Of Arthur, and to splinter it into feuds
Serving his traitorous end; and all his aims
Were sharpened by strong hate for Lancelot.

    For thus it chanced one morn when all the court,
Green-suited, but with plumes that mocked the may,
Had been, their wont, a-maying and returned,
That Modred still in green, all ear and eye,
Climbed to the high top of the garden-wall
To spy some secret scandal if he might,
And saw the Queen who sat betwixt her best
Enid, and lissome Vivien, of her court
The wiliest and the worst; and more than this
He saw not, for Sir Lancelot passing by
Spied where he couched, and as the gardener's hand
Picks from the colewort a green caterpillar,
So from the high wall and the flowering grove
Of grasses Lancelot plucked him by the heel,
And cast him as a worm upon the way;
But when he knew the Prince though marred with dust,
He, reverencing king's blood in a bad man,
Made such excuses as he might, and these
Full knightly without scorn; for in those days
No knight of Arthur's noblest dealt in scorn;
But, if a man were halt or hunched, in him
By those whom God had made full-limbed and tall,
Scorn was allowed as part of his defect,
And he was answered softly by the King
And all his Table. So Sir Lancelot holp
To raise the Prince, who rising twice or thrice
Full sharply smote his knees, and smiled, and went:
But, ever after, the small violence done
Rankled in him and ruffled all his heart,
As the sharp wind that ruffles all day long
A little bitter pool about a stone
On the bare coast.

There are some less obvious ways of embodying the passage of time in poetry than straightforward narratives: diaries or journals, records of the seasons, almanacs, calendars, and so on. Whichever method or model the poet chooses, the likelihood is that any modern long poem will have a strongly linear quality in terms of its overall structure. Even "collage" poems such as Michael Ondaatje's *Collected Works of Billy the Kid: Left-Handed Poems* (1970) follow a fairly straightforward timeline, taking us from the earlier events in the central figure or narrator's life to the later ones.

If we wish to avoid the obvious linear "timeline" or "argument" approach to structure, there are some non-linear alternatives to consider. Some poems are cyclical in structure: the end takes us back to the beginning. We could think of this as a mythic rather than logical approach to the representation of time. There are also some convenient models for non-linear structures: the season, the life cycle, the zodiac, the orbits of the planets, the motion of waves. Wordsworth's *Prelude* is famously structured around "moments of being" or heightened consciousness: we could structure our own long poem around the recurrence of a mood or image or activity we find significant.

Some long poems are as elliptical and paratactic as "Guinevere" is narrative and linear. John Thompson's book-length poem *Stilt Jack* (published 1978) is written in an Anglicized version of the ghazal form. Notice how the lines and sentences are linked by leaps of intuition rather than by the linear connections of logic argument or narrative. The first few cantos of this poem of thirty-eight cantos will give you a sense of Thompson's use of parataxis. The "Nashe" mentioned in Canto III is Thomas Nashe (1567–1601), an English playwright and satirist. Tu Fu (712–770) was a Chinese poet of the Tang dynasty era.

from *Stilt Jack*
by John Thompson

I

Now you have burned your books: you'll go
with nothing but your blind, stupefied heart

On the hook, big trout lie like stone:
terror, and they fiercely whip their heads, unmoved.

Kitchens, women and fire: can you
do without these, your blood in your mouth?

Rough wool, oil-tanned leather, prime northern goose down,
a hard, hard eye.

Think of your house: as you speak, it falls
fond, foolish man. And your wife.

They call it the thing of things, essence
of essences: great northern snowy owl; whiteness.

II

In this place we might be happy; blue-
winged teal, blacks, bats, steam

from cows dreaming in frost.
Love, you ask too many questions.

Let's agree: we are whole: the house
rises: we fight; this is love

and old acquaintance.
Let's gather the stars; our fire

will contain us; two,
One.

III

It's late. Tu Fu can't help me. There's no wind.
My blue shirt hangs from the cuffs on the line.

I can't talk to God. Tonight, I dug
three hills of potatoes. Sadness, what's that?

Give up words: a good knife, honed; and a needle
drawn across an iron bar, set in a matchbox.

Damn these men who would do my work for me;
my tomatoes redden by the window.

All spring and summer (this inch,
these noosed three moons) I fished trout.

One line of poetry dogs me; the newspapers,
the crazy world.

I'm thinking of you. Nashe. Rats on my window-sill.
The dirt under my fingernails.

Lord, lord. I'm thinking of you.
I'm gone.

You'll have noticed how dramatically the opening to the Tennyson poem contrasts with the first cantos of Thompson's suite of ghazals.

HOW IS A LONG POEM STRUCTURED?

There is no "default setting" for the form of a long poem in English. Milton's *Paradise Lost* is written in blank verse; Lord Byron's *Don Juan* (1818–24) in ballad stanzas; *The Atomic Poems* of Margaret Cavendish, Duchess of Newcastle (1653), and Alexander Pope's *The Rape of the Lock* (1712–14) in heroic couplets. Modern long poems are most commonly written in versions of free verse: poems such as T.S. Eliot's *The Waste Land* (1922) and Ezra Pound's *The Cantos* (published 1924–69) are highly paratactic and rely heavily on juxtaposition. David Jones's epics *In Parenthesis* (1937) and *The Anathemata* (1952) wander from visual rhythm to prose. Whitman and Allen Ginsberg and other writers of that tradition echo the form of a religious litany or chant. A.R. Ammons's *Sphere: The Form of a Motion* (1974) is in free-verse tercets while his *Tape for the Turn of the Year* (1965) is in his version of "open field" composition, as are Louis Zukofsky's *A* (published 1978) and, of course, Charles Olson's *The Maximus Poems* (1960–75). Several modern poets have made use of non-European forms such as the renga and ghazal, as Thompson's poem demonstrates. One would *almost* be correct in saying that the form of the long poem varies according to the fashion of the time, though there are always exceptions to this rule.

Most (but not all) long poems are suites; that is, they're divided into cantos. Cantos can be of any length, and each canto may encompass any number of lines and stanzas: there's no single template. Although the genre is open to the individual poet's creative approach to structure, most long poems are based on one of a limited number of formal strategies.

1.   A suite of lyrics (individual titles linked by a common persona and/or theme): For example, *The Father* (1992), a book-length suite by Sharon Olds, consists of individual lyrics about the author's experience of caring for her dying father. Special types of lyric suite include the **epistolary suite**, in which each poem is a "letter" to a particular auditor or a conversation in letters between two or more correspondents. Ted Hughes's *Birthday Letters* (1998) is an epistolary long poem consisting of lyric "letters" directed to the poet's late wife, Sylvia Plath. The **choral suite** consists of persona poems, each from one of a number of different speakers. The most famous example of a choral suite is *Spoon River Anthology* (1915), by Edgar Lee Masters. In that book-length suite, the voices of the dead who lie in a small-town cemetery speak about their lives. Each character is the subject of a poem, and the title of that poem is simply the name on his or her headstone. A suite of descriptive or ekphrastic poems is another option. Think of each lyric in the suite as a painting and the long poem as a gallery of such images.

2.   A **suite of cantos** (usually numbered sequentially or divided from each other by dingbats or design cues, such as the arrangement of each canto on a separate page): The omission of individual titles for the lyrics emphasizes the unity of the long poem as whole; numbers suggest a temporal flow and narrative drive while dingbats suggest a more pictorial approach in which each canto is part of a "gallery."

3.   A substantial continuous narrative (a lengthy narrative poem): As recently as the nineteenth century, these enjoyed a wide popular audience; twentieth-century modernism shifted the emphasis from narrative to image, and the vogue for narrative poetry faded away. The **documentary narrative** is a substantial poem based on events from history. Documentary narratives are often written in relatively short cantos and sometimes employ "collage" effects such as passages of prose or script interspersed among verse cantos; some documentary narratives even include photographs, clippings from newspapers or other historical documents, and so on.

4.   A **formal suite** such as the sonnet crown or **sonnet sequence**: Lady Mary Wroth (c. 1587–c. 1653) worked in both forms. A **sonnet crown** is a seven-sonnet sequence in which the last line of each sonnet is repeated as the first line of the next. The first and last lines of the sequence also mirror each other; this gives the sequence its crown-like circularity. Sir Philip Sydney's *Astrophil and Stella* (1591) and William Shakespeare's *Sonnets* (1609) are perhaps the

best-known examples of the sonnet sequence. Although that form is associated with the sixteenth and seventeenth centuries, quite a few relatively modern poets have worked in either or both genres. Elizabeth Barrett Browning's *Sonnets from the Portuguese* (1850) was a popular sequence in Victorian times, and John Berryman's *Dream Songs* (1964–69) and Robert Lowell's *Notebook* (1970) are twentieth-century examples that recast the sonnet as free verse. Fans of dark fantasy may be familiar with H.P. Lovecraft's sonnet sequence, *Fungi from Yuggoth* (1929–30).

5. A **collage poem** of various genres and forms, perhaps including lyrics, passages of prose, visual elements such as photographs or illustrations, clippings from newspapers or magazines, and other material.

6. An English-language adaptation of a traditional non-European form, such as the renga, haibun, or ghazal: The Japanese haibun is a poetic travel journal and would be a natural choice for poets who want to create a poetic record of their journeys. The renga, like the ghazal, presents opportunities for building long poems around highly paratactic shifts of perception.

7. An extended **chant** or **litany**: William Blake and Christopher Smart wrote long poems that relied heavily on anaphora and other forms of repetition and that featured long, rhythmic lines modelled on the parallel clauses of the King James Bible. Walt Whitman's longer poems brought that technique into American poetry, and modern American poets such as Allen Ginsberg and Robert Bly extended the tradition into the twentieth century. Whitman's "Song of the Open Road" (1856) and Ginsberg's *Howl* (1956) are classic examples.

8. A "borrowed" form from a non-literary genre: Canadian poet Robert Kroetsch's *Seed Catalogue* (1977) is modelled on just that—a farm-supply company's catalogue of available seeds. Any reasonably substantial document can, in theory, be used as the model for the structure of a long poem. The "hermit crab" strategy (see Chapter 1) can be a particularly fertile source of ideas for structuring long poems.

9. An experimental form, such as a "shuffle-able" deck of pages, a hypertext poem with hot-linked cantos, or an improvised performance poem or sequence.

Symmetry and Asymmetry

Like most art forms, long poems usually exhibit a high degree of formal symmetry, and looking for opportunities to develop that symmetry is an important part of drafting the poem. If we're writing a long poem that consists of several cantos, we'll probably need to look for symmetry and balance between various techniques, interweaving cantos that embody one technical strategy with cantos that embody a different technique: narrative cantos alternating with cantos that foreground description or rhetoric, say, or an interweaving of cantos narrated by two or more different voices. Alternating between speakers from canto to canto is one way of establishing **counterpoint**. Alternating formal strategies can also provide a sense of symmetry—cantos one, three, and five could be in free verse with short lines, for example, while cantos two, four, and six are in rhymed verse with long lines. Counterpoint can also involve shifting between modes: narrative and argument, perhaps, or narrative and pure image. You can often see symmetries more easily if you "map" the emerging poem visually (see Exercise 12/4).

A **fugue** is a musical composition in which motifs recur periodically. The effect of a fugue is one of interweaving: each motif becomes a "thread" that is woven through the composition. Hilda Doolittle's long poem *Hermetic Definition* (1972) uses fugue-like repetitions of phrases, images, and other motifs. The interweaving technique that characterizes the fugue can sometimes be effectively applied to poetry.

THE GENESIS OF YOUR LONG POEM: PERSONAL, HISTORICAL, OR MYTHOLOGICAL?

The process of poetic creation is to some degree subjective, but there are a few things we can say about the evolution of a long poem that should apply to most writers' projects.

Perhaps the first consideration when planning your project is the subject or source of the poem. Poets draw their *materia poetica* (material for poetry) from a wide range of different sources, some personal and some having to do with the wider world. A long poem can be, in essence, a collection of linked lyrics, and as such it can express the subjective world of the poet or speaker, though the long poem lends itself particularly well to larger, transpersonal themes in a way that the lyric normally does not. Some long poems concern the lives and exploits of historical or mythic figures. The traditional epic told the story of a hero or heroine: Ulysses, Aeneas, Roland, Adam, and so on. In the estimation of Milton's generation, the purpose of the epic was to present a man of virtue. None of this seems particularly sensible to our twenty-first century turn of mind: we tend to take our heroes with a large grain of salt, and both the specification of gender and the concept of virtue would likely seem anachronistic to us. We do have our own mythic figures, and sometimes poets build long poems around their legends.

The genesis of a successful long poem can be subjective and unpredictable. Some long poems begin their lives as short poems: the idea you had for a lyric outgrows the limits of that genre, and you find yourself adding cantos, experimenting with different techniques, and balancing motifs until your long poem finds its ideal form. Other poems require a more conscious and calculating planning process. First, you need to find a suitable concept. Here are a few suggestions:

1. *Research your family.* You may find some interesting stories salted away in your family's near or distant past. Browsing through letters or photographs can be a great source of inspiration, and excerpts and examples can even be included in your poem to create a "collage" effect, assuming you can get the requisite permissions.
2. *Research your community.* A "community," of course, can be a nation, an ethnic heritage, a trade, a subculture, or simply a group of friends. There are some good antecedents for basing your poem on local history. Often, there are episodes from the history of your city, town, or region that would make excellent material for a poem. Perhaps the classic example of a poem about a community is *Spoon River Anthology.*
3. *Research an historical figure.* Episodes from his or her life can be developed into sections in a long poem. You could create a dramatic poem consisting of monologues by the subject of your poem or juxtapose his or her voice with third-person narrative or monologues by his or her contemporaries.
4. *Research a pop-culture figure.* Twenty-first century people are perhaps less inclined to mythologize public figures from the worlds of politics, business, and the military than their nineteenth-century ancestors were, but pop-culture performers are pronounced "iconic" and "legendary" for the most trivial of accomplishments, and it's impossible to pick up a magazine in your doctor's office, browse the Internet, or pass through the checkout at a supermarket without being confronted with their surgically morphed faces. Developing the phases of a pop icon's rise and fall or the highlights

of his or her career into cantos within a lyric suite might provide a workable structure for a long poem. You could also juxtapose different observers' perspectives: the star's parents, perhaps, or the perspective of a worshipful fan or a cynical tabloid journalist.

5. *Research a mythic figure.* Ted Hughes's book-length suite of poems about the Native American trickster-figure Crow is a modern classic. Anne Carson has written a popular book-length suite of prose poems about a figure from Classical myth, a strategy that would have been common in earlier centuries but that seems quite innovative now.

6. *Record a journey or quest.* If you've taken a trip or risked an adventure, you could record the phases of the experience in a long poem. The poem might consist of a continuous narrative, or it might be divided into cantos, each of which addresses a phase or aspect of the adventure. A travel journal could be written as a sequence of poems or prose poems, or it could be adapted to verse from a prose original.

7. *Use a document from another genre as a template.* Base your poem on the structure of a menu, for example, or a project report or a sequence of tweets and Instagrams.

8. *Consider your life experience.* Perhaps you have lived with a chronic illness since childhood or have been the perpetual "newcomer" or "outsider" because you've moved every year or so. Or you could have a unique perspective on living in North America because you were raised in Europe or Asia. These long-term circumstances can make for interesting long poems.

DEVELOPING THE LONG POEM

When you're developing your poem, it can be useful to look at the evolving structure objectively and to try to see all its various elements. Here are some suggestions for analyzing your poem as it changes and grows:

- Imagine that you're pitching your long poem to an editor or publisher and wish to give him or her a sense of the poem's shape and structure. Try to generalize about the form (open field, litany with end-stopped lines, sequence of free-verse lyrics, primarily free verse with short lines, or something else).
- Evaluate the degree of formal symmetry employed in your poem. Is it highly symmetrical, using one formal constraint throughout,

or have you alternated two or three strategies? Is your poem completely asymmetrical, with each canto generating its own form? Would the poem benefit from being more symmetrical, or is it perhaps too rigidly patterned and in need of a touch of variety?

- List a few important images from your poem. Note any recurring motifs. If you had to identify one central metaphor or motif in your poem, what image would you choose? (Not all long poems revolve around a central motif—some are more open-ended and discursive.)

- Find ten to twenty-five unusual words that relate to your subject and (if applicable) persona or personae. Include foreign words, jargon, technical vocabulary, period or regional slang, or any other category of unusual words.

- Inventory your imagery. Could the poem be better organized so that any shifts in the field of imagery are highlighted by canto breaks (and possibly subtitles) and are thus more easily intelligible to your readers?

- Does your poem tell a story? Are the episodes from this narrative arranged in chronological order, and, if so, is that necessarily the best strategy for creating interest and drama?

- Does the subject of the poem lend itself well to regular stanza forms, or would it be more appropriate to vary the form from one canto to another? One good way of answering this question is to "listen to the poem" as you draft it and see if the language seems to cluster naturally into any particular form. Sometimes it's surprising how easily a poem can be moulded into regular tercets or quatrains and how much effect that simple strategy can have on the clarity of the poem.

- How many cantos are there (or should there be) in your poem? Are they roughly similar in terms of length and importance?

- Have you used subtitles, Arabic or Roman numerals, or some other type of section headings for the individual cantos? Check out some long poems that you admire, and see what the poets used to set off their cantos. Remember that everything in a poem has meaning, even the type of symbol you choose to demarcate your cantos.

- Consider the ideal presentation for your completed long poem. Factors may include page size, font, and layout (and possibly even medium). Would the poem be suitable for reading aloud to an audience? Could it be performed by a group of actors, each reading some cantos or sections? Would it lend itself well to illustration?

- Who is the ideal audience for your poem? If the obvious answer is "kids," then have a look at some book-length poems for children and see how the poets, illustrators, and book designers have presented their books. A couple of hours in the kids' section of your local public library should give you some great ideas. If your poem might appeal to folks who are more at home on the Internet than in a library or bookstore, consider how it could be mounted on a website or distributed through social media. It's usually easier to develop a poem if you have a growing sense of the intended audience.

WORKSHOPPING THE LONG POEM

Presenting long poems to a writers' group or creative writing workshop involves some challenges. It's usually impractical to present a long poem in its entirety for workshopping; it's more workable to submit a canto or a small selection of cantos on each of a few occasions.

One way of making the workshop experience as meaningful as possible is to begin by presenting a project proposal (see Exercise 12/1). When the workshop members have had the opportunity to read and discuss your proposal, they can feel that they have an investment in your project, and they'll also have a sense of where you want to take the poem and what you'd like to achieve. As they read and workshop successive cantos, they can suggest ways of rethinking the original inspiration outlined in your portfolio in order to exploit and develop new ideas and possibilities that begin to emerge through the drafting and revising process.

EXERCISES

Exercise 12/1: Long Poem Project Proposal

Write a brief (one-page) proposal for a long poem. List your subject and provide a tentative sense of the projected length of the poem. If you're participating in a writers' group or workshop, present a preliminary draft of your project proposal to your group. Be prepared to discuss your proposal informally. Then prepare a final draft of your proposal and distribute copies. If you decide to change your project substantially or to switch to another topic, submit a new or revised proposal.

PROJECT PROPOSAL

1. Author's name _____

2. Working title (and subtitle, if any) _____
    _____

3. (Approximate) projected length in pages, cantos, and/or lines:
    _____

4. Can you generalize about the scope and theme of the poem? Imagine that you're pitching your long poem to an editor or publisher and wish to give him or her a sense of the poem's shape and structure.

5. Is your poem "told" from one consistent point of view? If so, is the speaker a named character? If not, are you using a "choral" or "dialogic" technique? Do the style and diction change as we move from one speaker to another?

6. What are the formal strategies employed in your poem? Is it primarily free verse, blank verse, syllabics, or traditional rhymed stanzas? Does the form vary? Do you anticipate including prose passages or visual elements?

7. Discuss the source of material for the poem, including your knowledge of the subject and plans for research.

Exercise 12/2: Collage

Research an historical or pop-cult figure or an episode from history or current events and create a collage from your research findings. Your collage might include snippets from newspaper or magazine articles, copies of photos or paintings, quotations, song lyrics, excerpts from speeches or trial transcripts, and display ads, for example. Imagine this project as a bulletin board, and tack up anything that seems intriguing and broadly relevant.

Exercise 12/3: Journal

Keep a journal of a particular time of your life. You can start anywhere, but it's usually most effective to think in terms of an episode with a beginning and an end. Travelling provides good opportunities for journaling: you can record the interesting episodes from a trip; whether you keep a day-to-day journal as you travel or reconstruct the trip from memory at a later date isn't important. Consider the form of a journal or diary, and think about other ways you might record a journey—a series of blog posts, post cards, emails, or tweets, perhaps. As well as taking a trip, there are other episodes in our lives that lend themselves well to the journaling model: a period of illness, perhaps; a romantic relationship; a pregnancy and birth; or the memory of graduating from high school or college with all the attendant ceremonies, parties, friendships, and anxieties about dealing with opportunity and change. Your experience with sports or the performing arts might also make a good journal poem—take us through a tense playoff season, concert, recital, or tournament. The journal is necessarily narrative, but it's also episodic and lends itself well to a "fugue" structure in which different aspects of the theme are explored in the various journal entries and then arranged in counterpoint.

Exercise 12/4: "Mind Map" Your Long Poem Project

Draw a rough map of the structure of your poem. Use rectangles or circles to represent cantos, enclose them in larger figures to represent sections (if applicable), and then note the subject and speaker of each canto. Try to note the important images and metaphors in each section, and also note the stanza form, type, and number of stanzas in each section if you've made some of those decisions at this point in the drafting process. Draw lines connecting similar techniques used in different cantos and consider whether a counterpoint or fugue structure is a possibility.

Exercise 12/5: Long Poem Analysis and "Reverse Engineering"

Choose a long poem (10 pages or longer) that you've read and enjoyed and analyze its structure. Is it divided into cantos, and if so how many? Are the cantos subtitled, headed with numerals, or simply divided by horizontal lines or dingbats? Is the mode of narration (point of view) consistent, or does it vary from one canto to another? Try "mapping" the poem you've chosen, just as you did with your own poem in Exercise 12/4.

TAKEAWAY

- Modern long poems usually explore less ambitious themes and subjects than the traditional epic, but, like the epic, they provide a context for a more discursive or expansive approach to poetry than does the lyric.
- Like the epic, the long poem may (sometimes) focus on historical events and employ the public voice. Dialogic and choral approaches to narration are reasonably common, and the poem may be built around the exploration of history and popular culture. Writers of long poems—particularly of the "documentary narrative" subgenre—often background their poem with considerable historical research.
- Most modern long poems are in fact lyric suites consisting of several (the number may vary widely) discreet lyrics linked by a common subject or theme.
- Some long poems are, in stylistic terms, collages: they may combine verse lyrics, prose passages, photographs or illustrations, copies of print documents, and so on.
- Long poems sometimes use the "hermit crab" approach and borrow the structure and form of a non-literary genre.

TERMS TO REMEMBER

- chant
- choral suite
- collage poem
- counterpoint
- documentary narrative
- epistolary suite
- formal suite
- fugue

- litany
- lyric suites
- sonnet crown
- sonnet sequence
- suite of cantos
- verse autobiography
- verse novels

CHAPTER THIRTEEN

Alternative and Experimental Forms

In addition to the three traditional genres of poetry—lyric, epic, and dramatic—and the usual range of poetic forms, there are more recently evolved types of poems that don't fit any of the major categories.

A **prose poem** is just that: a poem written entirely in prose. Most poets try their hand at prose poems at some point in their careers: the lack of rhyme, lineation, and to some extent even rhythm or metre presents poets with interesting challenges, and poets welcome a technical challenge.

Prose poems usually rely heavily on descriptive imagery and figurative language. Like verse lyrics, they embody a preference for the concrete rather than the abstract. Prose poems are often witty and epigrammatic, another characteristic of the verse lyric. Obviously, writing in paragraphs rather than in lines and stanzas means that we lose some of the advantages of verse, and it's important to consider the techniques we can use to make our prose work as poetry. Taking away the opportunities for generating rhythm and complicating meaning afforded by breaking the language into visual units throws poets back onto the inherent musicality of English prose. Quite a few prose poems are written in parallel clauses linked by coordinate conjunctions ("and," "but," "or," "so," "for," and "yet"). That technique emphasizes the repeated structure of the clauses and can create a flowing rhythm; it's essentially the same strategy employed by verse poets such as Whitman, but without the line breaks at the end of sentences. Other prose poems feature the opposite strategy: short sentence fragments rather than complete sentences or clauses.

Some prose poems are brief narratives, often of the "metaphysical" variety. Others lean toward a more static, pictorial approach. It's no coincidence that surrealist poets like to work in prose; their poems frequently revolve around dream narratives, and the emphasis is usually on the visual dimension of the poem rather than the musical. There are also prose poems that foreground the language as material in much the same way that an abstract painting foregrounds the materiality of paint and canvas. The primary influence for "language centred" prose poetry is American modernist Gertrude Stein. Stein's poems use repetition and "word music" to such an extent that we may process the words as units of sound rather than as units of meaning.

The surreal, wildly imaginative imagery of Matthea Harvey's "Implications for Modern Life" is typical of modern prose poetry. Sina Queyras's "A Lilac Begins to Leaf" creates a narrative and then subverts it with paratactic shifts in context, another characteristic of the genre.

Implications for Modern Life
by Matthea Harvey

The ham flowers have veins and are rimmed in rind, each petal a little meat sunset. I deny all connection with the ham flowers, the barge floating by loaded with lard, the white flagstones like platelets in the blood-red road. I'll put the calves in coats so the ravens can't gore them, bandage up the cut gate and when the wind rustles its muscles, I'll gather the seeds and burn them. But then I see a horse lying on the side of the road and think *You are sleeping, you are sleeping, I will make you be sleeping.* But if I didn't make the ham flowers, how can I make him get up? I made the ham flowers. Get up, dear animal. Here is your pasture flecked with pink, your oily river, your bleeding barn. Decide what to look at and how. If you lower your lashes, the blood looks like mud. If you stay, I will find you fresh hay.

A Lilac Begins to Leaf
by Sina Queyras

Last night the memory of her mother walked out into the parking lot of the Long Rail Tavern at precisely five minutes to twelve. Where her tears fell, tiny puffs of dust rose. X-ray her now you will see her mother filing her nails. Her heart flickers off and on, random as a cat's paw on a pull chain, and neon. She will not fall to pieces here. Though at least if she did, she could now put herself together again. She remembers a superhero made of boulders. He could assemble and reassemble. She could get bigger, she thinks. There might be room for two. In her mind a lilac begins to leaf.

A **concrete poem** is a picture made of words (or words and other elements); letters in artistic fonts are arranged on a page to form a piece of visual art. Concrete poems are often playful and witty, and they represent an attempt to treat language as "concrete" material for the construction of visual images—hence the name. Concrete poetry was popular in the 1960s, and concrete poems still turn up in magazines and art galleries.

If concrete poetry bridges the divide between visual art and poetry, the **sound poem** locates itself between verse and pure music. The sound poem may belong to the history of avant-garde art, but it also recalls the earliest roots of poetry: sound poetry performances channel the chant-based poems and songs of our primitive ancestors.

Have you ever heard a child repeating one word or a short phrase over and over again? Little kids sometimes play with language and enjoy the sound of a word for its own sake without paying attention to meaning. If you repeat a word or phrase often enough, you may find that the meaning of the word is eclipsed by the sound: it ceases to be meaningful and becomes a meaningless knot of noise to your ear. The word you know is no longer familiar to you. This is a process called **defamiliarization**. When a word or phrase becomes sufficiently "defamiliarized," we begin to hear it as pure sound, as music rather than meaning.

All poetry—except possibly concrete poetry—is sound poetry. That is, all poems are intended to be enjoyed as music as well as understood as meaningful utterance. In this sense, every poem balances acoustic and semantic possibilities. In the works of some poets, the musical element is at least as important as the semantic. If we tip the scales even farther in the direction of music, we risk—perhaps intentionally—obscuring or losing absolutely the meaning of the work; its semantic level dissolves as units of meaning give way to units of sound. What we usually think of as "sound poetry" is poetry in which the semantic elements have been de-emphasized or eradicated in favour of the acoustic elements.

In order to understand the vocabulary of sound poetry, we need only to return to our discussion of "word music" and the range of acoustic devices employed in the composition of *all* poetry: repetition, alliteration, consonance, assonance, dissonance, sibilance, onomatopoeia, varieties of rhyme and half-rhyme, rhythm, and so on. Imagine a poet using one or more of these devices without reference to meaning or syntax. To get a sense of how a sound poem might work, take any syllable—the "o" from "boat," for example, and simply repeat it ten or twenty times, savouring its sound. Compose a musical piece consisting entirely of percussive consonant sounds. Or take a word, perhaps an onomatopoeic word such as "roar," and repeat it 176 times: that's what the Dadaist poet Tristan Tzara (1896–1963) did in his poem "Roar."

An **aleatoric poem** is composed by chance rather than design. Aleatoric poems can be composed (if that's the right word) in a wide variety of ways: dreaming up a method for chance generation is part of the fun. Some poets have cut up a page of prose and then scrambled the words or phrases and picked them out at random for use in a poem. Others have designed processes that involve the reader in selecting the language for the poem. Whatever the method of generation, the intent of the genre remains the same: to transfer the authority for the creative act from the poet to the reader.

Aleatorism is more often associated with music than with poetry, and some notable composers such as John Cage have dabbled in poetry. The Dada and surrealism movements in European in the late 1910s and and the 1920s saw chance generation as a way of harnessing the creative powers of the unconscious mind—or at least as a way of circumventing the rational bias of the conscious mind. The surrealists made use of techniques such as "automatic writing," in which the poet simply writes whatever comes into his or her mind, a strategy borrowed from Victorian spiritualism. The "Exquisite Corpse" exercise in Chapter 1 was a favourite of the Paris surrealists.

The Oulipo group of poets and mathematicians (see our discussion of constrained forms in Chapter 10) devised several systems for generating aleatoric poems. The **N+7 formula** requires the poet to "rewrite" a poem by replacing each noun with the seventh noun after it in a dictionary. If we apply the N+7 system to the opening line of William Shakespeare's "Sonnet XXIX," we accomplish the following transformation:

Original: "When in disgrace with fortune and men's eyes"

N+7 version: "When in dishcloth with fossil fuel and mendicant's eyehole"

As we've just seen, these aleatoric techniques can produce some amusing results. We'd be justified, though, in asking whether they can result in a poem with any depth of interest. Still, chance-generated poems can suggest opportunities for incorporating parataxis into more conventional poetry, and trying any new technique might be useful if you're feeling restricted by the usual formal strategies or are simply looking for ideas.

Poets of the early twenty-first century are living at one of those "cusp" moments in the history of language and culture. The availability of hypertext and hypermedia has opened up some intriguing possibilities for inventive poets, and the **hypertext poem** is a response to those opportunities. "**Hypertext**" links words to other words, documents to other documents; "**hypermedia**" links various media such as text, visual art, audio, and video. The terms were coined as recently as 1965 by media theorist Ted Nelson, but the ideas behind them are now commonplace—most of us access hyperlinked documents on our laptops, tablets, and cell phones every day.

Like the shift from oral to scribal and from scribal to print technology, the transition from print-and-paper texts to texts that can be hot-linked to other texts, other places in the same text, music, visuals, video, and so on makes possible dramatic changes in the way we compose and receive poetry. The potential of hypertext has been explored by a relatively small number of contemporary poets and remains a minor part of the world of poetry publishing; still, it's difficult to imagine that the extension of poetry into new media won't continue to develop over the coming decades.

Motion poetry, like hypertext poetry, relocates the poem from the printed page to a computer-based environment. Motion poems combine text with animation, so that the letters and words of the poem can move around the screen, appear and disappear, change font and colour, and so on. Like hypertext poetry, motion poems are still a relatively minor enterprise in the context of poetry publishing, but the possibilities are, as they say, endless.

If you're a fan of online or console-based gaming or if you simply have an interest in exploring new and exciting options in your creative life, you should consider looking into "new media" applications for writers. There are hypertext poetry magazines and discussion groups on the Internet, and mastering the basics of HTML or a related language isn't a major challenge for anyone with basic computer skills. This is a wonderful moment in history for writers; the old means of communication are still vital and will continue to be so, but now there are additional venues through which creative people can expand and develop their art.

We usually think of poetry as the creation of an individual, not of a group. Poetry is the most intimate of literary genres, and the idea of creating a poem with another writer runs counter to many poets' sense of the creative process as something private and personal. Song writers, on the other hand, quite often collaborate on the composition of song lyrics, with one lyricist bouncing ideas off the other. Where would modern pop music be without the collaborations of Paul McCartney and John Lennon, who often wrote different verses of the same song? Their pop epic "A Day in the Life," is an example of collaboration. Perhaps poets have something to learn from their music-industry counterparts.

Although collaborations among poets are relatively rare, there have been some fruitful partnerships. American poets Denise Duhamel and Maureen Seaton have published a few books of their **collaborative poems**, and a trio of Canadian poets (Kim Maltman, Roo Borson, and Andy Patton) publishes under the collective identity of "Pain Not Bread." Duhamel and Seaton have, on occasion, used the "Exquisite Corpse" technique we discussed in Chapter 1. "Florida Doll Sonnet" was written as an email correspondence, with each poet contributing two lines at a time.

Florida Doll Sonnet
by Denise Duhamel and Maureen Seaton

I love Fresh Market but always feel underdressed
squeezing overpriced limes. Louis Vuitton,
Gucci, Fiorucci, and all the ancient East Coast girls
with their scarecrow limbs and Joker grins.
Their silver fox husbands, rosy from tanning beds,
steady their ladies who shuffle along in Miu Miu's
(not muumuus) and make me hide behind towers
of handmade soaps and white pistachios. Who
knew I'd still feel like the high school fat girl
some thirty-odd years later? My Birkenstocks
and my propensity for fig newtons? Still, whenever
I'm face to face with a face that is no more real
than a doll's, I try to love my crinkles, my saggy
chin skin. My body organic, with no preservatives.

The Internet offers convenient venues for the creation of collaborative poems. A poem can be started by one poet and then emailed to several others, each of whom can add to, elaborate, and edit the growing manuscript. The whole group can participate simply by selecting "reply to all" when responding. Twitter, chat programs, and wikis are also possible ways of hosting the evolution of a collaborative poem.

A **found poem** is exactly that: a reasonably brief quotation from some extra-literary document that strikes the poet as being poetic, at least when it's wrenched out of its original context. The following poem is a collage of found elements. It consists of a list of injunctions and warnings of the sort that we often encounter when purchasing new appliances and equipment. The "found" elements have been modified a little to suit the context, which is a disclaimer that could preface a poem.

Disclaimer
by Stephen Guppy

This poem
May contain coarse language
And subliminal suggestions. It may not be suitable
For all family members.

This poem
Is for external use only. Avoid contact
With eyes and skin, and avoid inhaling fumes.
If ingested, do not induce vomiting.

This poem
Is provided "as is," without warranties.
Batteries are not included.

This poem
Is ribbed for your pleasure.
Align parts carefully, then bond.
Reproduction is strictly prohibited.
There are penalties for early withdrawal.

This poem
Has been formatted to fit your expectations
And pre-recorded for your time zone. Objects
Observed in these stanzas
May not be as significant
As they initially appear.

This poem should be used
As a supplementary restraint system only.
Always wear non-slip footwear and tie back long hair.
Do not activate during an electrical storm.

Do not read while operating
A motor vehicle or heavy equipment.
Do not read near an open flame.
Do not use intimately.
Do not use orally
After using rectally.
Do not exceed recommended dosage.
Failure to comply will void the warranty.

Action figure sold separately.

EXERCISES

Exercise 13/1: Prose Poem

Write a set of three or more prose poems. Prose poems differ from simple prose sketches in that they tend to emphasize image and metaphor rather than linear narrative. Some prose poems are narratives, but they're not stories: there's little or no sense of plot structure, and the characters are usually more symbolic than realistic.

If you're looking for an idea, try writing prose poems about some or all of the following subjects:

- sleepwalking
- thirst
- boredom
- the afterlife
- jealousy
- the gods
- coming home

Exercise 13/2: Collaborative Chain Renga

In its original Japanese form, the renga consists of alternating tercets and couplets of syllabic verse. In English versions, the renga can be a free-verse poem, but the alternating three- and two-line stanzas remain. The renga begins with a description of some aspect of a particular season, usually the season in which the poem is written.

For your chain renga, start with one poet writing the first (three-line) stanza and then passing the page (or sending an email, tweet, Facebook message, etc.) along to the next poet. Poet number 2 then contributes the second (two-line) stanza. If there are three poets in the "chain," the poem goes to poet number 3, who creates the third stanza (three lines again this time!); otherwise, the poem is returned to the first poet. Any number of poets can participate. In a workshop setting, it's fun to have everyone start his or her own chain, so that there are as many chain rengas being written as there are workshop members.

Set yourself a time limit or a final number of stanzas, and when you've finished your chain, try doing a group reading of your collaborative poem.

Exercise 13/3: Sound Poem Using Onomatopoeia

Write a sound poem about one of the experiences in the following list. Use no more than three English or foreign words, but make your poem at least twenty-five words long. In addition to those three words, use as many nonsense sounds as you wish.

- waking up in the dark
- waking up with a terrible hangover
- falling in love at first sight
- playing with a kitten
- kayaking through rapids
- diving into a very cold pool
- tuning a zither
- cooking a six-egg omelette
- blowing a gigantic bubble with bubblegum
- hang-gliding off a cliff
- walking a tightrope
- figure skating on thin ice
- boiling crude oil
- teaching a donkey to sing a scale
- swimming laps when you're very, very tired
- squeezing a lemon and drinking the juice
- waltzing with a chimpanzee

Exercise 13/4: Concrete Poem

Now that you've written a sound poem about the experience, convert it into a concrete poem. You can use your one or two words in the poem if you wish, but the emphasis should be on creating a graphic picture, not a bunch of words to be read. Instead of pure sound (or close to it), the poem will now be pure image (or close to it). Write a different concrete poem if you prefer.

Exercise 13/5: Aleatoric Poem

Devise a system for the random generation of poetry. Your system might involve writing words on scraps of paper and having workshop members pick them from a bucket and arrange them into lines. That's a simple method, but more complex options are possible. Using every tenth line in a textbook as one line in a poem would also work. Compiling tweets on a current hot-button issue and assembling them into a random-generated found poem could also be interesting. If you're into programming, you could try to formulate an algorithm for random generation and arrangement of language.

TAKEAWAY

- While we usually associate poetry with verse, poetry can also be written in prose paragraphs.
- Sound poems and concrete poems emphasize the auditory and graphic properties of language.
- Groups of poets can collaborate on the creation of a single poem.
- Aleatoric poems are generated by chance.
- Hypertext poems and motion poems are computer-based documents that adapt poetry to the digital environment.
- A found poem borrows language from non-literary sources and re-imagines it as poetry, the "poetic" quality often stemming from the context as much as from the language itself.

TERMS TO REMEMBER

- aleatoric poem
- collaborative poems
- concrete poem
- defamiliarization
- found poem
- hypermedia

- hypertext; hypertext poem
- motion poetry
- N+7 formula
- prose poem
- sound poem

CHAPTER FOURTEEN

Shaping and Polishing

Failure is the foundation for success,
and the means by which it is achieved.
—Lao-Tzu, Tao Te Ching

In the preceding chapters, we've been exploring strategies for building our poems from inspiration to completion. Once we've arrived at a complete and reasonably satisfying draft, there's still some work to be done. Most poems need editing and polishing before they're ready to be offered to editors and publishers or performed in front of an audience.

EDITING TO REFINE DICTION

Most of us are familiar with the *parts of speech*—nouns, pronouns, verbs, adjectives, adverbs, prepositions, conjunctions, and articles. These categories are useful, and any aspiring poet should be familiar with them. When we're writing and editing our poetry, however, it can be helpful to group these terms into larger categories: *content words*, *structure words*, and *colour words*.

Content words are the essential elements of any English sentence: the subject and the verb. The subject is usually a noun or a noun phrase (a group of words acting as a noun) or a pronoun (a word that takes the place of a noun—"it," "she," "they," "we," and "this," for example). In a poem, we're likely to choose the first of these options because phrases are relatively wordy and pronouns aren't very interesting. The verb or verb phrase is the "engine" of the sentence: it supplies the action or denotes the state of being. In a poem we'd probably choose a single-word verb over a verb phrase, and we might also eliminate a verb that simply expresses a state of being.

Colour words are modifiers—adjectives and adverbs. They add "colour" and specificity to nouns, verbs, or even to other colour words.

Structure words express spatial, temporal, or causal relationships (e.g., prepositions, conjunctions) or indicate a particular thing or differentiate between two or more things (e.g., article, relative pronoun, demonstrative pronoun).

You can often improve a poem simply by *deleting structure words*. Those little linkages are necessary in prose as they clarify the relationships between the important ideas that are signified by the "content words." In a verse poem, we have the additional resource of line and stanza breaks. The visual arrangement of lines and stanzas can take the place of the structure words. We can use graphic design instead of grammatical structures to show the readers how one idea or perception relates to another.

Colour words, like structure words, can often be eliminated from a poem. Loading our lines with modifiers is rarely a good idea. As we discovered in our discussion of diction, modifiers "prop up" nouns and verbs. They're often only necessary if we haven't chosen a noun or verb that's sufficiently precise. For example, in the phrase "an extremely tall, columnar, green-leafed deciduous tree," we've used four adjectives (tall, columnar, green-leafed, deciduous) and one adverb (extremely) in an attempt to compensate for the fact that the noun "tree" is much too general. There are many different species of tree, and though they may be broadly similar, they certainly aren't identical. We could, in this instance, have gone down the abstraction ladder and said "poplar"; having located the specific word we needed, we could then elaborate more interesting perceptions than the flat technical description we started with.

Table 14.1: Using Words in Poetry

categories	parts of speech	utility in poetry
content words	nouns and verbs	These words are the core elements of the English sentence.
colour words	adjectives and adverbs	Modifiers can be useful in poetry, but they often indicate that nouns and verbs should be more specific.
structure words	articles, conjunctions, prepositions, relative pronouns	These little words have no "content" and no impact on our senses; they're just the widgets that allow us to relate one idea to another.

LISTENING TO THE POEM

Once again, it's useful to think of the process of writing poetry as a dialogue between poet and poem and to listen carefully to whatever our emerging poem is telling us.

Writing poetry involves both conscious and unconscious creation. We may start with a conscious intention—to write a poem about an important event in our lives, perhaps, or about a moment that stood out in the day or even about some incident or character from history or myth. We gather our memories or do some research, and then we write a draft. This poem-in-embryo presumably records our intentions, embodying whatever images and ideas we wanted to explore. That's the conscious level of creation; the unconscious level consists of the images and phrasings that have bubbled up out of our subconscious during or before the drafting of the poem. In order to engage our abilities fully, we have to recognize that some parts of the poem may have come from the subconscious and may thus be "hidden" to our conscious minds. Unearthing those moments and building on them is essential to making the poem as good as it can be. Think of that process as "listening to the poem."

A Geiger counter is a machine used to detect radiation. When the gizmo is placed near a source of radiation, it flutters its dials or starts to chatter like an angry squirrel. When you're revising a poem, use your inner "Geiger counter" by reading through the draft and highlighting the strongest images, phrases, stanzas, and so on. Try to decide what part or aspect of it has the most energy and force. Then build on that vital central core. Every poem has a heart; you just have to use your skill to reveal it.

"Listening to the poem" requires approaching your draft with an open mind and being objective about its strengths and possibilities. That's a tough one for most of us—when we reread a new poem, we tend to see what we intended to write rather than what actually made it into the document. Getting a friend and fellow poet to read our drafts aloud might be helpful, and of course a writers' group or workshop full of enthusiastic readers is the ideal situation.

CHOOSING A TITLE

What should the title of your poem accomplish?

The title is the "shop window" of the poem. Browsing through a literary magazine, we may look for titles that catch our eye, and we may flip past poems with uninteresting titles. Once we've made the decision to read a poem, we expect the title to relate clearly to the body of the poem. Beyond that primary expectation, we may also enjoy titles that we can understand in two slightly different ways—titles that, for example, we understand superficially when we begin to read the poem and more deeply when we've finished reading.

Perhaps the most important thing a good title can do for your poem is provide the reader with a context in which to place the body of the poem. Think of your title as the "doorway" into the poem. A poem called "Elegy" gives us a general context for reading the poem. We know that an elegy is a poem written about someone who has died. We may be surprised, when we start to read the poem, to discover that it's really about the metaphoric death of a way of life or a ghost town; we may even find that the poem is ironic and comic, but in either case, the title has guided us toward a certain set of expectations as we enter the poem.

The more specific we make the title, the more help we've given our readers. Thomas Gray's "Elegy Written in a Country Churchyard" provides not just the idea of the elegy but also the setting (a country churchyard). Sharon Olds, in her poem "The Elder Sister," defines a biological and social relationship, and we have that idea in hand before we read the first line. When we begin to read a poem called "In Memory of W.B. Yeats," we know we're in the elegiac mode, and we're also drawing on whatever we know and feel about Yeats and his poetry. The author of the elegy, W.H. Auden, has provided us with a doorway that lets us walk into the world of the poem. He's also avoided having to clutter the body of the poem with an explanation of what and whom he's talking about. Gray did the same thing with his title: he doesn't have to tell us where we are, as the title has already done that job. A good contextualizing title can save a lot of unnecessary verbiage: it can make the poem efficient, and a poem should always be as efficient as possible.

Although there isn't an exhaustive taxonomy of poem titles, it's not difficult to list some of the more common types:

Formal Category Titles

Quite a few formalist poems are simply labelled as having been written according to the rules of one poetic form or another: "Sonnet," "Villanelle," or "Pantoum," for example. This approach draws the reader's attention to the formal qualities of the poem, but it tells us nothing about the poem's theme or its narrative aspect. If the form of the poem is its most interesting aspect, then a "form label" title is appropriate; if, however, the poem would have benefited from some indication of theme or subject in its title, then this approach leaves something to be desired.

Thematic Category Titles

Telling us that a poem is an elegy or a pastoral provides a set of expectations and helps to focus the reader's attention and clarify the theme. We're assuming, of course, that the reader is sufficiently literate to recognize those terms. Where readers of poetry are concerned, that's usually a fairly safe bet.

Painterly Titles

Poetry is often metaphorically linked to visual art, just as it's often linked to music. Giving your poem a title that's reminiscent of the titles that painters typically use for their canvases accomplishes a couple of things. First, the painterly title may provide a context. Calling a pastoral poem "Landscape" suggests the pastoral quality of the poem. (You could, of course, have accomplished the same objective by using "Pastoral" as your title, but notice that "Pastoral" conveys a more formal and traditional tone than "Landscape.") Second, a painterly title suggests that the poem is painterly—that it's primarily descriptive as opposed to narrative or argumentative. Naming the subject of a portrait poem has the same effect.

Musical Composition Titles

A title such as "Nocturne" may suggest an emphasis on the musicality of the language; if the reader is familiar with classical music, that title might also link the poem with a specific genre of music—the impressionism of late nineteenth-century composers such as Debussy, for example. Other titles associated with classical music might also suit some poems: "Overture," "Requiem," "Sonata," and "Fugue" all imply a theme or a structure. Titles can also reference more modern genres of music: "Blues," "Boogie-Woogie," "Improvisation," "Country Waltz," or "Speed Metal Stanzas."

Speaker's Name Titles

If you're writing a "persona" poem, it's reasonable to use the speaker's name as the title of the poem. Telling us who is speaking can make the difference between an accessible poem and a frustratingly obscure one, particularly if the speaker is an historical figure or a character from fiction or myth.

Ironic Titles

Any title can be ironic. Ezra Pound's poem "Portrait d'une Femme" (Portrait of a Lady) is accurate enough in that the poem is about a woman. On reading the poem, we may be surprised to discover that the "portrait" is more autopsy than ode, Pound having described the subject of the portrait in witheringly satirical terms. Giving a comic poem a title that might be suitable for an ode or even an epic can set readers up for an enjoyable reversal of expectations.

First-Line Lead-Ins

One way of starting a poem is to make the title the beginning of the body of the poem, so the first line completes a sentence or clause that the title begins. This technique can create a sense of informality and urgency, and it can also create some interesting ironic moments as we read from title to first line.

Incredibly Dumb Titles

Perhaps the dumbest title is no title at all. A poem called "Untitled" suggests a lack of imagination in the writer and wastes a great opportunity to add clarity, insight, and entertainment value to the poem. Laughably grandiose titles are almost as bad. Beginners sometimes make the mistake of giving their perfectly innocent poems overblown and inappropriate titles. If you call your poem "The Fate of Humanity" or "The Evils of War," you'd better be writing an ironic poem or else coming up with a startling original perspective on these vast issues. Stating the theme succinctly in the title and then verbosely in the body of the poem is another obvious mistake. A good title should contextualize the poem, not replace it.

The titles of literary works aren't subject to copyright, by the way, so you can call your poem "Ozymandias" or "The Love Song of J. Alfred Prufrock" without worrying about legal complications. You'll also be inviting your readers to compare your poem to its famous namesake, and you'll probably make most readers wonder if you've taken leave of your senses.

Checklist for titling poems:

- Always give your poem a title.
- Make the title original.
- Make the title interesting.
- Use the title to help the reader access and understand the poem.

CHOOSING THE RIGHT PLACE TO BEGIN

Fiction writers often work on the assumption that they'll eventually have to cut the original opening of the first draft of each new story: when you've finished a draft, they'll tell you, throw away the first page. Poets aren't usually quite so dramatic about their editorial strategies, but to some extent the standard advice for fiction writers applies to poets as well. Often, we wander into a poem rather than starting it at the best possible moment. Try running your finger down the page (physically or metaphorically) and looking for a striking opening line. Also, always apply the "less is more" rule: how few words would it really take to make the poem as effective and enjoyable as possible?

PUNCTUATION, CAPITALIZATION, ETC.

How do you punctuate a poem? Should each line begin with a capital letter? Should proper nouns be capitalized, just as they would be in prose? Should poets employ standard punctuation? Can numerals and ampersands be used in poems? These are some FAQs that students pose in poetry workshops. Thinking carefully about punctuation is important when you're polishing your poems.

The "default setting" for punctuating poetry is standard punctuation; in other words, unless we have reasons for doing otherwise, we generally use the same punctuation we'd employ when writing prose. "Default" does not mean neutral or transparent. Everything in a poem—word choice, lineation, typography, indentation, punctuation—communicates meaning: poetry is the medium in which language operates at its highest efficiency. By using standard punctuation, we're telling our readers that we wish to access and relate to a particular tradition: English with a logical structure and a familiar history. By not using standard punctuation, we're signalling a degree of freedom or deviance from the norm. Either way, we're communicating meaning by making that choice.

Some punctuation marks are more formal than others. In prose, we'd connect independent clauses with colons or semicolons; in a poem with a reasonably formal style and "voice," it might be appropriate to do the same. In a poem with an informal tone, running the clauses together or marking points of juncture between clauses with a comma might make more sense. (Note that in terms of standard usage, either of these options is an error—a run-on sentence or a comma fault.) The *ne plus ultra* of informality is the unpunctuated poem without capital letters. The lack of dots and hooks and the doffing of caps broadcasts an aggressive informality: the poem advertises itself as counter to all that is formal and capital "P" poetic and allies itself with voices beyond or outside the self-consciously literary world. The poet so militantly lower case that he or she cannot bring him- or herself to sign the poem with initial capitals is a familiar component of the modern scene. The alpha point in this continuum is pretty obviously e e cummings, but there's no dearth of imitators and disciples.

Hyphens and Dashes

Quite a few poets prefer dashes to more formal-looking markers such as colons or semicolons. The influential nineteenth-century American poet Emily Dickinson used dashes to connect short phrases rather than employing standard punctuation. The dashes gave her poems a sense of quick, electric flashes of insight.

Dashes are intended to set off parenthetical information, and the old cliché is that "parentheses whisper; dashes shout." Remember, a **dash** is not the same as a hyphen, and there are two types of dash in use. They differ in length. The "en dash" (pronounced "n" dash) is a little longer than a hyphen, and the "em dash" (pronounced "m" dash) is the longest of the three.

> hyphen -
> en dash –
> em dash —

- A **hyphen** (-) connects two words into a single compound word, usually two words before a noun, as in "a toll-free call." (Note that even though these two combined words may be two nouns, as in "dinner-dance companion," or a noun and an adjective, as in "toll-free call," they are modifying a noun and thus acting as adjectives.) In poetry, hyphens are used to join words into compound words ("word-jamming"), as in Hopkins's "couple-colour" and "fresh-firecoal-falls." Hyphens can also be used to split words between syllables ("word-breaking") for the purpose of enjambing lines.
- A short dash (–), called an "**en dash**," is primarily used to connect pairs of numerals in order to express a statistical comparison (the score in a football game, for example) or a range (from 63 to 75). To see how to produce an en dash, check your word-processing software to discover how to insert "special characters" using keyboard shortcuts. In recent versions of MS Word, you can accomplish the task by holding down CTL (PC) or Command (Mac) and hitting the "minus" key (-) on the numerical keypad.
- A long dash (—), called an "**em dash**," can be used instead of commas or parentheses to "set off" parenthetical statements. In poetry, these dashes can be used to connect ideas in quick flashes of insight. You can usually form a dash by hitting the hyphen key twice; if that doesn't work, check your software. In recent versions of MS Word, you can accomplish that task by holding CTL + ALT (Command + ALT for Mac) and hitting the minus sign (-) on the numerical keypad.

Capitalization

Traditionally, poets capitalized the first letter of the first word of each line. Many modern poets still follow that tradition. Some, however, prefer to capitalize only at the beginnings of sentences and proper nouns. Here are some of the common options:

- Capitalize only the first letter of the first word of each sentence and proper nouns. (In other words, use the same capitalization rules as you would for prose.)
- Capitalize the first letter of the first word of each line and the first letter of the first word of each sentence and proper nouns.
- Capitalize only proper nouns (usually used with the "no punctuation" or "eccentric punctuation" methods).
- Do not use capital letters, even for proper nouns (again, this style is usually used with the "no punctuation" or "eccentric punctuation" methods).

"And" or Ampersand?

Some poets prefer using the **ampersand** sign (&) instead of writing out the word "and." Again, there's a spectrum of formality and informality in poetry, and using ampersands usually locates the poem toward the informal end of the continuum. The choice between the word "and" and the ampersand mirrors the choice between formal and informal diction. As is often the case when we're writing poetry, the ultimate criterion is consistency: if we use ampersands in a poem, we're creating a convention and readers will expect us to stick with it.

Numbers

Similarly, using numerals seems less formal than writing out numbers.

> "Jack and two girls laughed and joked."
> "Jack & 2 girls laughed & joked."

Either method can be "correct," depending on the tone of the poem.

Summary: Options for Punctuating Poems

- Use standard punctuation. Periods go at the end of each sentence. Semicolons link independent clauses. Commas set off parenthetical elements and divide list items.
- Use standard punctuation except where punctuation is replaced by line breaks. (Use no commas or periods at the end of lines.)
- Use no punctuation.

- Use eccentric punctuation:
  - Dashes could replace commas or periods.
  - Ellipses can be used instead of commas or periods.
  - Colons could replace commas or periods.
  - **Interpuncts** (dots above the line such as · that one) can be used instead of commas and/or periods. The American poet Robert Duncan resurrected the Roman interpunct in some of his poems, and a few other poets have followed his lead. (In MS Word, you can insert an interpunct by holding down ALT and Shift and typing 9 on the regular keyboard.)
  - Use some combination of the above strategies.

Ultimately, the only firm rule when punctuating a poem is that the punctuation (or lack of same) should be consistent within that poem. Each poem establishes a kind of provisional convention for the use of punctuation. Varying conventions within a poem (or even within a chapbook or book-length collection) can seem awkward and confuse the reader. Apart from that, the only guideline is the writer's own conviction about the best way to engage his or her reader.

EXERCISES

Exercise 14/1: Editing for Precision

The following sentence contains three phrases: the noun phrases "the very old man" and "the very narrow road" and the verb phrase "ran extremely quickly."

The very old man ran extremely quickly down the very narrow road.

Each of the phrases in the sentence is too wordy. We could replace each phrase with one word: a precise, specific noun for the noun phrases and an equally good verb for the verb phrase. Here are a few possible revisions:

The *senior sprinted* down the *path*.
The *oldster dashed* down the *alley*.
The *codger bolted* down the *lane*.

Each of these examples boils a wordy phrase down to one precise and colourful word that's more specific than the phrase it replaces. Notice, as well, that while general terms such as "man," "ran," and "road" are only loosely descriptive, the new terms paint a more detailed picture. A "path" is a particular type of road—when we think of a path, we might think of a wilderness or rural setting, but when we hear the word "alley," we're more likely to imagine an urban locale. The words may be broadly synonymous, but their connotations differ radically. A "lane" could be either urban or rural, but its connotations suggest something better maintained and more orderly than a simple path.

Find rich, specific single words for *each* of the underlined phrases in the examples below. Repeat each part of the exercise at least three times, selecting different connotations for each iteration.

> A strong, harsh wind blew fiercely and fast-moving white waves broke very quickly against the long, sloping, rocky shore.

Exercise 14/2: Editing Diction and Style

Edit the following lines in order to improve both the diction and the phrasing and rhythm of the lines. Underline any words you consider dull, imprecise, or simply uninteresting. Substitute words that are more precise, original, and exciting.

> There are dark clouds reflected
>
> In the grey water of the still lake
>
> and the cool wet wind is blowing
>
> a little rain across the water.
>
> Some ducks with white feathers are swimming slowly
>
> toward the dark soft dirt shore of the lake.
>
> Their shadows are black as coal
>
> and seem to tremble in the clear white light
>
> that shines brightly through the branches of the trees.

Exercise 14/3: Eliminating Wordiness

Reduce each of these passages to as few words as possible without losing the core meaning or making the phrasing awkward. Don't add words; just delete anything that isn't necessary. You should be able to reduce the first three examples to five words or fewer; the remaining two should be boiled down to no more than ten words.

1. The auburn colour of the leaves of the elm trees.
2. And the winter frost frozen on the bare leafless boughs.
3. The daylight shining through the plate-glass windows of the house.
4. In summer, we used to like to lie on the sand on the beach and watch as the waves came in from the ocean in the heat of July.
5. After the winter had ended, several of the birds that had been nesting in the branches of the willows around the cottage in the grove of willows beside the stream.

Exercise 14/4: Finding the Heart of the Poem

Edit the following passage, deleting any unnecessary words. Try to make the poem more efficient by replacing verbiage with line breaks, indentations, or split lines. Select the best ideas and strongest phrases and arrange them into lines and stanzas, deleting everything that isn't absolutely necessary. Add words if you wish.

I've been watching the hummingbirds
feed from the blue-black flowers on the butterfly bush
They are hovering above their reflections on the koi pond
They are static in the summer air, their emerald-green breasts
and ruby-red throats glistening like the sequins on a jazz singer's gown.

The Mayans believed that the hummingbirds had been assembled
From the feathers and scraps of bone that were left over from the creation
Of all the other birds. They also thought that the sun was a hummingbird,
and that the hummingbirds were the spirits of their gods in disguise.

The hummingbirds make music as they dart back and forth
From one flower to another. Their wings are a blur
of darkness and their jewelled bodies shimmer like the soul
of the sunlight.

Exercise 14/5: Prose to Verse

Convert the prose passage below into a free-verse poem. Break sentences into lines where appropriate, keeping in mind both rhythmic and semantic considerations. Use enjambment, add stanza breaks if you wish to, and add or delete words to suit your new lineation. Look for phrases and clauses that could be made parallel, and then arrange the parallel passages into lines of verse that highlight the parallel structure.

Create at least two different versions of the poem, using a different strategy for breaking lines in each.

Our cat keeps killing rabbits. All spring she's been leaving their parts on the porch, conical rodent skulls neatly bisected, what's left of the truncated cortex still dreaming of the sweetness of swollen roots and tender green buds; fuzzy good-luck charms in Rorschach-blot blood; bunny-tails slick with saliva. It's my job, inevitably, to inter the dead. I do this reluctantly, scraping up matted fur, disjointed limbs, organ meat gleaming like ripe, ruptured berries from the driveway and sidewalks, then swilling blood from the concrete with the spray of a hose.

Once or twice, I've had to use the blade of the shovel to finish off the work the idiotic cat began. Taking aim at the soft, furred throat, I heave the primitive implement over my head, hesitate just long enough to focus my mind on its petty excuses, then blinking to banish the shiver of metaphor that threatens to wedge in my spine like a surgeon's hollow skewer, connecting the spavined rabbit's wounded twitch to my own body's quiverings, flinching from harm, bring the blade down like Abraham killing his son, for a god like a housecat, its blank tinfoil eyes reflecting not necessity, hunger, and fear, but the whim of the senses to hunt, hurt, and kill. The cat rolls and suns itself, watching.

TAKEAWAY: A CHECKLIST FOR EDITING POETRY

When you've got your draft together, take a moment to review the editorial strategies we've been discussing in the preceding chapters. The list that follows is by no means exhaustive, but it might help you to make sure that you've cleaned up any obvious clunkers and made your language as rich and efficient as possible. Don't feel that these are "rules" that have to be followed every time you write or rewrite a poem. Part of the fun of writing poetry is *breaking* rules, after all.

1. *Avoid abstract and general language.*
   The best language for poetry is the most specific and concrete. Always use the most specific word: never a "tree," always a "jack pine" or an "elm." When you're editing a draft, try to "bump up" the diction. Look for lacklustre, predictable, or unnecessary modifiers and general or obvious nouns and verbs. Make the diction as specific and original as possible. (See Exercise 14/1 for examples.)

2. *Eliminate "structure words."*
   "Structure words" are words that express spatial, temporal, or casual relationships (e.g., "here," "after," or "because") or that indicate a particular thing or differentiate between two or more things (e.g., "this," "whose," or "my").

   moving *through the* green rooms *of the* summer

   moving through green rooms of summer (articles deleted)

3. *Eliminate implied words.*
   In the previous example, the verb "moving" is implied by the preposition "through": the idea of going "through" something implies motion, either in space or in time. Consequently, we might be able to cut "moving" and tighten up the sound of the line without sacrificing the sense of the sentence.

   through green rooms of summer

4. *Eliminate unnecessary modifiers ("colour words").*
   Rather than using a noun and an adjective, find a precise noun that will do the job of an adjective-noun combination all by itself.

Substituting a strong noun for a weak noun propped up by an adjective makes our language more incisive. The same guideline can be applied to verbs and adverbs.

Also, avoid "easy" modifiers: "grey clouds," "towering buildings," "blue sky." Part of the enjoyment we get from reading poetry comes from the texture of the language. We can build up that texture by choosing original and interesting words.

5. *Avoid repeated subjects unless you're building a "chant" structure.*
   One subject can govern a string of verbs, so you can sometimes tighten up your lines by avoiding the repetition of the subject. You might, of course, wish to use the repetition as a structural device or to give your poem a chant-like quality. If that's not your intention, just delete every instance of the subject after the first one.

Example:

> She walked through the doorway from the garden,
>   holding a single white orchid.
> ~~She~~ held the flower to her lips.
> ~~She~~ began to eat the soft, fleshy petals.
> ~~She~~ spat out a couple of aphids:
> Romance, ~~she concluded,~~ is dead.

6. *Eliminate forms of the verb "to be."*
   The various forms of the verb "to be" pervade the language. In prose, they're usually hard to do without; in verse, they're often unnecessary. Verse isolates words and phrases so that simply placing a noun or noun phrase on a line asserts its ontological status: we can literally "see" that it exists. If we need greater emphasis, the visual arrangement of lines can do the job.

> The morning sun ~~is~~ amber on the causeway.

> The morning sun amber on the causeway.

> The morning sun
> amber on the causeway.

7. *Turn similes into full metaphors by deleting the words "like" or "as."*.
Similes are a type of metaphor: they work analogically, linking .
whatever we want to describe to something that's sufficiently
similar to make the comparison comprehensible. In prose writing,
it's often worthwhile to spell out the mechanism that joins the
tenor to the vehicle. "The winter sun is like silver on the waters"
might work without the linchpin "like," but we'd be wandering
into "poetic prose" or something akin to "stream-of-consciousness"
writing, which may or may not suit our intentions. In a verse poem,
however, we have the option of dropping "like" and letting the
visual arrangement convey the linkage:

> The winter moon
> silver on the waters

You can accomplish the same thing with a comma or a split line:

> The winter moon, silver on the waters

> The winter moon   silver on the waters

8. *Eliminate wordiness.*
Cut any words and phrases that aren't absolutely essential. *Always
treat words as if you had to buy them.* Be especially rigorous about
eliminating clichés and dead metaphors. The language of poetry
should come from direct perception; it should never consist of the
familiar locutions or borrowings from less-interesting writing.

9. *Look for opportunities to use structural techniques such as parallelism
and chiasmus.*
If there are several verbs in a poem, it might be effective to make
them parallel both grammatically (i.e., in terms of tense, voice,
and mood) and visually (e.g., by placing them at the beginnings
of lines).

10. *Inventory the images in the poem.*
Are they in the same "key"? Have you "followed" your imagery by
continuing to develop related images throughout the poem? Look
for the root metaphor of the poem and try to develop it consistently.
Good lyric poems are very often built around one strong central or
"governing" metaphor.

11. *Experiment with punctuation, and find or invent a convention that suits your voice.*

12. *Experiment with line forms.*
     When you've written down the ideas and images that come out of the initial inspiration for a poem, the next step is to begin to work on the sound of the poem. Try rearranging the lines and stanzas, experimenting with short lines or longer lines, varied line lengths or relatively regular ones. The best way to do this is to read the poem out loud, sounding each beat fully. Watch out for plodding, too-regular rhythms. Try to make the sound of the poem fit the sense of the poem. When you've completed a draft, try the "topography test." Turn your poem on its side and see if the arrangement of lines suggests symmetry or lack of it, and consider whether regular line lengths or widely varied line lengths are appropriate to your poem. Beware of single-word lines that don't justify that sort of emphasis, and also watch out for lines that rattle on forever and lose their rhythmic force—your verse poem may be devolving into prose.

13. *Use visual space.*
     The "white space" of the page is a field of composition for the poet and a system of notation through which she or he communicates the music of the poem. White space is a pause between rhythmic units. Centre-justifying lines suggests harmony and balance; make sure that those connotations are appropriate to your poem before deciding on this strategy. Beginning poets are often inclined to centre-justify everything for no apparent reason.

14. *Avoid or eliminate passages of pointless impressionism.*

             drips of water slowly
                 drip down the window-
             pane. It's
             raining

         (Yeah, okay. So what?)

15. *Avoid lists of "ing" words (called gerunds or participles).*

> Running down the alley
>> Turning   Burning
> Catching a fallen neutron star
>> Smiling!
> Sliding into second base
>> Falling through the webs of his memories
>> Drivelling
> on incessantly about nothing

16. *Look for opportunities to develop "word music."*
If you're writing a rhyming poem, you'd expect to spend some time looking for suitable rhyme words—you might even consult a print or online rhyming dictionary. You can apply the same technique to any poem, even if it's in free verse. Highlight key words (usually content words) in your draft, and then list a few words that rhyme, half-rhyme, alliterate, or just plain sound good with each of your key words. With luck, you may be able to work some of them into the poem, and, at its worst, the exercise may get you thinking about developing the musical side of the poem.

17. *Consider the mode of discourse.*
Does your poem foreground narrative, rhetoric (argument), or description? Could you clarify the intentions of the poem by focusing more clearly on one mode rather than mixing two or three? If you have mixed different modes (and you feel strongly that the poem benefits from this juxtaposition), then perhaps you should consider dividing the poem into cantos or at least be conscious of the need to orchestrate the modes logically.

18. *Avoid archaic or self-consciously "poetic" diction.*
There's a temptation, when we're writing poetry, to use formal or self-consciously "poetic" language. We find ourselves using words we wouldn't be caught dead using in conversation with our friends—"gossamer" or "eldritch," for example. Unless you're writing pastiche or parody, these archaic words aren't appropriate to the task.

19. *Make sure that the diction is appropriate to the speaker or the "voice of the poem."*

20. *Consider your audience.*

    Have you let your readers into the poem? Have you included allusions to personal matters that only your friends (or maybe even just you) will have any chance of understanding? There's nothing wrong with writing a private poem for a particular audience, but it's delusional to expect people from outside that charmed circle to be able to understand it.

TERMS TO REMEMBER

- ampersand
- colour words
- content words
- dash
- em dash
- en dash
- hyphen
- interpuncts
- structure words

CHAPTER FIFTEEN

Finding an Audience

It's hard to imagine a dedicated writer who doesn't want to be read. Writing, like speech, is a method of communication; few of us want to spend our lives talking to ourselves, and few poets are content to put their poems in a file and forget them. Finding an audience for our poems is a vital part of the writing life, and it's a venture—and sometimes an *ad*venture—that can be both rewarding and frustrating. Understanding the processes and protocols involved in publishing and performing your work can make the task easier than it might otherwise be.

MARKETS FOR POETRY

Formats for Poetry Publication

The usual trajectory of a poet's career begins with publication in print or online literary magazines and progresses to book or chapbook publication, with the possibility of inclusion in anthologies or textbooks along the way. Poems are published in a variety of formats, and productive poets may see their work in all or most of the popular options. The various formats are produced and marketed in different ways, but the target audience is almost always the same: readers who are passionately interested in poetry. That's a small demographic relative to moviegoers, gamers, or readers of popular novels, but it's a sophisticated and enthusiastic group. The folks who buy poetry magazines and books are generally well educated—formally or otherwise—and have high standards, so be prepared to offer them your best work. That said, there are some interesting options to choose from when you're sizing up formats and markets in which to showcase your poems.

A **broadsheet** is a single page with a poem—usually just one poem—printed on one side for distribution and display. Broadsheets are commonly printed on high-quality paper with an attractive design and typography, and they're often produced on old-school letterpress equipment. They're intended to be framed and hung just like paintings. Broadsheet production appeals to folks who want to preserve the time-honoured crafts of printing and paper making, and many broadsheets are beautiful and valuable art objects. The usual procedure is to publish the sheet in a limited edition, numbered and/or lettered and signed by the author.

A **chapbook** is a pamphlet of poetry. The average length for a chapbook is about two dozen pages, though some are only half that length. Chapbooks, like broadsheets, are produced by boutique publishers who take great pride in continuing the traditions of fine printing and elegant book design, and, like broadsheets, they may be issued in signed and numbered limited editions.

Poems are often selected for publication in **anthologies**. Inclusion in an anthology provides the poet with a second, often wider, audience than most literary magazines can provide, and it may also generate some publicity for the poet, as anthologies are more likely to be reviewed than single-author volumes. Publishers may put out a **call for submissions** to a new anthology, particularly if they're looking for poems on a particular theme or in a specific style. Lists of recent calls are available on the Internet; a search for the appropriate genre will usually locate one or two.

Most poets work towards publishing a **collection** of their work as a stand-alone book. Deciding which of your poems to include in a book or chapbook is an interesting and surprisingly challenging task; fortunately, it's one aspect of the publishing process in which poets usually work closely with their editors, many of whom have had considerable experience at orchestrating collections so that there's a clear sense of progression from one poem to the next or counterpoint between the various parts of the book.

Publishing in Magazines

At one time, it was common for newspapers and general-interest magazines to publish poetry as well as journalism. These days, the market for poetry—the *paying* market, at least—is almost entirely limited to literary journals. Journals are usually published relatively infrequently—quarterly or biannual publication is common—and they're often quite substantial, running up to two or three hundred pages bound as a book. Most literary magazines aren't big sellers, with distribution running anywhere from a few hundred copies to a few thousand, and even the most prestigious only pay ten or twenty $US a page, though there are a few exceptions. Many literary magazines pay poets by giving them a couple of copies of the edition in which their work appears. Publishing in literary magazines certainly won't make you rich, but it will make your poems available to an enthusiastic audience, and for most poets that's what really matters. It's also a good idea to build up a track record by publishing in journals before you approach a book publisher with a collection of your poems.

If you're into writing fantasy poems or science-fiction poems or "cowboy" poems, then you're probably looking at publishing your work in specialized genre magazines and performing at special-interest venues such as sci-fi conventions. Fortunately, quite a few genre markets publish some poetry in addition to short fiction, novellas, and journalism. Genre magazines pay by the word rather than by the page, but apart from that minor distinction, they operate in much the same way as literary magazines, and the same criteria apply.

Although poems don't show up in general-interest magazines as routinely as they did in the past, some of the popular magazines you'll see on your local magazine stand do print the occasional poem. *The Atlantic Monthly*, *The New Yorker*, *Harper's*, *Maisonneuve*, and *The Walrus* publish poems in every edition. Competition for those markets is intense, and they're probably not the best option for poets who are new to the publishing world.

Some poets are more resourceful than others where marketing their work is concerned, and they target specific specialty markets based on the subject of each poem they write. If they write a poem about bees, they submit it to a specialty magazine for apiculturists. Such magazines may not as a general practice be interested in publishing poetry, but once in a while they might like to print a poem as a sidebar to an article or simply as a change of pace.

Submitting your poems for publication can be a frustrating business. Every practising poet has heard the stories of collections or individual poems that were rejected twenty or thirty times before being published—and then, in some cases, being selected for anthologies or winning awards. To complicate matters, editors don't have time to offer constructive suggestions on work they aren't able to print, so writers remain in the dark as to the editors' reasons for rejecting their poems.

Don't be discouraged if some magazines reject your work. Editors genuinely want to publish the best work available, but their taste in poetry varies, and they're not superhuman: some are better judges of quality than others. They're also dealing with constraints of space and time: they only have so many pages to work with, and they may have a backlog of poems they've accepted and be reluctant to add to that stockpile. When you receive a rejection, take some time to reread and re-evaluate your manuscript, and then send it out again. Be sure that you've researched your markets carefully—submitting your work to markets that aren't normally interested in your style or genre is a waste of time.

Online Markets

Until fairly recently, online publication wasn't taken as seriously as publication in a print magazine. That prejudice was to some degree reasonable, as most poetry websites lacked the backing of universities and didn't have a track record of quality publishing or a tradition of peer review. Some websites, it has to be admitted, published low-quality work that should have been revised and improved rather than having been offered "as is" to the reading public. In recent years, established magazines have migrated to the Internet, some by launching online companion sites while continuing to produce a print edition, others by going fully online, and many new publications have opted for the online-only approach.

There's something exciting about seeing your work in a well-designed print magazine that comes through the mail and that's on display in up-market bookstores. Publishing your work online does have some distinct advantages for writers, however. Online submission is much more convenient than sending manuscripts through the mail, and it's also cheaper. The magazine editor gets your work instantly, and staff members will often reply more rapidly than they might if they had to deal with printing up their response and then fiddling around with return envelopes and trips to the post office. Online magazines may offer some free content to readers, and that ease of access can help to get your work to an appreciative public.

Given the relatively low cost of website authoring and hosting compared to the production and distribution of paper-based magazines, the migration of poetry publishing from the printing press to the Internet seems inevitable. It's possible, though, that we may see a corresponding rise in boutique print-publishing ventures that produce high-quality chapbooks and broadsheets.

PREPARING YOUR MANUSCRIPT

Professionalism in essential for success in writing and publishing, and submitting your work in the appropriate format is one aspect of being professional.

The first step in the submission process is to familiarize yourself with the market's requirements. Always read submission guidelines carefully. Some magazine editors or book publishers may stipulate a particular font or require an unusual format, and some markets are only open to submissions at specific times.

If there's no indication that the market has its own set of criteria, default to the standard format. Poems should be single-spaced and set in a plain (not ornamental or script) 10- to 12-point type. Use standard letter-sized white paper. Each sheet should include the poet's full name or last name only in the upper right corner followed by appropriate pagination. Margins should be one inch to one and a quarter inches on all sides.

We've already discussed punctuating poetry in the previous chapter, but there are also some mechanical conventions that can impact the way we present our poems.

Epigraphs and Dedications

An epigraph, like a good title, can help to contextualize a poem, providing readers with a useful clue to the subject and theme. **Epigraphs** are set in italics, **flush right** (against the right margin) or at least indented from the left margin. The name of the author is usually supplied directly after the quotation.

Poetry collections and even individual poems are quite often dedicated to someone. The dedicatee may be a friend or acquaintance who inspired the poem or a fellow poet whom the author sees as a literary comrade-in-arms. It's also common for poets to dedicate poems to people they *don't* know; a dedication to a senior poet, living or dead, for example, casts the poem as a kind of *homage*. A dedication of a single poem is usually set in italics and inserted flush right under the title, though in some cases the dedication may *be* the title, as in Robert Lowell's "Words for Hart Crane." Poetry collections often feature a separate "dedication page" as one of the preliminary pages or "prelims." The dedication of a book is typically centred about a third of the way down the page and again set in an italic font, though where books are concerned the publisher's graphic design people may overrule traditional guidelines.

Italics and Boldface

You can use italics when representing the narrator's thoughts, much as you might in a work of fiction. In the context of poetry, the distinction between internal thoughts and external speech is hazier than it is in stories or novels— the speaker of a poem is often giving voice to an internal monologue *throughout* the poem, so adding asides in italics isn't often necessary. There are, however, some poems in which a conflicted or simply complex narrator speaks to an implied auditor and then speaks to the implied reader in an aside—if that strategy suits your poem, signalling the shift by putting the asides in italics is probably a good idea. Foreign words (see following) and quotations are also usually set it italics.

Don't use boldface for emphasis or for dialogue, by the way. In fact, don't use boldface for anything in a poem: it's useful for highlighting words or passages in a prose document, but in verse it's obtrusive and annoying.

Foreign-Language Words

If you've read Ezra Pound or most of the other "high modernist" poets, you'll be accustomed to encountering words from languages other than English in the context of English-language poems. Pound liked to salt his poetry with ancient Greek, Latin, Italian, and both modern and medieval French, and he used Chinese characters in his *Cantos*. The typographical convention for using foreign-language words is simple: unless they're written in some orthographic system other than the Roman alphabet, put them in italics. (Some "foreign" words, such as "laissez-faire" are now considered part of the English language and are not traditionally in italics. If you are in doubt about a word's status, check a reputable dictionary to see whether that dictionary puts the word in italics or Roman type.) A more important issue is deciding whether your readers will be able to make any sense of foreign words. Even in a nominally bilingual country such as Canada, assuming that every reader will be functional in both official languages is probably a mistake. Poets take one of three approaches to the problem of comprehensibility: they provide sufficient context clues to make the foreign words accessible to all readers; they footnote each foreign word or phrase and provide a translation; or, like Ezra Pound, they simply assume that their poem should be accessible only to its ideal reader, who is either infinitely multilingual or willing to look up translations for anything he or she encounters. Most poets lack Pound's Olympian disdain for the common reader and prefer option one, providing a gloss in the text, or they simply avoid using foreign words in their poems. Footnotes work well enough, but they may seem too formal and "academic" for a book of poems or a poetry magazine. They also require us to shift our attention from the poem to the note, and whether we do this on the fly (in the middle of reading the poem) or after the fact doesn't make much difference; either way, it's a distraction. Reading poetry is an intimate experience, an almost physical encounter between speaker and reader, and anything that fractures that connection, even briefly, should probably be avoided.

LEGAL AND ETHICAL CONSIDERATIONS

A vital part of being a poet is understanding one's relationship to the tradition. We may flatter ourselves by insisting on the originality of our work, but, in fact, it's likely that much of what we create is filled with echoes of poems we've read. Being aware of the history of poetry and the ever-widening canon can provide us with opportunities for using allusions in our poems. It's important, though, to understand the legal and ethical ramifications of quoting another writer's words.

If you want to quote a phrase or line from someone else's work in one of your poems, the convention is to print those words in italics. Academic apparatuses such as footnotes or parenthetical citations can be obtrusive and can detract from the unity of the poem (see previous discussion about foreign words). If you're quoting from a living poet (or from any work that's still under copyright, for that matter), it's courteous to acknowledge that poet in an epigraph or in your title. Limit quotations to one or two brief phrases—a couple of lines at the most.

Quoting other writers involves you in the complexities of copyright law, unless of course the material you're quoting is no longer subject to copyright and thus "in the public domain." In the United States, any work first published before 1923 is in the public domain, though in some circumstances the copyright can be extended. In Canada, copyright applies until fifty years after the author's death. In the UK, the norm is to extend copyright to seventy years after the author passed away. Some jurisdictions provide for the "fair use" of brief quotations, but those laws vary from one country to another and are subject to interpretation. Your publisher or the magazine in which your work will appear should be able to give you some guidance on that issue. Be sure that you've researched copyright issues carefully before quoting from another writer's work.

It should be obvious that laws of libel and slander apply to poets: satirize living individuals at your own risk.

THE PUBLISHING PROCESS

Contacting Editors and Publishers

- Get to know the magazine or publishing house.
- Read the criteria for submissions carefully.
- Be polite.
- Keep your cover letter (or email) brief.
- Don't hassle people—they're busy. Online submissions portals will often allow you to go online and check the status of your submission; otherwise, be prepared to wait weeks or months for a reply.
- Don't pelt a magazine or publisher with manuscripts. Some editors will tell you how many submissions you can make in a calendar year in their guidelines; if there's no stated criterion, one manuscript per year is a reasonable rule of thumb.
- Most magazines will stipulate the number of poems they'll consider in a single submission; three to five lyric poems is the norm.
- Your submission should be accompanied by a cover letter. Cover letters should be kept brief. They usually follow the standard three-paragraph format for a business letter: state your business in the first paragraph, mention any relevant ancillary information (your previous publications, for example) in the second, and then close with a goodwill statement or a polite request for action. If the submission is in response to a call, or if it's directed to a specific

themed issue or anthology, be sure to reference that context in the
first two paragraphs.

- Write a brief (usually one-paragraph) biographical blurb for
yourself and keep it in an electronic file. When your work is
accepted for publication, your editor may require you to submit
such a blurb so that it can be printed on the back cover or flyleaf of
your book or on the "Contributors" page of a magazine. Blurbs are
also useful for publicity purposes when you're doing a reading or
when your book is being published.

- Keep a list of your publications. Publishers may want to know your
"track record" before they invest in publishing your work. It's also
a good idea to keep a record of all your submissions to magazines,
contests, anthologies, publishers, and so on. Record the title of
each poem and the date of submission; then you'll know how long
you've waited for a reply. When the poem or collection is ultimately
accepted or rejected, record that too.

Print and Online Submissions

Getting your poems to a magazine is reasonably straightforward procedure.
When print magazines were the only option, "snail mail" was the default
method of delivery. More recently, many print magazines permit online submissions, and quite a few print markets will only consider manuscripts that
arrive via email or through an online submission portal.

If you're mailing your manuscript and wish to have it returned if the
editor doesn't want to buy it, then you'll need to include a return envelope
with adequate postage. That's a bit of a hassle if you're submitting to a magazine with an editorial address in another country. You'll either need to track
down postage stamps from the receiver's country or include **international
reply coupons (IRCs)**. Some editors may specify that they don't want IRCs,
in which case you're left with the task of finding appropriate stamps. Get a
friend in the receiver's country to send you some or look for an online source.
Pack your manuscript in a reasonably sturdy envelope with your cover letter as
the top sheet, and address your envelope to the poetry editor. (As you'll have
researched the magazine thoroughly, you should probably know the editor's
name.) You may, depending on legislation in your jurisdiction, be able to claim
your mailing costs as a deduction against income tax.

Submitting your poetry online is more convenient than packaging it up
for mailing, but it may take a bit of getting used to. The world of online publishing is still in flux, and there are a few different methods of submission in
use. Again, it's important to read the magazine's guidelines carefully. Some

markets will ask you to save your manuscript as an electronic file in a particular format—typically MS Word or RTF (rich text file)—and attach it to an email message. Others are leery of attachments and want you to copy your poems directly into the message pane of your email. More and more magazines are only accepting submissions through an online submission portal. They'll provide a link to the portal's website, and you'll be asked to sign up and get a username and password before you can submit your work. Some online submission portals charge a nominal fee. Keep in mind that the vast majority of poems are rejected at least once before finding a home, so give some thought to the expense of submitting.

Exclusive or Simultaneous?

Some magazines and book publishers specify in their guidelines that they'll only accept "exclusive" submissions. Others are open to "simultaneous" submissions—in other words, it's okay with them for poets to submit the same poems to their magazine or publishing house and one or more others at the same time. In the case of **simultaneous submissions**, it's a courtesy to let the editor know if you're submitting to other markets. Many markets take a frustratingly long time to reply—literary magazines and small poetry presses don't have the resources to respond quickly to the (often enormous) number of submissions they receive—so simultaneous submissions are a great convenience for poets.

Self-Publishing

Starting your own magazine can be a great way of getting to know other poets. You'll also refine your editorial chops and gain publishing-industry experience that you can add to your résumé. Self-publishing a collection of poems can also be enjoyable, though distributing your books requires effort and creativity. If you participate in a reading series, you can try to sell your books at the reading venue. Self-publishing offers some important advantages to offering your work to trade publishers: you don't have to wait months or years while editors read and respond to your submissions, and you have control over the design and format of your book or chapbook. It's undeniable, however, that self-publication doesn't have the prestige of trade publication, and self-published books aren't always taken seriously by readers, other poets, bookstores, and publishers.

Contests and Awards

Literary magazines commonly try to increase their subscription base and balance their books by running poetry contests. Poets submit their work to the magazine and pay an entry fee, which usually covers a subscription to the magazine. The upside of this is that winning a contest could be exciting and might carry some weight with publishers when the time comes to collect your poems into a book. The downside is that the odds against winning are often very long. Consider whether you really want to subscribe to the magazine; if you do, then entering the contest is a bonus, but if you don't, then you might be wise to save your money.

Although quite a few poetry contests are bad investments, some are outright scams. Everyone who enters is proclaimed a "World Class Awesome Genius Poet" (or whatever the award is called) and offered the chance to purchase an expensive anthology, attend a convention, or purchase some other service. The contest is, in other words, just a come-on to get you to buy something, and the award is essentially meaningless. *Caveat emptor.*

PERFORMING YOUR POEMS

Poetry has always been an oral form, and even in our modern print and post-print culture, most poetry is intended to be read aloud. Every worthwhile poetry workshop provides opportunities for workshop members to get up and perform their work and encourages them to do so. Most communities include venues and organizations that host poetry readings. Just showing up is a good way of meeting other poets and readers of poetry, and taking the opportunity to perform your own poems is always a good experience.

Poets are more fortunate than some other performers in that we're usually performing in front of a sympathetic audience of dedicated poetry lovers. It's relatively unusual to run across a "tough room" or to have to deal with ambient noise or heckling. Audience members are patient and won't be put off by a few minor glitches, so if you bobble a line or trip over your tongue, just reread that passage and move on—there's no need to explain or apologize, and there's certainly no cause to be embarrassed.

It's a good idea to check out the facility before the reading if there's an opportunity to do so. See if there's a podium or lectern, and enquire about a PA system if you feel you need one. Little touches such as having a pitcher of water available can make a reading more enjoyable for the performer.

It's also a good idea to vary the tone of your reading. Too many dour, serious poems—however good they may be—will probably make your audience wish they were somewhere else. It's always a great relief to get a laugh out of the audience, so working in a comic poem or two isn't a bad idea. Most poets have a couple of funny poems that they trot out at every performance, and some poets specialize in comic readings—there are quite a few who could probably make their living doing stand-up comedy if they weren't too busy being poets.

Starting the reading with lighter stuff to break the ice and then progressing to more serious poems is a useful strategy. Saving the longer poems for later is also worth considering.

Take your time reading each poem, pausing a little at line breaks and at breaks between stanzas. If you're nervous, there's a tendency to rush through your poems; slow down and give your audience a chance to enjoy what you've written. It's common for poets to introduce each poem with a brief preamble, but the key word should always be *brief*.

Some poems lend themselves well to duet or choral performances. If it's appropriate to the style and form of your work, rope in a few friends (it's great if you know some theatre folk), and try an ensemble presentation. Performing your poems with musical accompaniment can also be fun, though it's best to keep the arrangement fairly sparse and to do a careful soundcheck before performing—it's easy for a poet to be drowned out by enthusiastic musicians.

Although poetry audiences are a committed and sympathetic bunch, they're also human: expecting them to sit and listen for more than forty minutes or so isn't realistic. If you've got a fresh-off-the-press book or a sheaf of newly minted poems to share with your audience and the reading is going well, there's a temptation to prolong the performance, but that's rarely advisable. Wrap things up by thanking the audience or opening the floor to questions and discussion, and then spend a little social time with any audience members who choose to stick around.

The end of a reading is a good time to offer your books or broadsheets for sale. Your hosts may provide a display table and appoint a volunteer to take care of sales for you. Often, though, it's down to you to sell your books or broadsheets, so bring along some copies and be prepared to make change—and don't forget that you'll need a pen to sign the books.

EXERCISES

Exercise 15/1: Finding a Market

Research markets for your poetry. Find at least three magazines that would, in your opinion, be appropriate for your style and genre. Note the submissions guidelines for each magazine and whether the market pays. If you're participating in a writers' group or workshop, share your information with your colleagues.

Exercise 15/2: Drafting a Submission Letter

Write a draft submission letter for at least one of the three markets you've located. Keep your letter brief and informative.

Exercise 15/3: Organizing a Poetry Reading

Organize a poetry reading for your writers' group or workshop, or at least draft a plan for such an event. Suggest a venue in your region that's suitable for an intimate performance and that keeps costs minimal. Design a poster and suggest other means of generating publicity. Consider an alternative format such as a reading that's made available through social media, and be specific about methodology and practicality.

Exercise 15/4: Performing Your Poem

Using your long poem from Chapter 12, or any of your longer poems, orchestrate a choral performance. Record your performance and make it available through your blog or Facebook page as a podcast. Alternatively, make a video of yourself reading a few of your poems, and post it on your page or website.

Exercise 15/5: Proposing a New Poetry Magazine

Write a brief proposal for a new poetry magazine. Consider your mandate—what sort of poetry you want to publish and what you want your magazine to accomplish. Discuss the magazine's format—print or online, number of pages, frequency of publication, means of distribution, and anything else of significance to its production. Include a brief statement of your proposed general submission guidelines, as well as a sample set of guidelines for a themed special edition.

TAKEAWAY

- Poetry is published in a variety of formats, including broadsheets, chapbooks, anthologies, and stand-alone collections.
- Professionalism is essential to success in publishing. Poets should familiarize themselves with submission formats and publishing protocols.
- Most poets begin their publishing careers by submitting their poems to print or online magazines.

- Starting your own poetry magazine or micro-press is a good way to make contacts and learn about the publishing business.
- Poetry has always been an oral form, and performing your work is a vital part of the writing life.

TERMS TO REMEMBER

- anthologies
- broadsheet
- call for submissions
- chapbook
- collection
- epigraphs
- flush right
- international reply coupons (IRCs)
- simultaneous submissions

Permissions Acknowledgements

Kim Addonizio. "The First Line Is the Deepest," from *Lucifer at the Starlite*. Copyright © 2009 by Kim Addonizio. Used by permission of W.W. Norton & Company, Inc.

Richard Arnold. "October Aspens," from *Fuse*. Leaf Press, 2002. Reprinted with the permission of Richard Arnold and Leaf Press.

James Arthur. "Ode to an Encyclopedia," reprinted with the permission of James Arthur.

Ken Babstock. "Tarantella," from *Airstream Land Yacht*, copyright © 2006 by Ken Babstock. Reprinted with the permission of House of Anansi Press Inc., Toronto: www.houseofanansi.com.

Elizabeth Bachinsky. "For the Punk Rock Boys," from *Home of Sudden Service*. Nightwood Editions, 2006. Reprinted with the permission of Nightwood Editions, www.nightwoodeditions.com.

Stephanie Bolster. "On the Steps of the Met," from *Two Bowls of Milk*. Toronto: McClelland & Stewart, March 1999. Reprinted with the permission of Stephanie Bolster.

Jericho Brown. "Tradition," reprinted with the permission of Jericho Brown.

Suzanne Buffam. "The New Experience," from *The Irrationalist*, copyright © 2010 by Suzanne Buffam. Reprinted with the permission of House of Anansi Press Inc., Toronto: www.houseofanansi.com

Jennifer Chang. "Pastoral," from *The History of Anonymity*. Copyright © 2008 by Jennifer Chang. Reprinted with the permission of The University of Georgia Press.

Lynn Crosbie. "Xtraordinaire (722 Queen Street West) 1994–96," from "Alphabet City" in *Queen Rat*. Copyright © 1998 by Lynn Crosbie. Reprinted with the permission of House of Anansi Press Inc., Toronto: houseofanansi.com.

Sean Thomas Dougherty. "Dear Tiara," from *Sasha Sings the Laundry on the Line*. Copyright © 2010 by Sean Thomas Dougherty. Reprinted with the permission of The Permissions Company, Inc., on behalf of Copper Canyon Press, www.coppercanyonpress.com.

Tyehimba Jess. "Hagar in the Wilderness," from *Olio*. Copyright © 2016 by Tyehimba Jess. Reprinted with the permission of the author and Wave Books.

Nelly Kazenbroot. "When You Wear Clothes," from *Wild Life*. Windsor, Ontario: Netherlandic Press, 1995. Reprinted with the permission of Nelly Kazenbroot.

August Kleinzahler. "The Strange Hours Travelers Keep," from *The Strange Hours Travelers Keep*. New York: Farrar, Strauss, and Giroux, 2003. Copyright © 2003 by August Kleinzahler.

Deborah Landau. "I Don't Have a Pill for That," from *The Uses of the Body*. Originally published in *Poetry*, January 2015. Copyright © 2015 by Deborah Landau. Reprinted with the permission of The Permissions Company, Inc., on behalf of Copper Canyon Press, www.coppercanyonpress.org.

Stephanie Lenox. "After Uncle Fred Nearly Dies, We Send the Tape to America's Funniest Home Videos," from *Congress of Strange People*. Airlie Press, 2012. Reprinted with the permission of Airlie Press.

Rebecca Lindenberg. "Catalogue of Ephemera," from *Love, an Index*. McSweeney's Publishing, 2012. Reprinted with the permission of Rebecca Lindenberg and McSweeney's Publishing.

Mina Loy. "Moreover, the Moon — — —," from *The Lost Lunar Baedeker: Poems of Mina Loy*, edited by Roger Conover. Copyright © 1996 by the Estate of Mina Loy. All rights reserved. New York: Farrar, Strauss, Giroux, 1996, 1997.

Cassidy McFadzean. "The Magician Wove," from *Vallum* 10.1 (2013). Reprinted with the permission of Cassidy McFadzean.

Don McKay. "Astonished," from *Strike/Slip*. Toronto: McClelland & Stewart, 2006.

Janet McNally. "The Wicked One Goes to the Makeup Counter," from *Some Girls*. Copyright © 2015 by Janet McNally. Reprinted with the permission of The Permissions Company, Inc., on behalf of White Pine Press, www.whitepine.org.

A.F. Moritz. "Busman's Honeymoon," from *The Sentinel*, copyright © 2008 by A.F. Moritz. Reprinted with the permission of House of Anansi Press, Toronto: www.houseofanansi.com.

Aimee Nezhukumatathil. "Red Ghazal" from *Miracle Fruit*, published by Tupelo Press. Copyright 2003 Aimee Nezhukumatathil. Used with permission.

Cecily Parks. "Aubade with Foxes," from *O'Nights*. Copyright © 2015 by Cecily Parks. Reprinted with the permission of The Permissions Company, Inc., on behalf of Alice James Books, www.alicejamesbooks.org.

Benjamin Péret. Excerpt from "Wink," translated by Keith Hollaman. Bellevue Press, Binghamton, New York: 1983.

Alexandra Teague. "Hurricane Season," from *Mortal Geography*. Copyright © 2010 by Alexandra Teague. Reprinted with the permission of Persea Books, Inc., New York, www.perseabooks.com.

John Thompson. "Canto I–III," from *Stilt Jack*. Copyright © 1978 by John Thompson. Reprinted with the permission of House of Anansi Press, Inc., Toronto: www.houseofanansi.com.

Paul Tyler. "Manitoba Maples," from *A Short History of Forgetting*. Gaspereau Press, 2010. Reprinted with the permission of Gaspereau Press.

Pauline Uchmanowicz. "Elements of Style," from *Inchworm Season* (NWVS, #72). Finishing Line Press, 2010. Reprinted with the permission of Pauline Uchmanowicz.

Priscila Uppal. "Sorry, I Forgot To Clean Up After Myself," from *Ontological Necessities*. Exile Editions, 2006. Reprinted with the permission of Priscila Uppal.

Karen Volkman. "Laughing below, the unimagined room," from *Nomina*. Copyright © 2008 by Karen Volkman. Reprinted with the permission of The Permissions Company, Inc., on behalf of BOA Editions, Ltd., www.boaeditions.org.

Ocean Vuong. "Aubade with Burning City," from *Night Sky with Exit Wounds*. Copyright © 2016 by Ocean Vuong. Reprinted with the permission of The Permissions Company, Inc., on behalf of Copper Canyon Press, www.coppercanyonpress.org.

The publisher has endeavored to contact rights holders for all copyrighted material, and would appreciate receiving any information as to errors or omissions.

Index of Key Terms

abstract nouns, 97–98, 117, 250
abstraction ladder, 98–101, 117
abstractions, 55, 70, 71, 98
accentual verse, 155–56, 157, 159, 168, 206
accentual-syllabic verse, 159, 168
acrostic, 186, 194
aleatoric poem, 229–30, 235–36
allegory, 84, 86–87, 90
alliteration, 21, 119–22, 124, 130, 137,
    155–56, 180
alliterative verse, 155–56, 168
allusion, 41, 72, 84–85, 90, 92, 109, 261
ampersand, 245, 255
amphibrach, 142–44, 147, 148
analogical, xvi, xviii, 27, 74, 77, 84, 90
analogy, 56, 71, 75, 77, 78, 79
anapaest / anapaestic, 22, 114, 142–43,
    147, 148, 175
anaphora, 196, 198, 200, 208, 209, 218
animistic, 84, 90
anthologies, 257, 263, 268
antimetabole, 199, 209
apostrophe, 18, 41, 44, 51, 53, 65
ars poetica, 11, 16, 32
assonance, 120–24, 125, 126, 127, 130, 196,
    203, 229
aubade, 6, 16, 161–62
auditor, 18, 26, 37–38, 40–41, 49, 51, 53,
    217

ballad / ballad stanza, 21, 28, 141, 171,
    175–77, 193, 194, 212, 216
blank verse, 22, 34, 141, 150, 180,
    216, 224
blason, 7, 16
blues stanza, 171, 194
bridge, 177, 194
broadsheet, 256, 257, 266, 267, 268

caesura, 153, 155, 161, 168, 196
call for submissions, 257, 268
canonical, 131, 148

canto, 12, 24, 31, 68, 86, 138, 140, 165, 168,
    210, 214, 216, 217, 218, 219, 221, 222,
    223, 225, 226
carpe diem, 7, 16, 187
cascading rhyme, 139, 148
cento, 187, 194
chain renga, 188, 194, 234
chain rhyme, 138–39, 146, 148, 171
chant, 18, 34, 44, 145, 175, 192, 196, 197,
    216, 218, 226, 229, 251
chapbook, 210, 257, 268
chiasmus, 196, 199, 200, 209, 252
children's verse, 21, 34
choral poem, 46, 53
choral suite, 217, 226
chorus, 25, 120, 131, 177, 194
cinquain, 173, 190–91, 194
circumlocution, 80–81, 90
clause-generated lines, 150, 167, 168, 204
clichés, 1, 13, 24, 49, 112–13, 117, 133,
    134, 252
collaborative poems, 188, 231, 232, 236
collage poem, 19, 187, 208–09, 210, 211,
    214, 217, 218, 225, 226, 232
collection, 257–58, 260, 268
colour words, 237–38, 250, 255
concrete images, xvi, 4, 33, 54, 55, 59, 68,
    69, 71, 78, 93, 96, 98
concrete nouns, 97–98, 100, 117
concrete poem, xiv, 228, 235, 236
confession, 18, 19, 34
confessional poem, 36, 53
connotation, xiii, 66, 89, 92–93, 105,
    113–14, 117, 247
consonance, 120, 122–28, 130, 137, 144,
    180, 196, 203, 229
content words, 237–38, 254, 255
counterpoint, 144, 202, 211, 219, 225, 226
couplet / couplet quatrain, xvi, 21, 119,
    145, 149, 170, 171, 173, 178, 188, 194,
    199, 203, 207, 216
cowboy poetry, 21, 34, 257

Index of Poets and Poems

From the Publisher

A name never says it all, but the word "Broadview" expresses a good deal of the philosophy behind our company. We are open to a broad range of academic approaches and political viewpoints. We pay attention to the broad impact book publishing and book printing has in the wider world; we began using recycled stock more than a decade ago, and for some years now we have used 100% recycled paper for most titles. Our publishing program is internationally oriented and broad-ranging. Our individual titles often appeal to a broad readership too; many are of interest as much to general readers as to academics and students.

Founded in 1985, Broadview remains a fully independent company owned by its shareholders—not an imprint or subsidiary of a larger multinational.

For the most accurate information on our books (including information on pricing, editions, and formats) please visit our website at www.broadviewpress.com. Our print books and ebooks are also available for sale on our site.

On the Broadview website we also offer several goods that are not books—among them the Broadview coffee mug, the Broadview beer stein (inscribed with a line from Geoffrey Chaucer's *Canterbury Tales*), the Broadview fridge magnets (your choice of philosophical or literary), and a range of T-shirts (made from combinations of hemp, bamboo, and/or high-quality pima cotton, with no child labor, sweatshop labor, or environmental degradation involved in their manufacture).

All these goods are available through the "merchandise" section of the Broadview website. When you buy Broadview goods you can support other goods too.

broadview press

www.broadviewpress.com

The interior of this book is printed on 100% recycled paper.